MediaGuardian

On Air

A Career in TV & Radio

Edited by **Chris Alden**

Copyright in text © Chris Alden
Copyright in database © Guardian Newspapers Ltd 2005
Austin cartoons © David Austin

The Guardian and MediaGuardian are
trademarks of the Guardian Media Group plc
and Guardian Newspapers Ltd.

Guardian Books is an imprint of
Guardian Newspapers Ltd.

A CIP record for this book is available from
the British Library

ISBN: 1-84354-207-2

Distributed by Atlantic Books
An imprint of Grove Atlantic Ltd
Ormond House
26–27 Boswell Street
London WC1N 3JZ

Cover Design: Two Associates
Text Design: www.carrstudio.co.uk

Data researched and updated on behalf of Guardian Newspapers Ltd
by Toni Hanks

Disclaimer
*We have taken all steps possible to ensure the accuracy of the data in
this directory. If any information
is incorrect, please send an email with updated
details to* mediadirectory@guardian.co.uk

Printed by Cambridge University Press

Contents

How to use this book

Many people dream of a career in TV or radio, but not everyone succeeds. This book gives you the lowdown on how to tip the odds in your favour: how to target and find the role for you, and how to go about getting it.

To help you, we have split the book into four sections. One, what broadcasting is: to give you an introduction to the world of TV and radio. Two, the jobs: read through this section to get a comprehensive sense of the different kinds of people who work in TV and radio. Then three, how to get the job: we suggest you read this once you have worked out what job it is you want. Finally, we list all the phone numbers and websites you need to get there, in section four.

Section 1: what broadcasting is
Before you start looking for a job in TV or radio, you need to know what you are letting yourself in for. So in this section, we tell you exactly that.

What skills and personality must you have to work in TV or radio? The answer, of course, is that there are many different jobs for different kinds of people, whatever medium you choose. So on page 10, you will find a summary career flowchart to help you get a sense of what skills and personality you might need to do each job. You can use this flowchart to help you decide what kind of a career is right for you. We also offer a guide to the major employers.

Section 2: the jobs
The bulk of the chapter is a guide to explaining what these different jobs are – from TV to radio production, technical roles to presenting, broadcast journalism to script editing, graphic design to post-production. We tell you in greater depth what specific skills you need to do them; and we provide tips on how your career might progress. But don't just take our word for it: we include first-hand experiences of more than 25 people in the broadcasting industry.

Section 3: how to get the job
Once you have a good idea of what job you want, it is time to turn to Section 3: the 10-step plan on getting it. The plan is not long: we have cut out the self-help padding as far as we can, to leave you with simple, step-by-step practical advice on research, networking, tapes, CVs, interviews and more – in short, everything existing broadcasters

have painstakingly done before they "stumbled" into the jobs they have now.

To get the most out of the plan, follow it in conjunction with the advice in Section 2 that relates to the job you want: there will be more specific information on many parts of it there.

Section 4: TV & radio contacts

Finally, we offer the meat and drink on which everyone in the media thrives: contacts. At the back of the book are phone numbers and websites for every TV and radio station in the country, plus production companies and post-production facilities. We also include the names of people in top jobs. Ancillary organisations that can help you in your career – unions, diversity associations, and of course the trade press – are also listed.

Follow the advice in this book, and we confidently predict that you will land that career in TV or radio – but only if you are talented enough, hard-working enough and lucky enough too. And if you still haven't succeeded after approaching the task in an organised and practical way, then take our advice: turn to page 82 of this book.

What broadcasting is

About TV and radio

What is it like to work in television and radio? That, of course, depends on you. There is a huge range of jobs in broadcasting – from the creative roles, such as writing, producing and directing; to the technical roles, such as lighting, camera and sound; and the specialised broadcasting skills, such as journalism and presenting. You could do any one of these jobs, and each will give you a different perspective.

Nevertheless, the following general points should be helpful. Broadcasting is an informal industry: until you are in a management role or appearing on camera, you are unlikely to go to work in a suit. It is flexible, too: you will often move from company to company in search of work, as the number of programmes on your CV is the best way to judge your experience. Perhaps predictably, it is a tough place to work: you often put in long and unpredictable hours to make a programme the best you can, whether you are a producer who is running the show or a runner performing errands for the crew. But it is also fun: ideally, you should be in TV or radio because you feel pride in the programmes you are helping to produce, and because of the sense of camaraderie of being part of a successful crew.

But broadcasting is still a business; and as a business, it is not averse to getting the most out of its workers where it can. According to the sector skills council for broadcasting, Skillset, more than half of people in TV work short-term, freelance contracts; this means when you get a job, it is often only for the programme or series you are working on. That makes it hard to survive: whether you are a director or a camera operator or a production manager, you are constantly in competition with other workers, and constantly under pressure to prove yourself. In radio, the situation is similar, although just over half of workers are employed. So you need to be able to cope with insecurity, have a good business head, and be constantly adapting to cope with new technologies in a fast-changing workplace. Multi-skilling, too, is becoming more of a given – this is especially true in radio, where production teams are smaller and budgets are correspondingly tight. The more skills you have at your disposal, the more likely you are to land that freelance gig.

Finally, if you do end up in the wrong career, either inside or outside broadcasting, remember that it is never too late to move. Because people in the media tend to switch jobs so much, an employer won't usually hold it against you for not sticking your last

Career Flowchart: TV and radio

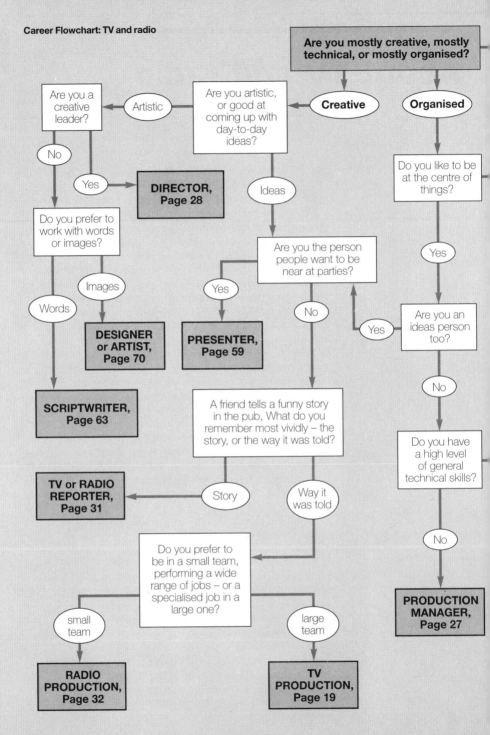

Are you mostly creative, mostly technical, or mostly organised?

Are you artistic, or good at coming up with day-to-day ideas? ← **Creative**

Organised

Artistic → Are you a creative leader?

Ideas

No

Yes → **DIRECTOR, Page 28**

Do you like to be at the centre of things?

Do you prefer to work with words or images?

Are you the person people want to be near at parties?

Yes

Yes

Images

Words

No

Yes → Are you an ideas person too?

DESIGNER or ARTIST, Page 70

PRESENTER, Page 59

No

SCRIPTWRITER, Page 63

A friend tells a funny story in the pub, What do you remember most vividly – the story, or the way it was told?

Do you have a high level of general technical skills?

TV or RADIO REPORTER, Page 31 ← Story

Way it was told

No

Do you prefer to be in a small team, performing a wide range of jobs – or a specialised job in a large one?

PRODUCTION MANAGER, Page 27

small team

large team

RADIO PRODUCTION, Page 32

TV PRODUCTION, Page 19

10

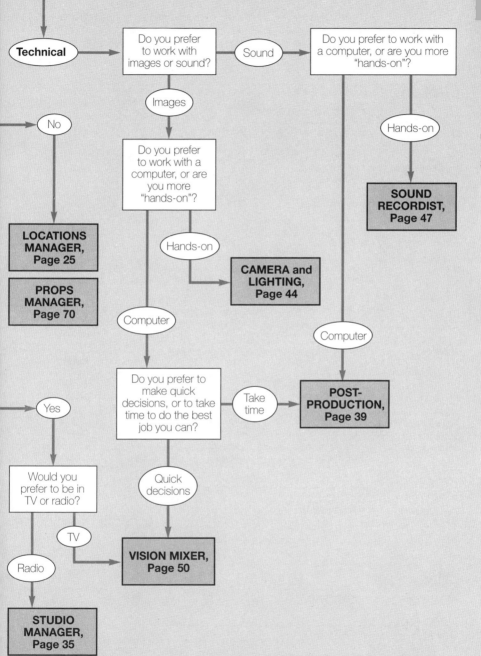

Technical → Do you prefer to work with images or sound? → Sound → Do you prefer to work with a computer, or are you more "hands-on"?

Images ↓

Do you prefer to work with a computer, or are you more "hands-on"?

No →

Hands-on →

SOUND RECORDIST, Page 47

Hands-on →

CAMERA and LIGHTING, Page 44

LOCATIONS MANAGER, Page 25

PROPS MANAGER, Page 70

Computer ↓

Computer ↓

Do you prefer to make quick decisions, or to take time to do the best job you can? → Take time → POST-PRODUCTION, Page 39

Yes →

Quick decisions ↓

Would you prefer to be in TV or radio?

TV →

VISION MIXER, Page 50

Radio ↓

STUDIO MANAGER, Page 35

Main TV & radio employers

	Who they are	Turnover	Ownership	No. of staff	UK offices
BBC	National terrestrial TV, national & local radio	£3.5bn	Public broadcaster	29,000	London & nationwide
BSkyB	Satellite channels	£3.2bn	News Corporation (Rupert Murdoch)	10,400	Middlesex
Capital Radio	Local radio group: Capital, Choice, Century, XFM	£115m	Plc	700	London & nationwide
Channel 4	TV station	£769m	Semi-public	900	London
Chrysalis	Local radio group: Heart, Galaxy, LBC	£250m	Plc	1,000	London, Birmingham, the North
Emap Performance	Radio & TV: Kiss, Magic, The Hits, Kerrang	£16m	Emap plc	5,300 company-wide	London
Endemol	TV production company	£41m	Telefonica, Spain	800 inc freelancers	London
Five	TV station	£252m	RTL Group	250	London
GWR	Classic FM, local radio	£129m	Plc	850	London & nationwide
ITN	TV news production company & channel	£100m	ITV (40%), Daily Mail & General Trust (20%), Reuters (20%), United (20%)	800	London
ITV plc	TV broadcaster with production arm	£3bn	Plc	5,500	London & nationwide
All3Media	TV production company	£100m	Independent	100 permanent, 300 fixed-term	London & Glasgow
RDF Media	TV production company	£45m	Independent	350 in UK, US	London
Scottish Media Group	Scottish TV, Grampian TV, Virgin Radio, production companies	£188m	Plc	?	Glasgow, Aberdeen, London
Scottish Radio	Radio stations: mostly Scotland & Northern Ireland	£41m	Plc	1,100	Mostly Scotland and Northern Ireland
Talkback Thames	TV production company	£131m	RTL Group	800	London
Tiger Aspect	TV production company	£46m	Independent	80 permanent 3,000 freelancers last year	London
Trans World International	TV production company	not disclosed	IMG	470	London
TV Corporation	TV production company	£62.4m	Plc	300 full-time permanent	London
Ulster TV	Independent TV franchise	£54m	Plc	315 throughout Ireland	Belfast

job out for more than a year; and if you have experience in the "real" world, meanwhile, it could be useful background knowledge for TV or radio.

Think about yourself

So what skills or personality do you have? You could start out in a programme-making role, such as producing and directing; an organisational role, such as programme management; a more technical position, such as camera, lighting, film editing and vision mixing; or you could be a presenter, a writer, or both. This chapter outlines all the jobs in turn, so you can find a job that suits you.

To help you, on the previous page is a career flowchart that you can use to find your niche: simply start at the top and work down, where you will find short explanations of the kinds of job you might do. The chart then refers you to the in-depth guides to each role that form the bulk of this chapter. We would recommend that whatever the result of the flowchart, you do read this entire chapter to get an idea of the different kinds of work that go into making a TV or radio programme happen.

TV or radio?

Having trouble choosing between TV and radio? Think carefully – the differences are more than just the fact that one has pictures and the other doesn't. If you live outside London, for example, you might not have much of a choice: the vast majority of TV jobs are in the capital, whereas thanks to the success of local commercial stations, radio offers a wider range of positions outside. Other than that, it is worth noting that in TV, you will often work for a larger team, handling bigger budgets, for greater potential reward, but will often be freelance or on a short-term deal; whereas in radio you will work for a smaller team, often paid less and handling smaller budgets, but are more likely to have a permanent job. In some parts of broadcasting, meanwhile, it is common practice to start off in radio and then, if you wish to, move on to TV later in your career. These include journalism, scriptwriting and presenting – see pages 51, 63 and 59 for more details on these.

The landscapes of TV and radio are quite different. The TV market is dominated by a small number of large broadcasters. The three most powerful are the BBC, the nation's public service broadcaster; ITV, the largest commercial broadcaster (ITV plc controls 11 of the 15 regional franchises); and BSkyB, the major satellite broadcaster. The two smaller players are Channel 4, which commissions most independent programming, and Five, which has been the subject of much takeover speculation in recent years. Each of these companies separates its "broadcasting" divisions, which handle scheduling, commissioning and finance, from the departments that make the programmes. This is because broadcasters' production departments are in competition with the independent production sector ("the indies"), which also makes programmes, particularly for the BBC,

ITV1 and Channel 4. A number of small post-production (editing and special effects) studios are also independent. Finally, there are hundreds of channels of varying sizes which broadcast on digital terrestrial, cable and satellite; taken together, these channels reach a large audience, but taken individually their audiences are often negligible.

Radio, by contrast, is more localised. National stations are more or less dominated by the BBC – but local radio stations are dominated by the commercial sector. There is still a fairly large number of major commercial players in radio – GWR, Capital, Chrysalis and Emap are the biggest – but the relaxation of ownership rules in the Communications Act 2003 left the way clear for consolidation. Smaller radio stations include hospital radio, student radio and access radio (see glossary, page 32), all of which provide good ways into the industry for people who are just starting out.

Equal opportunities

In principle, anyone who is talented or hard-working enough, or some happy combination of the two, will get a job if they are good enough. In practice, though, there are problems. Skillset reported in 2004 that just 7.4 per cent of people in film and TV are from ethnic minority. The BBC, for its part, has hit its own quota of 10 per cent, set under the ex-director general, Greg Dyke. Women make up just 38 per cent of the workforce: they were only a significant majority in certain roles, such as make-up and hairdressing (94 per cent), wardrobe (80 per cent) and cinema cleaners (71 per cent); only 13 women made it into the MediaGuardian 100 list of the most influential people in media.

Disability is another area where broadcasting could do better. Only 1.1 per cent of people working in film and TV are disabled, according to Skillset; but after the media secretary, Tessa Jowell, called on broadcasters to recruit a representative number, the BBC responded by launching "disabled quotas". The corporation said it wanted at least one disabled character in each high-profile BBC1 series, one disabled contestant in 50 on high-profile quiz shows, and one disabled person in high-profile factual and leisure shows such as Changing Rooms and Bargain Hunt. It also pledged to boost the numbers of disabled people on its other main channels.

The jobs

Television production

Many people who want to be in TV say they want to be in production. But this still encompasses a huge range of skills. Are you an ideas person, or better at translating ideas into action? Are you good at research, or at organising complex projects? There are roles for many different kinds of people, at all different levels of seniority, and in different television genres.

Even before you start a career in programme-making, you should be aware that there are three main career paths: **producing**, **directing** and **production management**. If your strength is coming up with ideas for projects and planning them from the development stage to production, then you should aim to be a producer. If, on the other hand, you are more technically creative – someone who wants to plan the camera shots, do the storyboarding, and make the production work best on the day of the shoot – then you should plan to be a director. If, finally, you are well organised and good at handling budgets and contracts, then you might aim to be a production manager – itself a route into producing.

Whichever route you choose, you will probably be working freelance much of the time, or on a succession of short-term contracts. You will probably have done at least two or three freelance jobs at one level before you think about getting jobs at a higher level; and sometimes, if the money is good enough, you will work at a lower level from one

 Glossary of terms: **television production**

Barb The Broadcasters Audience Research Board, which measures television audiences.

continuity Ensuring the visual detail of each shot matches the next one.

dry hire Hiring equipment from a facility without the crew to operate it.

EPG Electronic programme guide. Used to navigate around multichannel TV.

format
1. Framework idea for a programme, that can be sold on by a production company.

2. Technical specification for video or film.

gallery Control room of a studio, where the director and vision mixer may work.

HD High-definition. Premium-quality picture format, widely used in the US.

multichannel TV that includes more that just the five analogue terrestrial channels.

multiplex A single digital terrestrial transmission, comprising several channels.

Ofcom Super-regulator for the broadcasting industry.

Pact Producers' alliance for cinema and television. Highly successful lobbying body for independent production companies.

serial Continuous story broken up into episodes.

series Set of self-contained programmes.

you did before. See Section 3 for advice on freelancing and on building your experience and CV.

Bear in mind that, even at an early stage in your career in television production, the **genre** you work in is a major choice in itself. Although producers and directors work a lot of short-term contracts, they do not generally hop between roles in different genres – for example, from documentaries to drama and back again. As part of your career research, make time to watch a lot of different kinds of television genres, to get a sense of where your future may lie; and try to do different kinds of work experience too. The choices you make now may prove invaluable later.

Finally, you need to decide what **kinds of company** you want to work for. Your answer may be that you don't really mind – you just want to work in TV. Nevertheless, you will find that working for the programme-making division of a national broadcaster, for example, is a world away from working in an independent production company; and even in the indie sector, there is a huge difference between working for a top-20 firm such as RDF and a tiny company that only makes 20 hours of television a year. Again, you need to work out what is best for you.

Bottom rung: the runner

Well, you have to start somewhere. As a runner, you are the broadcasting world's dogsbody – the person who runs the errands, puts props in place, does the filing and makes the tea. The pay is terrible, the hours are long, there is little job security, and much of what you do will be seemingly meaningless chores. What more appropriate introduction to working in TV could there be?

That said, being a runner is a great way to start your career – because the key to getting on in broadcasting, beside experience, is your ability to work in a team. Starting at the bottom, you need initiative, energy, enthusiasm, and good organisational and communication skills; attributes, in other words, that will benefit you through your entire career. So whether you can succeed as a runner says a lot about your ability to succeed in the long term.

As a runner, you quickly learn that in television production, the success of the team is more important than your personal pride. There are so many different kinds of people who make up a production – from the producer and assistant producer, the director, the line producer and production managers, and the technical team – that there is no room for big egos: not when you are bottom of the heap, at least. And because television production is such an insular world – a cottage industry, at many levels, where people work many different short-term contracts and bump into each other again and again – you will find that when you get a reputation, it sticks. Sure, it's hard to be affable when you're tearing around on wild-goose-chase errands for a hotshot young director. But if you go about your job with professionalism and dignity, then you stand in good stead to move on.

The runner

Name: **Adam Cooper**
Current job: **film student and TV runner**

What was your first paid work in TV?
None as yet: the only paid work I have had has been for corporate videos. At the moment I am still doing jobs for love – that is to say, for no pay (except expenses) – but it is necessary to gain experience.

How did you get it?
The majority of work that I get is through contacts and recommendations. The last job that I had I was brought in by the first assistant director whom I had worked with previously on various projects.

What did the job involve? what was it like?
It was a TV pilot produced for an independent company. It was a relatively short shoot (over one weekend), but very intensive. On that particular shoot I was tending to focus mainly on continuity and script supervision, as well as assisting the art department and doing all the usual jobs that help make the production run smoother.

What were your educational qualifications at the time?
At the moment I am currently finishing a bachelors' degree in film. The course is predominantly theoretical and critical, but there is a practical element and having a working knowledge of how film/TV production works is an advantage. At the end of the day, no course can fully duplicate a working environment – they can only prepare you.

What experience did you have before starting work?
Before my first running job, the only production experience I had was making my own student films.

How did your career progress after your first job?
My career is still in its infancy – yet after my first job I was approached by the same producer again each time work became available, and I am able to work as much as my university workload will permit.

What advice would you have for anyone thinking of a career in TV?
First of all, be persistent. Runners are 10-a-penny, so it can be hard getting a foot in the door, but keep at it and eventually you will get somewhere. Enthusiasm and a good attitude are really important: it's what employers will remember you for. One of the runner's main duties is to look after the crew – a good runner should anticipate when drinks/ snacks are needed, and by doing so will ensure that the crew doesn't have to continually stop and start and hold up the shoot.

On-set etiquette is perhaps more tricky to pin down. This is something that you will pretty much have to figure out for yourself, as each working set is different. But the three main things to remember are: not to get in the way, but always be at hand; never be late; and always do your best. It's all well and good having the connections, but if you're not any good then you won't get called back.

> " The three main things to remember are: not to get in the way, but always be at hand; never be late; and always do your best

Once you are working as a runner, you are in a perfect position to work out whether TV is really for you. If you find yourself getting worried about your long-term job security, that's fine – you can still go off and do that accountancy course instead. Think it's all too much like hard work? Hell, go and finish your PhD. But if you find yourself chatting to other people in the team, asking how they got into the industry, dreaming of your future career as producer, director or production manager – in short, enjoying yourself a bit too much – then welcome home. Whichever way it turns out, working as a runner will have been more than worthwhile.

Producing

Once you have worked for a runner at an organisation, be it at a large broadcaster or at an indie, then you should have an idea of which main career path – producing, directing or production management – is for you. That said, bear in mind that many jobs at the bottom of the "producing" path, particularly assistant producer, will also prepare you for directing; and that many production managers go on to have careers within producing or at the higher echelons of a broadcaster.

The researcher

All TV production thrives on good ideas. As a researcher, you are the person who has to come up with the ideas that solve the day-to-day problems of TV production – by finding the best talking head for your documentary, the best guest for your reality show, and the best clips and pictures that your current affairs show can afford. As a result, you need to have a wealth of knowledge at your fingertips – not only about television, but also about the field in which your production is working, and the law.

On documentaries in particular, this means you will be charged with much of the background "journalistic" responsibility. So as a researcher, you need to have a certain amount of broadcast journalism skills. These include a high level of curiosity, confidence when interviewing members of the public, relentless pursuit of the facts, and the ability to write and structure stories – both in the office and on location. Like all members of the production team, you should also be good at thinking visually, thinking through how every idea will look when it is finally shot.

Above all, though, you need to be good at the research. It is said of broadcast journalists that they don't necessarily know everything there is to know about a subject, but they always know someone who does: as a researcher, the same applies to you. Not only do you have to know your way around Google and a wealth of reference volumes, but you need to be good at building personal contacts, which you will add to your growing contacts book. You will normally be the first point of contact for any potential contributor, the person who briefs them during shooting, and even the interviewer; so you will need to be friendly and affable, even as you are working out how best to get what you want on screen. You may also find it useful to buy the latest edition of the MediaGuardian Media Directory: its contacts book at the back lists 6,000 phone numbers, including every major public institution in the country, plus charities, campaign bodies, unions and FTSE 100 companies.

Part of your job, mostly in documentaries but also in other genres, may also be to negotiate with film and picture libraries for clips and stills. In such negotiations, you need to know what "rights" or licences you are buying – so a good knowledge of copyright law is essential. Similarly, as you are the person who is supposed to get the facts right, it is in your interest to know about libel too. Most courses will teach you these essential skills.

Being a researcher is good experience for being a producer or assistant producer: coming up with ideas for parts of a project will inevitably lead to project ideas themselves. It may also be good experience for being a documentary director, as you will probably interview contributors with a lightweight DV camera. As in other parts of the industry, initiative and enthusiasm are well rewarded.

The researcher

Name: **Lindsay McCoy**
Current job: **researcher, BBC1 Politics Show**

What experience did you have before starting work?
Before I started working at the BBC I had worked for a number of MPs and MSPs, I worked for a political party and I had been parliamentary officer for the Disability Rights Commission. I had not worked in broadcasting before.

How did you get your first broadcasting job?
I saw the job advertised on the BBC website and applied.

What is the job like?
The job involves researching story ideas, providing research for films, and preparing interview briefs for our main interviews for the programme on Sunday.

What were your educational qualifications when you applied?
I studied literary studies at Glasgow University.

What are you doing at work this week?
This week I am working on a film about the byelections in Leicester South and Birmingham Hodge Hill on July 15 2004. I will also be working on the interview briefing for the programme this Sunday.

What advice would you have for anyone thinking of a career in TV?
My advice would be to get as much work experience as possible at university, to learn something from every job you have and have some fun along the way.

The assistant producer

The assistant producer, or AP, is the next stage up from being a researcher. Many of the essential "journalistic" skills are the same, and every AP should be well grounded in research; but as an AP you are more experienced, and you will take more responsibility for the overall production values of a programme. You will probably do more interviewing, so you should be good at asking the open-ended questions that get interviewees talking on camera; you will be guiding presenters on how to write their links, so you need to have developed your written skills and your tact; and you will do some small-scale directing, so you need a fair amount of technical knowledge about cameras and lenses, and will need to manage your own locations.

Largely, though, you will spend more time planning and producing content to budget and deadline. You will, of course, assist the producer and director in the overall project; but you will also be let loose on parts of the production, or "inserts", to be shot on location. This is the fun bit, because you get to be the boss; it also means you are responsible for ensuring that this small part of the production comes in on time and to budget, and to a quality that will impress. So you need to be good at planning shots; thinking on your feet on location; and planning what the final edit should look like before you take it to the post-production team, including any music you may select. By this stage of your career, you will probably be working long hours.

Because you need such a good mixture of creative, technical, editorial and management skills to be an AP, it is the obvious jump-off point from producing to directing.

The producer

As a producer, you are the boss of a television production. Everything, in theory at least, is your responsibility – and in order to meet it, you will need a good mix of creative and business skills.

These skills are nowhere so important as at the beginning of any project, when – whether you are working on an indie or at the programme-making division of a broadcaster – you may be the producer responsible for seeking funding for your programme ideas. The most bankable skill is the ability to target ideas at the audience that a broadcaster wants to meet; but you also effectively need a "business plan" for each idea, because you need to know how much they will cost to make. So you need to know the cost of selecting the right creative team; of the locations you want to use; of the shooting itself; and of post-production. All these are creative decisions for which you need the relevant technical knowledge, but they also need to be made with an eye on the budget: an effective producer will strike the right balance between production values and cash.

Those core principles aside, there are many different types of television producer. You may be a **development producer**, whose main skill is coming up with programme ideas – in a job like this, you are ultimately chasing that holy grail of broadcasting, a "returnable format" that can be sold to broadcasters around the world. You may

The freelancer

Name: **Claire Eades**
Current job: **freelance producer and presenter**

What was your first job in broadcasting?
My first job was on a BBC Radio Five Live outdoor pursuits programme.

How did you get the job?
After finishing university I applied to a production company for work experience. I figured this was a good way to get in and gain some practical experience. I got a six-week placement, working within radio production. My placement was then extended to a paid contract.

What did the job involve?
The job involved researching and finalising programme ideas, sourcing contributors and locations, writing scripts, briefing presenters and recording and directing presenters out on location. It was a great opportunity for me to gain hands-on experience – it was challenging, as I was new to broadcasting, but a fantastic opportunity to be given so much responsibility.

What were your educational qualifications at the time?
I had just completed a BA (Hons) in English literature and American studies.

What experience did you have before starting work?
During my final year at university I went into London Weekend Television, to view a programme as research material for a paper I was working on. I decided then that I would like to use my research skills within TV, and applied for a work placement at LWT. I was given a placement on a factual programme, which proved to be valuable training and helped me get my placement at BBC radio.

How did your career progress after your first job?
I gained a place at the National Film and Television School on a funded course, learning all aspects of film and television production.

After that I worked on various film productions as a script supervisor, before moving into TV drama.

I crossed over into factual entertainment to gain experience producing, before moving back into TV drama as an associate producer. So I now have experience within a variety of roles – researcher, producer and development producer, presenter – across a variety of genres, including documentary, drama and factual entertainment.

> **"**
> Breaking into broadcasting can be daunting, but if you persevere, have self-belief and are committed, you will succeed

I recently went travelling to Hawaii and was a guest producer/presenter for Hawaii Public Radio. I am now developing my own programme formats.

What are you doing at work this week?
This week I am scripting a pilot programme for a new travel show and starting pre-production on a new film project.

What advice would you have for anyone thinking of a career in broadcasting?
Stay focused on what you want to achieve. Breaking into broadcasting can be daunting, but if you persevere, have self-belief and are committed, you will succeed. Make sure you have a clear idea of your own strengths and abilities and apply for work experience within the area you want to work.

be a more **creative producer**, who prefers to work closely with the director on story ideas. You may be a **line producer**, whose role is similar to that of a production manager. You may climb the career ladder and become a **series producer**, with several programme producers working for you; or at a more senior level, an **executive producer** who manages programme-making at an indie or a broadcaster, often within the confines of a genre. By this stage in your career, you won't really be needing this book.

The drama producer

Name: **Mark Redhead**
Current job: **head of drama, Hat Trick Productions**

What was your first job in broadcasting?
Researcher at LWT on talk shows.

How did you get the job?
I replied to an ad in the Guardian.

What did the job involve? What was it like?
Choosing, interviewing and preparing guests for chat shows. Joan Collins was my first guest – and I had to carry her handbag, which was the size of a suitcase. I got us lost in the maze of the London Studios; she was very unamused. It was intellectually undemanding, but was fun and my boss had a really disciplined system so it was actually good training in how to construct and produce performances for camera.

What were your educational qualifications at the time?
I had a degree in English.

What experience did you have before starting work?
I'd done six months touring a Shakespeare play round the UK and the US as an actor and musician. I'd then trained as a journalist on a provincial newspaper, which was miserable, but door-knocking grieving families in search of a photo and a few quotes is a toughening experience.

How did your career progress after your first job?
I wanted to do something more demanding and when a project emerged to do a TV trial of Richard III I managed to persuade the head of department to let me take it on, and I researched and ultimately produced the show which was shot in a day and ran for three hours on C4. Then I tried Lee Harvey Oswald (using actual witnesses), a stint on the original yoof show Network 7 (to get out of studio), producing and directing documentary series on subjects including Climate Change and the Monarchy, before turning to drama as a producer. Productions include The Murder of Stephen Lawrence, This Is Personal, Bloody Sunday, In Denial of Murder and Bodies.

What are you doing at work this week?
Viewing a cut of episode six of Bodies, a medical series written by Jed Mercurio; meeting with an Irish detective in Dublin; and discussing God with Frank Cottrell Boyce.

What advice would you have for anyone thinking of a career in broadcasting?
Journalism worked for me: it gave me experience of people and of stories and useful skills that have served me well and it gave me the drive to get out and on.

The executive producer

Name: **Richard Shaw**
Current job: **executive producer, Lion Television**

What was your first job in TV?
Waving a PD150 in the general direction of Sandi Toksvig on location in Phoenix, Arizona, as she learned how to ride a horse in preparation for her entry in the All-Women Professional National Finals Rodeo. The horse was deeply reluctant, her riding coach wore bottle-thick glasses, and the ground she hit as she fell to earth was hard as hell. Toksvig was airlifted by helicopter to Phoenix City Hospital leaving me (and my PD150) in the desert with a very worried Dude Ranch owner and a horse happily munching on a cactus.

How did you get the job?
I came up with the idea that Sandi participate in the All-Women National Finals Rodeo in New Mexico. It was a spur of the moment thing. I persuaded her to go – not that she took a great deal of persuading: she thought it would be fun, if a little bit mad. We were friends. We persuaded the directors of Lion Television to fund us and they, equally madly,

thought it would be fun too. I resigned the job I had at the time and we went.

What did the job involve?
It was a nightmare. And it was the most fun I had ever had, and also the most worrying. There were a lot of very scary professional women rodeo riders. Many of them had bigger beards than me. The hospital bills were also very large. I was producer/camerman/researcher and chief sandwich-getter. Sandi was writer, presenter and all-round cowgirl. Entirely unprepared and hopelessly out of my depth, I researched, production managed, produced, filmed, coached, wheedled, begged, borrowed and stole to make it work.

What were your educational qualifications at the time?
I was 38. I had given up a lucrative career in the performing arts to make a career swap into TV production. I had no qualifications and had done no courses. I barely knew where the start button was on the camera.

What was your career history outside TV?
I had worked in the performing arts for 17 years. In addition to working for The National Theatre and the Arts Council of Great Britain, I was the deputy chief executive of English National Ballet for eight years and the director of public affairs for the

Royal Opera House Covent Garden during the refurbishment and over the reopening. After a year of the new building's operation I had had enough of the world of classical music and wanted something completely different. So I came to the stable, balanced, happy, sensible world of television.

How did your career progress after your first TV job?
I worked for the BBC making the Holiday Programme, again with my trusty PD150. I've tried ever since to persuade John Comerford – executive editor, travel, at the BBC – to give me a longer-term job there, and although he's always been charming and personable he's also been elusive. I'm still on his trail. John commissioned me to go off with Saga Holidays to make segments about old people in Mallorca, Yosemite, or Palm Springs. Then I joined Lion Television. I started producing and directing for BBC4. We did books and Big Reads and literary travelogues and then more books and more travelogues. And that's what we're still doing.

What are you doing at work this week?
Casting the next 10-part travelogue for the autumn of this year. Putting together the team for the next Magazine Programme. Balancing the budget for the next large series. Re-cutting the last series into 10-minute shorts for

Don Cameron, BBC4's head of scheduling. Pitching something to PBS. Attempting to find an intern for our New York office who knows who Charles Dickens is. Reading Martin Chuzzlewit. Writing a press release for the company's arts output for the autumn. Suggesting to the boss who should direct a documentary about guns. Going off on three recce trips. Going to see Franny Moyle at the BBC. And fantasising about my next Big Project which will never get commissioned because it's far too weird – but it's nice to dream.

What advice would you have for anyone thinking of a career in TV?
Do it. But isn't what you think. It's unstable and can be hand to mouth, and the egos can be both fragile and enormous and the politics complicated. Go and see people whose work you like and badger them until they give you their attention. Be prepared to work long hours and for relatively little reward. Retain your sense of humour. If you are planning to do it half-way through your career, be prepared for it to take some time to happen and have something to fall back on while you develop your new contacts. And never use your friends as subjects for documentaries.

Production management

If your skills lie in organisation rather than in content creation, it is possible to climb through the ranks in production management. If so, you could be a **floor manager** who manages production within a studio; a **location manager**, who finds and secures locations for producing; or at a more senior level, a **production manager**, who handles budgets and contracts for producers.

Floor manager

If you have ever been to a television studio to see a programme being made, then you will probably have noticed the floor manager in action. He or she is the one running around the set, clipboard in hand, making sure everything is in place and everybody knows what they are doing. To do the job, you need to be direct but unflappable, and won't mind going about your day's work under studio lights, often in full view of a hundred or more strangers. You will also be organised and have a good sense of timing.

To get a job as a floor manager, you may simply have worked as a runner, and gone on to become an **assistant floor manager** or similar role; you may have worked as a researcher; or most suitable of all, you will have experience in theatre stage management.

Because of the organisational side of the job, being a floor manager is good experience for being a production manager; but because it is a very hands-on position, it's also good background if you want to become an assistant director.

Location manager

Location management is a practical, problem-solving job. When the production team dreams of a location for a scene or a sequence – such as a street market, a smoke-filled boozer, or a Gothic castle – it is your job to turn that visualisation into a reality. So you need to have your creative side, to be able to pick out the perfect location among the hundreds of options; and you need your persuasive side, to get the powers that be to let you use it. Finally, you need to sort the paperwork and manage any problems that arise on the day of the shoot.

Like many jobs in television, good location management is about building and nurturing contacts – be they with local authorities, the police, or the owners of buildings and estates – so that when a crisis does arrive, you know who to call to get it sorted. Good organisational skills are a must: if a cast and crew turn up on the wrong day, it could cost a fortune. Because you are often travelling from location to location, working hours can also be long.

The production manager

Name: **Phillippa Tooth**
Current job: **production manager for IPM, filming "6ixth sense with Colin Fry",
series 6 & 7**

What was your first job in broadcasting?
Production coordinator for ARTV/CNN.

How did you get the job?
Through a mutual friend and two successful interviews.

What did the job involve?
Supporting the production manager in all aspects of production, from booking worldwide crews, assisting in scheduling, booking equipment, assisting in post-production, booking editors and managing the digitising of all the rushes. It was a very hectic schedule, filming two programmes weekly in different worldwide destinations for transmission 52 weeks of the year via CNN. It was hard work but also enjoyable; we all worked together as a team and it was a wonderful working environment.

What were your educational qualifications at the time?
I went to college as a mature student at the age of 20, and did a BTec national diploma in media studies, for which I gained a distinction.

What broadcasting experience did you have before starting work?
I didn't. I had three years previous experience in corporate production, hoping to make the switch into broadcasting. Actually in retrospect it probably held me back: it was difficult making the switch from corporate into broadcasting.

How did your career progress after your first job?
As it was hectic and the schedule very demanding, I learnt very quickly; and when the current production manager left I took over their role until they found a replacement. After six weeks they still hadn't found a replacement and I had proved myself to be the best candidate for the job, so they promoted me to production manager.

What are you doing at work this week?
Setting up for a two-week studio shoot at Flextech studios in Maidenhead, organising the relevant crew employing five producer/directors, five assistant producers, and two editors for a 12-week contract, as well as looking for a replacement member of staff to look after post-production. Setting up the audience team and ensuring they hit their daily targets for audience numbers, producing a 12-week production schedule and a deliverable TX schedule for Living TV; liaison with the studio manager and confirming all crew for the studio shoot. Budget meetings with the executive producer.

What advice would you have for anyone thinking of a career in TV?
Be very clear on the position you want to gain, say in five years' time, and try to follow the correct path – so if you want to be a producer/director then ideally you should start as a junior researcher and work your way up. It is also important to research and identify the type of programmes and production companies you would like to work for and make. Be committed, be realistic, stay determined and focused. Determination provides the will to succeed.

Production manager

As a production manager, you are responsible for the practical side of producing, and are effectively at the producer's right hand. Your job is to manage everything that requires organisation – principally budgets and scheduling, but also freelances' contracts, locations, castings, and health and safety. As bosses seek ever greater efficiency in television production, so production managers are in ever greater demand.

Similar positions include **line producer**, a management/production role; the **production assistant**, who assists the producer and director directly; and **production coordinator**, which is a more junior role than production manager. As a freelance, you may find yourself working in different roles as demand dictates.

Directing

There is only one real reason to follow the directing route: to become a director. As a director, you are the primary creative force behind a television production – the visual storyteller, who interprets a script or idea and turns it into a series of images to which the audience will respond. Not surprisingly, many people want to be in the chair, but few actually get the chance. To become a director, you might aim in the short term to become an assistant director, perhaps on a large production, where you can watch an experienced director in action; but at the same time it is good to have experience of directing your own small-scale creative projects, be they short films or even theatre.

Assistant directors

On a typical production, a television director will have two or three assistants. These generally perform organisational and scheduling tasks for the director, and may also direct inserts or other small parts of the programme. They are called, for the sake of hierarchical clarity, the 3rd, the 2nd and the 1st AD, or assistant director.

The **3rd assistant director** is a junior role, but requires good organisational skills. Your main role is to assist the first assistant director, and brief everyone during large and complex shoots – so you need to relay cues and be aware of what guests and cast are doing at all times. Other than that, you help keep things running smoothly, with runners to help you out.

The **2nd assistant director** is more of a coordinating role. In this position, you are involved in general pre-production tasks – coming up with schedules, and helping guests and casts to prepare. On large productions, you are responsible for booking extras and supporting cast. You need a high level of organisation skills – and be tactful and calm in a crisis.

The **1st assistant director** is the main assistant to the director. Your main role is to understand what the director wants for the production and to establish how it will apply in practice, drawing up a timetable for the day of the shoot. Working with your assistant directors, you will then relay the director's instructions to guests, cast and crew, in an attempt to chivvy everyone along so you shoot everything that's needed.

The director

Do you have the creative vision to tell a story in pictures? Do you have the leadership skills to get a whole production team working toward that vision? Do you understand cameras, lighting and sound? Are you able to withstand the pressures of budget and deadline to get the best possible creative result? In short, can you call the shots? If this is you, you could be a television director.

The *sine qua non* of directing, of course, is storytelling. Whether you are in news or factual, documentaries or drama, then as a director you need to have a good eye for a story. It is impossible to give a full rundown of storytelling techniques in this short space, but, in

---

☑ Get the Job: **TV production**

Employers

TV channels, stations, production companies

Before the interview

• Get multichannel TV
• Watch many hours of TV, especially in your genre and the output of the company you are applying for
• Read Broadcast and Televisual magazines
• Subscribe to email newsletters
• Come up with four or five killer ideas for programmes
• Read reviews of last night's TV programmes

What you need to demonstrate at interview

• Curiosity – so ask questions
• Knowledge of TV
• Enthusiasm
• Willingness to work hard and fit into a large team
• Problem-solving skills
• Ideas, ideas, ideas

What to discuss at interview

• Reality DIY: what's the next big TV trend?
• Public service: what future for the BBC?
• Digital revolution: how will the analogue switch-off shape the market?

Questions to ask

• What programmes has the team worked on before?
• How long is the contract?
• How much will I be paid?

The freelance director

Name: **James Hawes**
Current job: **Several: consultant director to BBC Network, advising on cross-genre projects and programme development; creative director at 2AM Films, an indie; directing a drama feature about Britain's least likely terrorist**

What was your first job in broadcasting?
Researcher at the BBC on TV review programme Did You See..?, chaired by Ludovic Kennedy

How did you get the job?
A BBC producer (Peter Dale – now head of factual at Channel 4) filmed elements of a theatrical production I had put together . He put me in touch with the team at Did You See..?

What did the job involve? What was it like?
I had to watch endless TV shows! Great first job. I was given specific research tasks to do – ranging from thinking of potential panel members; contacting them and writing up their biogs etc, to developing material for short films about broadcasting issues.

What were your educational qualifications at the time?
Usual batch of O- and A-levels, and a law degree.

What broadcasting experience did you have before starting work?
None.

How did your career progress after your first job?
I managed to get experience as a researcher on a range of other factual shows across the BBC's output, from docs to features and current affairs. Moving to the illustrious Crimewatch about a year after I began at the BBC, I began directing the reconstructions. From there I moved on through documentaries, directing an hour-long film written and presented by Prince Charles on the challenges facing the environment – and slowly moved into documentaries with a drama element.

I left the BBC after seven years to pursue a drama directing career, and have remained freelance ever since. I make it a rule to mix my work in drama and documentary projects, for all the terrestrial channels, in UK and US. I enjoy the contrast of drama and documentary work, and I enjoy exchanging skills between the disciplines. The combination of experience makes me a bit different to everyone else in the market. And that counts.

What are you doing at work this week? ,
I am meeting with a producer and writer on a feature script that is in funded development; reading a number of scripts that have been submitted to me to decide on their merit for further development; holding a large cross-genre development meeting for the BBC Network development role in BBC Glasgow; a series of meetings about ongoing and upcoming projects; liaising with a director currently shooting a feature doc in Canada. Oh – and attending the 20th anniversary party for CWUK!

What advice would you have for anyone thinking of a career in TV?
Develop broad interests. Don't get hung up on a media studies course as the only way in. Do something that proves you mean business – it may be in student or fringe theatre, college or local radio or journalism, or making your own film. It is a hugely competitive environment, and you have to stand out. A great deal of the job is about initiative and lateral thinking. Get off your arse and do something! Especially with the affordable technology now available, there is no excuse for a film-making enthusiast not to make their own film.

When you get your first gig, make yourself indispensable. Listen loads and don't say too much. Enthusiasm is great, cockiness is a pain in the arse. You really don't know it all.

general, viewers respond best to development – be it the emotional development of a Faking It contestant, the character development of a fictional heroine, or the plot development of an action thriller. Viewers want to be taken on a journey: directing is about presenting that journey in moving pictures.

Next you need the technical skills to realise your vision. It helps if you know how to operate a camera yourself: these are skills you might have picked up as an AP or as an assistant director, but which you should probably be practising from the second you first pick up a video camera at home. Not only will these skills help you to visualise the final result, but they will also help you understand the restraints under which the technical team are working. In any case, you need an encyclopaedic knowledge of the technical requirements of the shoot: be it the format you are shooting on, the microphones you are using,

The indie owner

Name: **David Liddiment**
Current Job: **creative director, All3Media; former head of programming at ITV**

What was your first job in broadcasting?
Promotions scriptwriter at Granada TV.

How did you get the job?
I answered an ad in the Guardian (true, honest).

What did the job involve?
Writing continuity scripts and making programme trails. It was a great first job in TV, because it involved the whole schedule and meant that I met all programme makers from all departments very quickly, and it gave me an insight into how TV worked.

What qualifications did you have at the time?
A degree in English. No specific media qualification – none existed back in 1970!

What broadcasting experience did you have before you started work?
I set up a student radio programme with BBC Merseyside.

How did your career progress after your first job?
I became a researcher, then trainee director – directed for 7 years, then producer, executive producer, head of department and finally director of programmes. Granada in those days believed in generalists, so you were expected to work in any genre - the head of comedy had been editor of World in Action! It was actually possible to have a career at one TV station.

What are you doing at work this week?
Writing my regular column for MediaGuardian; attending a development meeting at Cactus TV, part of All3media where I am creative director; and flying to New York to meet a prospective director for the Old Vic's new production of The Philadelphia Story.

What advice would you give to someone starting out in broadcasting?
Watch/listen to a lot of TV/radio, have a point of view about it, believe in yourself and be persistent.

the effect of the lighting on the artistic result, the weight and the flexibility of the cameras, and so on. These technical skills may be best learned on a course.

Finally, remember that the pressures on a director are often intense. There might well be a producer and a production manager on hand to nag you about budgets, a location manager to sort out where you're going to be, and a host of researchers and assistants to make sure everyone knows what they are doing – but the major decisions on the day of the shoot are down to you. Every incorrect call – be it a failure to check the weather, a technical error, or simply spending too long on one shot and getting short of time – will cost the production money and detract from the story you are trying to tell. So you need to be well organised, charismatic enough to bring the team with you, but also prepared to be flexible in pursuit of your creative goals; if you are all these things, you should be able to handle the inevitable stress.

The controller

Name: **Dawn Airey**
Current Job: **managing director, Sky Networks**

What was your first job in TV?
Graduate management trainee, Central Television (ITV).

How did you get the job?
I applied for a place, and went through an arduous interviewing/boarding process with many others.

What did the job involve?
Anything and everything – including cleaning the toilets and working in the canteen! Very hard work.

What were your educational qualifications at the time?
An MA (Hons) in geography from Cambridge.

What broadcasting experience did you have before starting work?
None.

How did your career progress after your first job?
Rapidly! After eight years at Central, I joined ITV Network as controller, network children's and daytime TV; then Channel 4 (controller, arts and entertainment); helped set up Channel 5, as director of programmes, then as CEO – and am now at Sky as MD, Sky Networks.

What are you doing at work this week?
Addressing the annual Australian Broadcasters Association conference in Canberra.

What advice would you have for anyone thinking of a career in TV?
Be prepared to work very hard, over long hours, for little compensation. Make yourself indispensable and BE NICE TO PEOPLE!

Radio production

Radio production is a very different world from TV production. Roughly the same number of people work in each sector; yet although there are just over 100 major TV stations in Britain, there are more than 300 radio stations. It doesn't take much maths to work out that in radio, you work as part of a smaller, more multi-skilled team, often with close links to its audience or community.

There is one main way to get a job in radio production: to do **work experience**, either on a hospital radio or student radio station near you, or on a placement at a bigger station. Hospital or student radio in particular thrive on the contributions of volunteers, and are good places to demonstrate your initiative, skills and programme ideas; producers actively look for such experience when looking over your CV. With hospital radio experience in the bag, you might get work experience or low-paid work at a commercial or BBC station: the Commercial Radio Companies Association's website, www.crca.co.uk, contains a frequently updated file of placements; while there is a similar resource on the BBC website at www.bbc.co.uk/jobs. See page 77 for how to get the best out of broadcast work experience.

Another significant route into radio production is to be a **broadcast journalist**: many of the skills of a producer or researcher

⬆ Glossary of terms: **radio production**

automation Computerised mixing or broadcasting.

community radio Formerly "access radio", a new type of licence for non-profit community broadcasting. Commercial employers might see it as a threat.

fader Slideable button on a **mixing desk**, for altering audio levels.

levels Measure of the decibel range of audio, in an editor or on a **mixing desk**.

mixing desk Device used to alter audio levels of different channels of sound.

multiplex A single digital terrestrial transmission, comprising several channels. There are two national and about 50 local multiplexes.

Ofcom Super-regulator for the broadcasting industry.

radio spectrum The total capacity of radio frequencies that can be received. A small part of the electromagnetic spectrum, which is made up of a range of phenomena including gamma rays, X-rays, UV radiation and visible light.

Rajar Radio Joint Audience Research, the company that calculates radio audience reach and share. Its results are known as the "Rajars".

reach In Rajars, number of people aged 15 or over who tune to a radio station within at least a quarter-hour period over the course of a week, and have listened to the station for at least five minutes within that quarter-hour.

RSL Restricted service licence. A licence for small stations such as sporting event transmissions, and hospital and radio stations. Useful stations for those getting into the industry.

share In Rajars, the percentage of all radio listening hours that a station accounts for within its transmission area.

are similar to those of a journalist, and many people do get into broadcast journalism via newspapers and magazines. As a journalist, your skills in understanding your market, interviewing people and handling breaking news stories are all transferable to radio production.

As you progress, give thought to what **kind of employer** you want to work for. If you start in local radio, you may work on the BBC or at commercial station, broadcasting in analogue and digital or both; some may be large operations with a huge reach, while others may be tiny labours of love. You could be at a music-based station, a speech station, or a bit of both. As in television, you also have the opportunity to work for an independent production company; though indies in radio are much smaller enterprises than their television counterparts.

There is a fairly small number of true production roles in BBC and commercial radio – although, paradoxically, job titles can vary widely. Here is a guide to the main distinctions between the different production positions; they exclude presenting and broadcast journalism, which are covered separately on pages 59 and 51.

Broadcast assistant

As a broadcast assistant, you are at the bottom of the heap in radio production. Your precise duties can vary a great detail, especially between speech and music stations: but broadly speaking, you are there to provide vital production and administrative support for the programme-making team. The smaller the production team you work for, the broader the experience you are likely to get.

First, you need to be able to cope with the wealth of paperwork and other administration that a radio station creates. Your duties will involve updating the running order, keeping records of what is broadcast when, managing contracts, and so on – anything that the producer may require. You may also answer the phone-in lines, which means making vital decisions about the callers who are trying to get on air: do they sound interesting enough, or are they about to cause trouble for the station? In order to do your job well, you need to be organised, reliable and trustworthy, and unafraid to ask questions about what you don't know.

You will also become involved in the more technical and creative sides of programme-making. You should get the chance to work with simple scripts – which means you need concise written English, and a good sense of what works best for your target listener. You may edit audio files using software such as Adobe Audition; so it is a good idea to have been on a course, or at least practised in advance by downloading a free audio editor from a website such as Download.com. Finally, you may take on some of the roles of a radio researcher, such as researching stories, briefing guests – and even interviewing them yourself. In order to get on, you need to take the initiative, ask questions, and above all be constantly coming up with ideas.

The producer/presenter

Name: **Beccy Pinfield**
Current job: **assistant producer, Virgin Radio Drivetime and Virgin Radio's evening show, Most Wanted; traffic and travel presenter, Virgin Radio Drivetime.**

What was your first job in broadcasting?
Receptionist at Virgin Radio.

How did you get the job?
After four weeks of unpaid work experience, Virgin Radio needed holiday cover on reception for two weeks, and they asked me if I'd mind. During that two weeks, one of the receptionists moved departments; so I ended up covering for a couple of months before being made permanent. I accepted the receptionist's job in the hope that one of the runners would move on so that I could do that instead, but that didn't happen for a year!

What did the job involve? What was it like?
Basic reception duties. But it was a good way to discover who did what and how the company worked, as well as being able to build relationships with other people across all the departments.

What were your educational qualifications at the time?
I started work experience the week after I'd handed in my finals – I did an English language and literature degree at King's College London. I also had 10 GCSEs and 4 A-Levels. I never did any kind of vocational course, even though I knew I wanted to go into radio. This was partly because at the time, my school didn't offer any kind of media studies courses, but it was also because I really loved English and wanted to do a degree in that! I always assumed that work experience was more important, so I put the emphasis on that instead.

What experience did you have before starting work?
I got a four-week placement after my GCSEs with BBC Radio, which was invaluable. It also confirmed that this was the career path I wanted to follow. I then got as involved as possible in my university radio station, although this wasn't fully up and running at the time.

How did your career progress after your first job?
After a year of working on reception, one of the two runners left. I'd always made it clear that I wanted to be a runner, so I moved jobs. The other runner and I organised working split shifts so that we could both build assistance on

shows into our working day, so I ended up running on the breakfast show in the mornings as well as being a station runner for the rest of the day. I also came in at the weekends to help out on specialist shows, learnt how to tech-op pre-recorded shows and how to edit audio, and occasionally read the traffic and travel bulletins. I also co-presented and produced a show on a digital station in my spare time. I was made the permanent traffic and travel presenter for Drivetime this January, and have recently been promoted to my current job on Drivetime and Most Wanted.

What are you doing at work this week?
In the mornings, I mainly organise interviews, deal with competition admin and edit things for Most Wanted. Every day follows a similar pattern once the two shows start, including reading the traffic and travel bulletins every 20 minutes, fetching CDs, and making tea.

What advice would you have for anyone thinking of a career in broadcasting?
Generally, the best idea is always to get as much work experience as possible, as at entry level this is really the only concrete thing employers have to go on. Some work experience placements even

Researcher

Primarily a BBC role, researcher is the next stage up from a broadcast assistant – although because production teams are so small, there can be a great deal of crossover between the two. You need to be able to do everything that a broadcast assistant does – but in addition, you need to have developed your research and technical skills.

These research skills are critical to your success. This means more than just finding out information: it means understanding what the listener wants from the station, and coming up with creative ideas that fit the brief. For a music station, you should of course immerse yourself in the kind of music the station and programme play, as that is the main way they define their identity. For music and speech stations alike, you need to find the contributors and guests who will give you the most entertaining clips or the liveliest debate – be they experts in economics or members of a hip-hop crew. To do this, you will need to find out everything you can about your subject in the shortest possible time, so you need good internet skills; and you need to be good at building contacts, which you will add to your growing contacts book. (See also the latest edition of the MediaGuardian Media Directory for its list of 6,000 essential contacts.) You will interview your contacts using simple audio equipment – often just an MP3 or MiniDisc recorder, with a suitable mike – so you need to be good at asking open-ended questions and putting people at their ease; and in a live broadcast, you will cue in contributors as they go on air, so you need to be focused and good at giving instructions.

Finally, you will spend more time writing scripts and links at your producer's request – so like a broadcast assistant, you need to be good at writing concisely, in a way that suits both your presenter and the listener. To do this safely, you should also understand basic media law.

Studio manager

Studio management is a highly technical production role – roughly equivalent to post-production in TV, but based in the studio and therefore more central to the process. As a studio manager, you need to be an all-round expert in the technology of sound, with expertise in using high-end multi-track audio software; so good computer skills are a must. But you also need to be creative: you will edit and mix audio clips, adding the flourishes that give the station its distinct identity, especially on a music station; and you will be responsible for more complex sound recording. On a live programme, you may be responsible for handling the on-air desk, under instructions from the producer.

The demand for studio managers has declined in recent years, thanks to the rise in digital technologies; but because multi-skilling cuts both ways, there are other jobs for you too. There is a certain amount of production management involved, which means making sure everyone within the studio knows what they are doing; and you may also get the chance to do some basic research and come up with programme ideas.

"

I ended up running on the breakfast show in the mornings as well as being a station runner for the rest of the day. I also came in at the weekends to help out on specialist shows, learnt how to tech-op pre-recorded shows and how to edit audio

require you to have work experience already, which is a bit unfair! The other thing would be to make sure you are capable of doing the job you're trying to get. There's never any shortage of people really keen to help out behind the scenes, but this is far more likely to go somewhere if you have the technical ability to back it up. You also need to be prepared to work for little or no money for at least the first year, or to work on a temporary basis for a while before something permanent comes along.

In commercial radio, many of the roles of a studio manager may be performed by a **technical operator** or assistant.

Producer

As a producer, you are responsible for almost everything in radio production. There is no distinction between the work of a "producer" and "director", as there is in TV: so in the absence of pictures, you are both the management boss who targets programme ideas to the listener, and the creative boss who inspires the team and makes the ideas work.

What kind of "producer" you are depends a great deal on whether you work on a speech or music station – but there are many tasks both have in common. You will spend most of your time coming up with programme ideas, drawing up running orders, writing scripts and interviewing contributors – although you will have researchers,

The local radio editor

Name: **Pauline Causey**
Current job: **managing editor, BBC Radio Cornwall and BBC Cornwall website**

What was your first job in broadcasting?
Reporter, Marchersound, Wrexham

How did you get the job?
I replied to an ad.

What did the job involve? What was it like?
Covering news bulletins and news reporting at an ILR

newsdesk. Working in a small team and learning how to pronounce Welsh place names.

What were your educational qualifications at the time?
A postgrad diploma in radio journalism.

What broadcasting experience did you do before starting work?
Hospital radio, work experience, "hanging out" on Saturdays and a year's broadcasting training at college.

How did your career progress after your first job?
I went to Signal Radio, Stoke on Trent, then into BBC local radio as a reporter.

What are you doing at work this week?
Working with my colleagues on West and South West radio stations, to recruit a shared programme presenter; some one-to-one meetings with team leaders and presenters.

What advice would you have for anyone thinking of a career in broadcast journalism?
Make sure you know the programmes/output of the organisation you want to work for. Do all you can to get work experience. Once you've got a work experience foot in the door, listen to, talk to and help everyone you're assigned to work with – even the person showing you how to make the tea knows something you can learn from.

☑ Get the Job: **radio production**

Employers

Radio stations, independent radio producers

Before the interview

- Listen to hours of radio, especially in your genre and the station you are applying for
- Check the station's audience share and reach
- Get digital TV and radio
- Catch up with what you missed by listening on the internet
- Come up with four or five ideas for features or programmes
- Read reviews of radio programmes for the past week
- Practise using an audio editor

What you need to demonstrate at interview

- Curiosity – so ask questions
- Knowledge of radio and news/music
- Willingness to "muck in" with whatever jobs need doing
- Ideas, ideas, ideas

What to discuss at interview

- Musical truth: the CDs you own
- Week that was: what's in the news at the moment
- Role model: your favourite DJs and broadcasters
- Breakfast wars: who will win in your region

Questions to ask

- What is the last person in this job doing now?
- What formal training is available?
- How much will I get paid?

"

Make sure you know the programmes/ output of the organisation you want to work for

Pauline Causey

journalists and broadcast assistants to help you out in this, of course. Thanks to the rise in digital audio technologies, you will do a lot of the everyday audio editing, mixing and recording that were once done by a studio manager. You will also need to know how much programmes cost to make, and be good at handling budgets.

Finally, as a producer, you are the person responsible for getting the most out of those most difficult-to-manage members of the production team – presenters. This is the job which, in TV, would be left to the director; but as a radio producer, it is down to you. So you need to put together clear pre-production briefs, and have the tact and the assertiveness to get everybody pulling in the same direction.

Not all producers work for a broadcaster: if you are experienced enough, you may instead work freelance for a radio production company, which means you will be coming up with programme ideas and pitching them to commissioning editors at radio stations – particularly national BBC stations, such as Radio 4 or Radio Five Live.

"

You'll meet some fantastic people, but don't expect great pay or any thanks for a while!

Pete Simmons

The programming boss

Name: **Pete Simmons**
Current job: **group head of programmes, Chrysalis Radio**

What was your first job in broadcasting?
I was a tech op at Metro Radio in Newcastle.

How did you get the job?
Persistent contact with the station, and helping out on Saturday afternoons during their sport show. Be prepared to work for nothing!

What did the job involve? What was it like?
It was a big learning experience, working with presenters, journalists, and engineers. It launched me into the political world of radio.

What were your educational qualifications at the time?
I was vastly over-qualified, having hidden in university too long. I had a degree in music

from Newcastle Uni, and an MA from Durham in electronic music.

What broadcasting experience did you do before starting work?
None, but I had trained between universities as a recording engineer at a great studio in Birmingham and had experience in every aspect of that job from multi-tracking, disc cutting and dubbing on to film to making the tea!

How did your career progress after your first job?
There were a lot of opportunities once I moved to Capital in London. So I quickly moved into production in news as senior producer for The Way It Is, made documentaries, helped set up Capital Gold Sport,

became head of sport and eventually programme controller, 95.8 Capital FM.

What are you doing at work this week?
Working across all our brands – Galaxy, Heart, LBC, digital radio – on a huge variety of programming, sponsorship, research, marketing, people and even engineering issues that occur day to day.

What advice would you have for anyone thinking of a career in broadcasting?
Do it – there is nothing more rewarding. You'll meet some fantastic people, but don't expect great pay or any thanks for a while!

Post-production

Television production does not stop when the cameraman goes home. There is still plenty of work to be done in post-production: editing the footage down to size, putting it in the right sequence, adding sound and any special effects, and so on. If this interests you – that is, if you are creative but also good with technology, the sort of person who enjoys playing with the editing facilities on your home video – then you could consider post-production as a career.

Within post-production, there are two main career paths: to be a picture editor, who edits the footage of a broadcast; or to be a sound editor, who creates the final soundtrack, adding any music and other effects. In each role, you will be employed either in-house at a large broadcaster, such as BBC Resources; or you will be at one of a growing number of independent post houses, which are often small outfits employing no more than 10 people: see page 118 for a list.

If you want to get into post-production, the best approach is to work up from the bottom, picking up the technical skills you need as you go along. This means working for very little at first: like production companies, many post-production facilities are run on a shoestring, and so employ runners to do all their fetching and carrying; see page 77 for what this will usually involve. While you are in the office, you should ask someone to show you around editing

---

⬆ Glossary of terms: **post-production**

actuality Scenes or audio recorded during the shoot, not added later.

Avid Company that makes editing software.

CGI Computer graphics.

clean feed Version of a programme without the presenters' commentary added.

colour grading Adjusting a programme for overall colour balance. Made more simple by digital editing systems.

compositing In visual effects, the art of "layering" multiple shots on top of each other, adjusting the light and colour accordingly.

Flame Visual effects system, manufactured by a company called Discreet.

foley The art of creating audio effects from scratch in a studio.

Lightworks Company that makes editing software.

linear Traditional, cut-and-paste editing – fast going out of fashion.

non-linear Systems that allow you to shuffle the order of scenes while editing.

offline Lower-resolution editing – the bit where you make creative decisions for clients' approval.

online Higher-resolution editing – becoming more popular as hardware becomes more powerful.

post house Post-production facility

rough cut Result of offline editing.

rushes Unedited tape direct from the client each day.

suite Room where you do the editing; normally small, with one kind of editing system inside.

timecode System used to help you find where on the tape you are.

software such as Avid, Lightworks or Final Cut; that way, you will be able to list familiarity with these products on your CV.

After being a runner, you will usually be employed as an assistant editor, which means you are effectively doing the technical job under the instruction of a more senior editor.

Editor

Being an editor in post-production is a tough, stressful job. You will commonly be presented with hour upon hour of raw TV footage – shot either in film or, more commonly these days, one of a number of video formats –which you need to get down to size, on deadline, with all the scenes in order and all of the technical imperfections ironed out. You will often spend long hours working in a darkened room, surrounded by technology, to hit your deadline – knowing that the better you do your job, the more credit the director will ultimately take. That said, you will end up with the satisfaction of knowing that you had control over the final cut of a television programme.

If you want to be an editor, your first goal is to master the technology. Traditionally, most editing had to be "linear" – a process by which you had to record on to a tape from start to finish, so if you changed your mind about something you did at the start, you were in trouble. As a newcomer to the industry, though, it is more useful to be familiar with methods of "non-linear" editing: that is, software that enables you to move scenes and images from place to place at leisure, before you combine them into a whole. Examples include Avid, Lightworks, and the cheaper Final Cut Pro. When working in these programs, you may either be working offline, which means you are producing a lower-quality "rough cut" for the producer's approval, taking up less storage space on a computer; or you are working online, which means you are putting together the "final cut" for broadcast. Offline is perhaps considered the more creative process. You might also be familiar with other software: such as Adobe AfterEffects, which allows you to slot different images into a single composite shot.

Remember, most editing software will be beyond the budget of the average individual, and there are few courses available – hence the need to get work experience, or be a runner, to pick up the skills you need.

Whatever software you are using, an important part of the job is to have a sense of a television programme's creative structure, and its pace. If you are working in drama or documentaries, this is particularly vital: storytelling is all about timing, and both the writer and the director will have worked hard to develop a story that maintains the viewer's interest from the opening credits to the close. Your job is to hack down the shots that disrupt this creative tension, and give greater emphasis to those that reinforce the necessary mood. Needless to say, the more television you watch, the better at this you will become.

Apart from your creative and technical skills, you also need to be a certain kind of person to be a good editor. You will be someone who

> "
>
> Don't ever forget it's skills that drive the kit, not the other way around
>
> Rob Miller

wants to take creative responsibility for the success of a project, but doesn't mind passing the credit to others; you need to have an organised mind; and you need to be good at working to a brief. Finally, you need to be calm enough to cope with the odd interminable shift in the editing suite.

The picture editor

Name: **Rob Miller**
Current job: **part-time picture editor, BBC news & current affairs; freelance producer/director, Shooting Pictures**

What was your first job in broadcasting?

Trainee assistant picture editor in news.

How did you get the job?

I saw it advertised in the MediaGuardian, had two interviews, and was part of an intake of 30 people from what I believe were thousands of applications.

What did the job involve? What was it like?

A lot of tapes: running tapes into transmission, running tapes for editors to work with and preparing tapes for editing with. Also taking satellite feeds and being a general dogsbody.

What were your educational qualifications at the time?

I had an HND in advertising and editorial photography. I had worked for a year for a small production company as assistant photographer, however, they also produced films and tape/slide presentations so gained some post-production experience there.

How did your career progress after your first job?

I became an editor after about three years. I did that with news for a couple of years, and then got involved with the BBC's big push into multi-skilling. This meant some journalist training, resulting in an attachment as an assistant producer on Business Breakfast. Multi-skilling also extended to camera and sound work: I undertook a three-month attachment as a sound recordist as part of a two-man news and current affairs crew in 1996. Then I went part-time to do a postgrad in drama directing at the Northern School of Film and TV. It was something I had been interested in pursuing for some time. On completion I stayed in part-time editing to pay the mortgage, and started helping on short films in various capacities – eventually getting involved with Shooting Pictures, where I now produce and direct corporate films. We are currently developing our first TV project with has been optioned by the BBC. Last year I also did some lecturing on documentary film-making at a college in west London.

What are you doing at work this week?

I have just completed A Failure of Intelligence, the Panorama which was broadcast last Sunday evening. This weekend I'll be working on The Politics Show.

What advice would you have for anyone thinking of a career in broadcasting?

Courses can be a start: however, they outnumber jobs by about 100 to one. DV has revolutionised – perhaps democratised – production. For under £1,500 you can shoot and edit something of near broadcast standard; however, don't ever forget it's skills that drive the kit, not the other way around. Sometimes the bean counters forget that, so practise to get your craft skills and then you will make programmes worth watching.

The post-production engineer

Name: James Evans
Current job: camera technician and post-production engineer at Lion Television

What was your first job in broadcasting?
I was on the sound crew at Granada Satellite Broadcasting at the Old School in Manchester, where I gained a huge amount of experience in live and pre-record programme making.

How did you get the job?
As soon as I left uni, I sent CVs to all the production companies I could find addresses for. Most of them wrote back saying there was no work but they would keep my CV on file. They weren't lying. I got a call from Granada Satellite about six months later, asking me to come for an interview. Two interviews later, I got the job. I was lucky though because they were paying very low wages and hence took people with very little experience. About 10 of us were hired at the same time, and we were all fresh out of uni. It made for a great atmosphere.

What did the job involve?
I started on the studio floor, miking presenters and guests for various shows, setting up backup mics, making sure there was adequate foldback on the floor, and learning as much as I could about the other departments. I also helped out any other departments. I then started playing in stings etc in the sound booth, and when I'd learned enough, I was given the chance to mix the odd live and pre-recorded show. I was in the fortunate situation of having a boss who believed in giving people chances, and he was happy to let me do things that would usually take years to get to. It was a fantastic job because it was a very young team and we were all learning at the same time. There was always a great atmosphere and a good social life. It was a job that actually put a smile on my face in the mornings.

What were your educational qualifications at the time?
I did a degree in music technology and and audio systems design with popular music at Derby University, so I knew all about sound applications, mics, mixing desks, and the theory.

What experience did you have before starting work?
I had done work experience during my time at uni on the sound crew for Emmerdale in Leeds. I also had a technical job in the student union nightclubs, setting up and operating light and sound systems, so my CV read quite well in terms of technical experience.

How did your career progress after your first job?
Very varied! I went straight from Granada to Planet 24 in London where I was the technical floor assistant on the Big Breakfast.

I then went to Panama for two months to do Survivor, where my job covered everything in production and post-production. I assisted every department, and got my first taste of post-production engineering and Avid assisting.

After the Big Breakfast came off the air, I had two jobs for shopping channels on a more or less freelance basis covering sound, graphics, VT, vision mixing and vision engineering. After a few months, I went to work for 2nd Sense in Elstree, where I was a post-production dubbing assistant. I did everything from learning how to edit audio and mix professionally, to building a new suite – even building the soundproof internal walls. From there I went on to Lion Television. At peak times we run 17 Avid suites, and I am responsible for maintaining these suites and keeping the editors happy! I am also responsible for all the camera equipment we have here. I have found my niche and this is the job that I will be staying in for a long time.

What are you doing at work this week?
This week is a rare quiet one, so I am taking the time to solve any minor problems we have in the edits, rigging a new edit for sound, and getting up to date with camera maintenance and repairs. Beats a desk job any day!

Computer graphics editor

A growing sector of television production is CGI: that is, computer generated imagery. CGI has been around for a couple of decades now, but thanks to rapid advances in digitisation, is still perceived as a relatively new field. If you want to progress in this sector, you should approach one of the post-production facilities with CGI expertise (see the list on page 118 for what different post houses do). The job is highly specialised and becoming increasingly glamorous, so expect a great deal of competition.

Sound editor

In post-production sound, your job is to put together the complete soundtrack of the television programme. The basic principle is that you take the recorded sound from the production, solve any errors or problems with it, synchronise it with the footage after picture editing, and then add other sound as necessary: be it music, library sound, or – depending on the budget of the production – original effects.

As in picture editing, you will need a high level of technical skills: you will need to know how to use a multi-track audio editor, for which the best training is again to seek work experience and learn on the job. In addition, you need great attention to detail – you might need to rerecord dialogue, for example, if any of it turns out to be unintelligible or incorrect; and you should be prepared to put in some painstaking hours synchronising your work.

One of the most important skills of the sound editor's job is to understand how different sounds, especially the music, can alter the pace and mood of a television programme – building tension or dissipating it as appropriate. Like the picture editor, you are ultimately working to the director's overall vision, even if you might not spend much time working with the production team from day to day.

Up the career ladder

If you are a successful editor in post-production, there are only a few ways in which your career will traditionally progress. You could move up to a senior level in a facilities house or your in-house team, in which case your job will very quickly become more about project management and developing the business; many of your decisions will be about which emerging technologies to buy into, so it will be important to keep abreast of developments. Even if you want to remain an editor all your life, you will often have to learn a lot about technology just to stand still; technology changes fast, making today's standard tomorrow's anachronism.

Finally, you could use some of your picture editing skills as a way into other parts of the industry – particularly directing.

"

Make sure you are always willing to help people ... if you don't get on with someone, others will know about it before they know you

What advice would you have for anyone thinking of a career in broadcasting?
Don't think it's going to be glamorous. It takes serious hard work and often extremely long hours. Your social life has to be very flexible and you often have to cancel engagements for the sake of your career. Also, think very hard about exactly what area you want to aim for. Make sure you are always willing to help people, and don't hold grudges. Remember that the industry is extremely incestuous, and if you don't get on with someone, others will know about it before they know you. Be as sociable as possible. The more friends you make, the better your career prospects.

Technical roles

No television or radio production would get made without its technical staff. Every camera needs to be operated, every shot needs to be lit, every sound needs to be recorded; and in every gallery (the control room), a team is needed to keep the show on the road.

If you want to perform one of these technical roles, the most important qualification is experience. The jobs usually have a clear, hierarchical career progression for you to follow: you start at assistant level and work up, usually from production to production. This makes work experience doubly important, although an engineering qualification will no doubt assist you in most jobs. Remember, many technical roles in TV and radio are in fact "technically creative" jobs: so not only will you need an intimate knowledge of the equipment you are using, but in using it, you will have a greater or lesser degree of artistic input into the finished result.

Some points to mention. First, because you will often be freelance – as between a third and a half of all technical staff are – you will often be responsible for training yourself, particularly at the start of your career. Take a look at the BBC website in particular, to get a sense of the different kinds of training that are offered. Second, the technical roles in lighting, camera and sound are still overwhelmingly dominated by men: in sound, according to the sector skills learning council, Skillset, the proportion of women is below one in 10.

Camera

As a camera operator, you have arguably the most important technical role in TV. If TV is about moving images, then you are the person who actually creates them; the person whose job it is to capture any shot that is dreamed up by the rest of the production team. To do the job, you need to have a strong sense of visual

↑ Technical glossary of terms

baby legs A tripod used for low-angle shots. So-called because of its little legs.

best boy Assistant to the gaffer in a lighting team.

blonde Powerful light, usually coloured yellow for easy identification.

boom Long pole on which a microphone is held.

cherry-picker Tall crane for high-angle shots.

crane System for elevating a camera and its operator.

dolly A movable camera platform, on wheels or rails.

focus puller In a complex shot, someone whose job is to keep it in focus.

gaffer Lighting electrician.

grip Operates camera-moving equipment.

redhead Standard light, usually coloured red for easy identification.

rigger Member of the equipment maintenance team.

composition; have up-to-date technical knowledge about lighting, cameras and lenses, the different shots they are capable of and the formats you will be shooting on; and in most roles, you will need quick reactions and a strong sense of initiative if you are to interpret the director's ideas into a successful series of scenes.

You are never "just" a camera operator. If working on a drama, you are interpreting the director's creative instructions for every shot; if shooting a live event, then you are acting partly according to a plan and partly on your own initiative, depending on what is happening and when; and if working with a broadcast journalist, then you are an important part of the journalistic team.

To get started in your career, the most important thing is to build your technical experience. It might help to do a course: this would help you to put together a showreel, using a lightweight camera; but it is more important to get work experience – usually

The lighting cameraman

Name: **Mike Coles**
Current job: **freelance lighting cameraman**

What was your first job in broadcasting?
I got a job as a camera assistant with CBS News in London, after doing part-time work for them in their cutting rooms when I was a student.

How did you get the job?
Contacts I had made when doing the part-time assistant editing work.

What did the job involve? What was it like?
The camera assistant job involved travelling around the world looking after equipment, assisting the producer/cameraman and doing some shooting.

What were your educational qualifications at the time?
I had just graduated from the Royal College of Art film school.

What experience did you have before starting work?
Only working on student films as cameraman, plus the assistant editing.

How did your career progress after your first job?
I stayed with CBS for 18 months, and then worked on contract for the BBC film unit at Ealing, eventually joining the staff and then leaving to go freelance in 1977.

What are you doing at work this week?
I am in the fourth week of a drama for Channel 4, whose theme is IVF treatment.

What advice would you have for anyone thinking of a career in broadcasting?
If you are interested in the technical side, try and get a start in a facilities house or post-production company. If you are interested in the production side then try to get jobs as runners or researchers or assistant directors – and keep trying!

as a runner in a production team. With luck, and if you get on well with people, you should be able to secure a job as a **trainee camera operator**, perhaps on a short-term contract. After that, your career might progress up through **camera assistant** to **camera operator**, although your precise route will depend on the size of the productions you are working for. On very large productions or films, for example, jobs for assistants can be highly specialised.

After years of experience, you may be in a position to become the senior operator on a crew: in this role, you will manage the complex job of planning all the camera shots, in conjunction with the director and the production management team. You might also aim to be a **lighting cameraman**, a specialised creative role in which you take responsibility for the visual mood of a factual programme – a programme about Islamic art, for example, might require very different colour balancing to a documentary about an inner-city sink estate; and often the precise result will depend on the editorial message the director is trying to convey. At this level, some camera operators branch out by starting their own camera and facilities businesses.

There is also one manual/technical job connected with the camera team: the **grip**, whose responsibility is to manage the equipment which enables a camera to move – for example, high up on a crane, or on rails down the side of a running track. Given the size of a typical production team, health and safety awareness is a particularly important part of the role.

Lighting

As a lighting operator, you have a slightly less creative job than camerawork – though there is still a creative side to the job, especially in senior roles. In this department, you are responsible for the enormous wealth of electrical lights that may be used to work on a production, be they in the comfort of the studio or on a gloomy day on location. To do the job, you are likely to be a qualified electrician or electrical engineer.

Again, the best bet is to build your experience. You could start off as a **lighting assistant**, which basically means running errands and climbing the scaffolding to help the lighting operator; in this job, you will see at first hand what the different members of the lighting team do. As your career progresses, you will set up the equipment, and operate the lighting consoles as necessary. After years of experience, you may finally become a **lighting director**, whose role is similar to that of a lighting cameraman (see previous section).

On films, the lighting operator may be called the **gaffer**, and the assistant the **best boy**: as is clear from the nomenclature, these jobs are still mostly done by men.

There are also two manual/technical jobs connected with lighting (and indeed other parts of production): the **rigger**, who sorts out the necessary scaffolding, and the **crane**, who operates a crane. Again, health and safety awareness is an important part of the job.

Sound

Sound is an essential element of both radio and television. In radio, of course, it is the whole point of the broadcast: while in television, the job of recording sound and maintaining vital sound links is crucial to the success of the team. As in other technical roles, the way to get on is to increase your experience by working through the ranks.

In television, your first job will often be as a **sound assistant**. This is effectively your apprenticeship: you may help to carry and set up equipment as necessary, ensure presenters can receive earpiece instructions from the gallery, and other everyday tasks. You will often then progress to becoming a **boom operator** – that is, the person who holds or controls a microphone, usually on an extendable "boom

The sound recordist

Name: **Al Green**
Current job: **freelance sound recordist and sound editor**

What was your first job in broadcasting?
Sound assistant on the detective series, 99-1.

How did you get the job?
A placement from film school – then I worked on the second series, for low money.

What did the job involve? What was it like?
Assisting the sound recordist and boom operator. It was quite uninvolving at times, and I wasn't really that good at it. But I got to work with very experienced and

talented technicians, who I learnt a lot from.

What were your educational qualifications at the time?
I had just left film school (NFTS). I was already educated to degree level, but in sociology.

What experience did you have before starting work?
I did an evening class, an advanced TV workshop at Sussex University – a good introduction, but limited. I managed to get into film school on the back of that.

How did your career progress after your first job?
Slowly. I wanted to do documentary-style work, and took a long time building up the contacts and work.

What are you doing at work this week?
A sound dub on a film I did the recording for. It's about a blind motorcyclist who broke the

world land speed record for the blind – 165mph!

I just got back from making a documentary for the Discovery Channel in Namibia, about the Himba tribe.

I also did a corporate shoot for a government agency, and a comedy video. it's been really varied.

What advice would you have for anyone thinking of a career in broadcasting?
I've always tried to work with people I like, and I've avoided doing jobs that I didn't feel were what I wanted to do. I've ended up doing temping if I didn't have any film work, rather than chasing work with clients that I didn't feel were right for me. That makes for slow progress, maybe, but it could be worth it in the long run.

47

The vision mixer

Name: **Ben Burdon**
Current job: **supervising senior vision-mixer, BSkyB**

What was your first job in TV?

Coming from a theatrical family, I always found myself "backstage" – whether it was helping to move the scenery at a summer season show on a pier at Blackpool, or running around at Thames TV in Teddington calling the artistes. But my first real job in TV must have been as a runner on the newsdesk at the newly formed Sky News in 1989.

What was it like?

"Teas and coffees, anyone?" It was a foot in the door. For a student who had one more year to go at university, it was a summer spent making contacts and finding out as much about the industry as possible. I really needed to get my head into my college books, but I knew that the time spent at Sky would be far more beneficial for my future career.

What were your qualifications at the time?

O-levels, A-levels and a degree in English and European literature from Essex University – but ultimately the time I spent bunking off to the computer labs, and late nights tinkering with a raft of the earliest personal computers, have proven the greatest educational resource for me.

What broadcasting experience did you have before your first job?

I ticked all the usual boxes at university: helped with the campus radio station, was involved with the embryonic video camera club, appeared in university stage productions. Everything that you should have on a pristine college leaver's CV, and therefore everything that everyone else has on their own CV! So I can only put it down to the fact that I was able to drop a few pertinent Sky names that my CV was saved from drowning in a sea of paper, and landed me an interview and a permanent version of the same job that I had left at the end of the previous summer.

How did your career progress?

I took it as a compliment that most people at Sky News asked me when I was moving on from running. I wrote and voiced packages for Sky News, mostly soft sports stories or fodder that could be dropped as easily as the proverbial dead donkey. Yet my path was diverted from journalism by the bright lights of the vision-mixing desk and the lure of the graphics computers. The studio was manned by a skeleton crew after midnight, and this afforded me the opportunity to vision mix for the overnight director, and I spent several months learning the intricacies of what is now, by comparison, a very basic Grass Valley switcher.

But it wasn't until one night in August 1991 that both Boris Yeltsin and I became big news stories in our own different ways. I was sitting at home watching live on Sky News the drama unfurling in the USSR as Yeltsin stood on the turret of a tank in defiance of a coup attempt in front of the White House in Russia. It occurred to me that it was unlikely that the evening vision mixer would have had a break during such a busy night of news, so at 1am I got into my car and drove to work. Sure enough the vision mixer had been going for eight hours solid and she was almost in tears because she had not been able to move from the desk. When the head of news asked the head of studios how they were going to get another vision mixer to come in at 2am, I took a deep breath and held up my hand. My heart was racing but I managed to mix for three hours, guided by the head news director until the morning VM took over. The next day I was called to talk to the head of news, and was rewarded with his thanks and a trainee vision mixer's position.

I spent four more years in Sky News and became the senior vision mixer. After that I moved around several companies until I found myself back at Sky, this time in the studio operations department heading up a team of 16 staff VMs.

What are you doing at work this week?
There's no Premiership or Champions League football to cover at the moment, but looking after the needs of a team of vision mixers keeps me extremely busy. This week I have organised training sessions for some of our junior staff, upgraded and tested the software in one of our mixers, attended meetings about the new football season, and met with the British head of a Japanese electronics company to discuss the future of vision mixing equipment. And late on Friday, at the end of a busy week when everyone else gets to wind down, I shall be cutting the final of a "million dollar" poker tournament – 18 cameras frantically covering every movement of six professional poker players, only Sky would

attempt to cover such an event live! – But I suppose that's why I put up with the hours.

What advice would you give?
As a graduate in English/European literature who is practically obsessed by computers, my advice would have to be to keep your options and your mind open. Try to be attuned to the creative processes behind the programming as well as the intricacies of its technical requirements.

"

"Teas and coffees, anyone?" It was a foot in the door

Ben Burdon

arm", often dangling just out of shot. Next, you may be a **sound recordist** – the person responsible for actually recording the sound in synchronicity with the camera: to do the job, you need a good understanding of the directions in which different microphones will record, and what recording levels you should use in different conditions. Finally, you may be a **sound supervisor** or **sound director** – that is, the person creatively responsible for the overall sound of a large production.

Sound editing, meanwhile, is usually handled in post-production; see page 39 for the full range of post-production roles.

In radio, job titles are very different from TV. Because sound is the essence of radio, and radio teams are very small, a lot of the everyday sound recording is handled by the production team. The **studio manager**, for example, is a technical/production role, roughly similar to that of a technical operator in television – see page 35 for more advice on that. A **radio engineer**, meanwhile, is responsible for managing a full range of computer and technical equipment, and providing back-up where necessary; to do the job, you will probably be qualified in electrical engineering.

In the gallery

Within the gallery (the control room) of a TV production, there are usually a number of general technical roles. Job titles include the **technical operators** and their assistants, whose role is to perform a huge range of different functions – usually preparing, operating and managing the software that monitors the picture quality, records sound and so on. To do the job, you need excellent computer skills and will normally have an engineering qualification.

The most complex gallery job is performed by the **vision mixer**, who usually works on a complex TV production such as a rolling news service or a sporting event. As a vision mixer, you are the person immediately responsible for what appears in screen at any time. At a football match covered by many cameras, for example, your job is to switch from camera to camera as the action progresses, under supervision of the director – so you need quick reactions, good eyesight, and a good working relationship with the rest of the production team. You will also be responsible for putting on screen the different graphics that the production might use.

One of the benefits of gallery work is that you will usually be employed by a studio or broadcaster to work on a range of different productions; according to Skillset, only about one in seven people in "technical and studio operations" are freelance.

Broadcast journalism

So you want to be a broadcast journalist? Congratulations: you've been seduced by the most demanding, most competitive part of the media there is. Wherever you want to work – in radio or TV, local journalism or national, for a commercial broadcaster or for the BBC – it will be a tough challenge for you to break in.

Why is broadcast journalism so hard to get into? Because broadcast journalism is really two jobs: journalism, and broadcasting. This means that not only do you have to be brilliant at finding and researching stories – a people person, in other words, with an insatiable curiosity about the world you live in, and a growing contacts book of everyone you've ever come across at work – but you also need to be a good storyteller, who is comfortable on air or on camera, and can find the language, sound and pictures to get your points across. Most people find it hard enough to do one well; but to do both takes rare talent – not to mention the commitment and determination to do it all again the next day and the day after that. Little wonder that editors and producers are picky about those who apply.

Ways in

If you want to get on in broadcast journalism, your first major goal should be to find a job as a **reporter**. This is because most production in broadcast journalism is done by the people who find the stories themselves – so there is no separate journalistic "production route", other than becoming a radio researcher or similar (see radio production). The traditional way to start off is as a reporter in local radio; this is probably still the best grounding for a career in TV, as it gives you the chance to get the broadest possible experience as early as possible in your career. Other entry points these days include 24-hour news channels and news agencies; and of course many broadcast journalists are in fact experienced newspaper reporters.

To get yourself that coveted reporter's job, you have two main options: you can find work experience, and you can do a course accredited by the BJTC (Broadcast Journalism Training Council). Of these, only the work experience is absolutely essential: editors and producers are looking for signs that you have been in a broadcast environment before, and can also demonstrate your passion and commitment to radio or TV. To maximise your chances of getting work experience, the best thing to do is start small: hospital radio is the traditional starting point, but in recent years there has been a marked increase in the number of student and community radio stations too. You could also apply for a placement at a BBC local radio station (see www.bbc.co.uk/jobs); but remember, the larger the broadcaster, the greater the competition, so the more formal the process you will normally have to get through. See page 72 for how to get the best out of work experience when you get it.

A BJTC course also comes highly recommended, not only because it teaches you basic broadcast journalism skills, but because it will help you get work experience. There is a wide range of courses available: turn to page 165 of this book to have a flick through what is on offer, and to page 78 for a guide to getting the best out of it. Remember that new courses are always appearing: City University, for example, started a "current affairs journalism" course in 2002, for students who want to produce more in-depth, analytical reports. Whichever course you choose, make sure it covers enough of the basic vocational skills that you think you will need.

There is also a highly competitive BBC broadcast journalist trainee scheme.

Over the last few months I've been accosted by the American secret service, had my hair set on fire by a hot air balloon and got stuck down Europe's deepest mine

Jonathan Swingler

Radio reporting

Although radio and TV reporting are very different worlds, they share important common ground. Most of the basic skills you need to be a reporter will enable you to get by in both – so if you want to be a TV reporter, you should certainly read this section too.

The first skill you need in any local radio job – and indeed, when applying for any job in journalism – is to understand the needs of the audience. So you need to be **steeped in media**. So keep up to date: you need to be someone who reads all the local newspapers and catches all the local news bulletins; this way you will know what issues are exercising local people most. Make a point of recording all the different local radio bulletins in your area; that way you will get a sense of who the typical listener to each programme is. Follow the national press too: many story ideas that you come up with may be local takes on issues of national concern.

In order to initiate and follow up story ideas, you also need good **research skills**. You should know how to use wire services, cuttings files, libraries, the internet and more, so that you are reading not just today's news but the archives of what has gone before. Even more importantly, you need to be constantly building personal contacts, be they on the phone, over lunch or in the pub: so keep a contacts book, and keep it backed up. Remember everyone is a potential contact; whether they are a friend of a friend, or someone a colleague may know. You can buy the latest copy of the MediaGuardian Media Directory, which lists 6,000 of the everyday phone numbers that journalists and researchers need. A BJTC course may also be helpful with contacts, as it gives you an overview of how public life works, and which public officials do what.

One of the most important skills you need in local radio reporting is the ability to **conduct an interview**. Before you get any job, you should be well practised at interviewing using simple equipment such as a portable microphone and digital recorder. This could be done over the phone, but people tend to open up more if you have time to interview

The radio reporter

Name: **Jonathan Swingler**
Current job: **reporter, BBC Radio Cleveland, on board the BBC Bus**

What was your first job in broadcasting?
The first time I ever got paid for hanging about a radio station was at Scot FM. I'd been sent out to report on anticapitalist protestors kicking up a fuss on the streets of Edinburgh. So what did I find? Nothing. But as I was about to phone the editor, the bomb squad were kind enough to turn up and close off the main street. One of the shops had received a suspicious package and so within a few minutes I was doing a live report on the lunchtime news programme. Looking back on it I probably sounded a bit overexcited – a good imitation of Alan Partridge on speed. Of course the "bomb" turned out to be nothing.

How did you get the job?
I'd done some work experience so I'd been given a few paid shifts. Working freelance is a little like treading water, but it does give you the opportunity to work in a few different places.

What did the job involve? What was it like?
I'd only worked a few shifts there. At the same time I managed to get a bit of freelance work at BBC Radio Scotland, which was all good experience.

What were your educational qualifications at the time?
I was doing a politics degree at Edinburgh University so it wasn't anything specifically aimed at broadcast news. After the freelance work I did a postgraduate course in journalism at Cardiff University.

What experience did you have before starting work?
I mucked about on student publications for a while. It was a good laugh interviewing bands playing at the student union. I had no formal training at first but you quickly pick up skills on the job.

How did your career progress after your first job?
During my postgraduate course I worked as a reporter for BBC Radio Newcastle, and after that I worked as a TV reporter for Tyne Tees Television. I was then offered a job on the BBC Bus at BBC Radio Cleveland. It's absolutely mad but great fun. Over the last few months I've been accosted by the American secret service, had my hair set on fire by a hot air balloon and got stuck down Europe's deepest mine.

What are you doing at work this week?
Being hyper! We've just won two Sony Awards, one of which was a gold for our coverage of George W Bush's visit here in November 2003. Plus I've been doing a bit of research on stories I'll be reporting on next week.

What advice would you have for anyone thinking of a career in broadcasting?
Get to know the industry well, make contacts, listen to lots of radio, watch lots of TV news and know what you want to do. Editors receive stacks of vague emails from students saying they want to work in the media, so you need to be precise on what you can offer a station.

them in person. Before conducting any interview, though, you should do as much research as you can about your subject, and then prepare open-ended questions that will get your subject talking. During the interview, you need to be good at coaxing out interesting answers: so if the subject is reticent, you need to be good at putting them at their ease with background questioning; but if they are evasive, you need to be strong enough to ask the incisive follow-up questions. If the interview is recorded, you should be thinking at this stage about what the final broadcast is going to sound like: you need to be a good listener, so that you can ask further questions as they suggest themselves to you. Whenever the interviewee says something interesting enough to use later, note the position on the disc or tape; and try not to wrap up the interview until you have the material you need.

You probably won't have good enough recording equipment to do it at home, but to be a good radio reporter, you also need to be good at identifying the background sounds that illustrate the point of your piece – such sounds will enliven even short pieces of radio journalism.

Once you have recorded an interview, you need to be able to edit it. Editing is primarily about selecting those passages of the audio that get the subject's point across faithfully, in the shortest possible time. This can be time-consuming work: but it is also instructive, because it is inevitably when you edit a piece of audio that you begin to notice the questions you should have asked. On the technical side, it is useful when looking for work experience to have practised editing interviews on your computer at home: to do this, you could download an audio editor from a website such as Download.com. Connect your digital or analogue recorder to your computer with a cable from any hardware store.

Although not all broadcast journalists have the skill, it is also useful to have shorthand. Sure, most of your interviews will be on tape – but there may be times when a contact either refuses to be recorded, or you don't have the right equipment with you. In these cases, having a good standard of Teeline shorthand is an invaluable backup. The downside is that shorthand takes a long time to learn properly – many journalism courses or evening classes teach it, or you can buy a coursebook and practise at home.

The final skills, and the most high-profile, are writing, editing and talking; in short, the **storytelling**. To be a good writer for radio, you need to be able to sum up the point of any story – the who, what, where, when, how and above all why – in as few words as possible. Unlike in newspapers, these might not necessarily be in the first words of your report – it is usually better to "set up" your key points to maintain interest right through to the end, as you would when telling a story in conversation; and also, just as in conversation, it is good to use lots of short sentences instead of one long one. Remember, good journalism is about putting the listener first – so you must always ask yourself: if I were the listener, what would I want to know? Never underestimate the listener's intelligence. Links and cues, meanwhile, are a skill of their own: you need to write them in such a way that whet the appetite of the listener, without giving away the point of what is to be broadcast next. In each case, you may only have a few seconds to get your point across: so your English must be concise and direct. Use active verbs when you can, cut out the adjectives and adverbs, and don't say anything that doesn't need to be said, or raises questions to which you can't give a satisfactory answer.

Finally, you need to be comfortable on the radio, and have a good broadcasting voice. Read the presenting section on page 59 for tips: although, to sum up, the key is to know who your typical listener is, and always have him or her in mind both when writing and when on air. If you have a voice creamy enough to drag a cat from its food, so much the better; but even if you don't, your listeners will appreciate it if you take the time to speak with poise and clarity. This, of course, means you have to be even better at editing your words down to make your broadcast fit the time available: but it is far better than rushing or garbling your broadcast, which will only confuse your listener.

TV reporting

TV reporting has one very significant difference to radio reporting: pictures. To be a good TV reporter, you need to be good at telling stories in images as well as in language; which means you are not merely reporting on the news, but you are often also showing the news and setting it in context with your report.

This emphasis on pictures will have a great effect on your working life as a TV reporter. First, you may find that your news values alter from those of a newspaper or radio reporter: put simply, a story is less of a story if you do not have the pictures to tell it with. Second, you have to be prepared to work long hours: if you are going to get the pictures you need, then you always need to be in the right place at the right time – and then you may have to spend time editing your packages or doing live pieces to camera. Third, you need to be good at working in a team; you may have a camera crew working with you, in which case you need to be able to both lead them journalistically and take advice from them too; but even if you are shooting your own pictures, you still need to be in constant communication with the programme editor to make sure you are getting the kind of sequence he or she wants.

Visual storytelling is not an easy skill to learn. Before working in TV news, it is helpful to have had some experience operating some kind of lightweight camera yourself; at least this will give you a sense of the complexity of the job. Broadly speaking, you need to find the pictures that at best show the news first-hand, or at least illustrate the story you are trying to tell. Then, you will employ different kinds of shot in order to give your sequence a sense of visual development. So a wide shot of a location will set the scene for the viewer, and give a sense of perspective to your piece; a close-up will give a sense of immediacy, so the viewers feel as if they are experiencing the scene almost at first hand; and a medium shot, somewhere in between, will give enough width to show individual action. The skill, which you must master to be a good TV reporter, is to build these different kinds of shot into a unified whole.

Pictures, of course, are nothing without context. So in TV as in radio, you need to have clear, concise writing skills and a good broadcasting voice; but this time your words must work in conjunction with the images the viewer sees. Your writing does not have to be as explicit as it would be for a radio report; you can let the pictures tell the story where they can, but you must never keep the viewer guessing as to what a picture is or means. Other than that, reread the section on radio reporting: many of the same principles apply to TV.

The reporter/presenter

Name: **Caroline Richardson**

Current job: **assistant editor, BBC South Today, reporting and presenting bulletins for TV**

What was your first job in broadcasting?
Broadcast journalist, BBC Radio Stoke.

How did you get the job?
I went there on a college placement - they then gave me freelance shifts which soon became a permanent staff post.

What did the job involve?
Mainly reporting to start, then bulletin reading. It was very hard work, for low pay, for a tyrannical editor with very high standards. An excellent training ground – and one that has set me up with the stamina and skills that keep me going today!

What were your educational qualifications at the time?
I had just finished my postgrad diploma in broadcast journalism at the London College of Printing. I also had a degree in French and politics.

What broadcasting experience did you do before starting work?
Apart from the college attachment at BBC Radio Stoke, I had done some work experience at BBC Midlands Today and at the commercial radio station in Birmingham, BRMB. I was also a trainee researcher on DayTime TV for the year before my postgrad course, to earn money to pay for the course.

How did your career progress after your first job?
I stayed at Radio Stoke for three years, then saw adverts for journalists at BBC South. I went to BBC Radio Solent as a radio journalist reading bulletins – then had an attachment in the TV newsroom for South Today (they share the same building). I went back to Solent as news editor for three months, then back to TV to start production

shifts of smaller lunchtime and late-night bulletins. I became a district reporter and starting presenting news bulletins. I have recently been promoted to assistant editor, newsgathering.

What are you doing at work this week?
Presenting live from Portsmouth in the run-up to the D-Day commemorations in France.

What advice would you have for anyone thinking of a career in TV?
Get plenty of work experience. Listen to criticism and feedback. Be tenacious and thick-skinned.

Don't plot your entire career – doors will open in unusual places, and unexpected opportunities will present themselves, so don't let them pass you by. Remember, not everyone can be the Washington correspondent!

The regional correspondent

Name: **Michelle May**
Current job: **north of England correspondent, Sky News**

What was your first job in broadcasting?
Freelancing for Channel One TV in Liverpool, briefly. I think freelancing is good way in. My first contract job was as a part-time journalist for Lite AM radio in Manchester.

How did you get the job?
For Lite AM, I was living in Liverpool looking for work and sent my CV to lots of radio stations. They took me on quite quickly.

What did the job involve? What was it like?
It was very early morning till around 2.30pm. It was a very small radio station with few news resources. I would work alone writing a few stories up from wires, IRN and from local sources – then read the national and local news on the hour and sport on the half-hour. It was good money and helped me develop news judgement and improve my voice. It started as just a weekend job, but gradually I got more shifts. The early starts were painful, especially as I was commuting from Liverpool – but I really enjoyed it.

What were your educational qualifications at the time?
Nine GCSEs, three A-levels; BA in journalism, film and broadcasting from Cardiff University; postgraduate diploma in broadcast journalism from Cardiff Journalism School, Cardiff University.

What broadcasting experience did you do before starting work?
The Cardiff diploma organised great work experience opportunities during the course. I spent time at BBC Wales and Channel One London where I worked as a VJ for two weeks. The course was very practical with lots of package making.

How did your career progress after your first job?
I started freelancing for regional Granada TV news whilst also working for Lite AM. After six months I got a job as an off-screen journalist for Granada. This was all the responsibilities of a reporter, but my face wasn't allowed on TV! After 18 months I applied successfully as on-screen Liverpool reporter. I gave up Lite AM and Granada moved me to the main Manchester office where I stayed for another three years doing lots of major stories and occasionally newsreading. I particularly enjoyed live TV, and answered a Guardian ad for Sky News. I was thrilled to be taken on as north of England correspondent in January 2004.

What are you doing at work this week?
Very varied. So far, reports and lives in Oldham on Gordon Brown's comprehensive spending review, and a fun piece on Harrison Ford's canal holiday in Wales!

What advice would you have for anyone thinking of a career in TV?
If you're sure, then start as young as you can. My first job was as a teenage runner at my local newspaper – a background in print media is well respected. There are so many people wanting to get into TV – you need to get as much experience as possible.
Be flexible: I moved to the north of England without work because I knew it was a busy news patch and was prepared to risk it.
Although it is not always essential, I would recommend a journalism qualification.
Know that it's not glamorous! It's hard work and long hours but extremely rewarding, and everyone you know will quiz you about your job!

> Know that it's not glamorous! It's hard work and long hours but extremely rewarding

Needless to say, to be a TV reporter, you also need to be confident in front of the camera. That doesn't mean you have to have a pretty face: it just means you have to be an effective on-screen communicator, who is just as happy reporting on live TV as you are putting a recorded package together. Above all, you need to be yourself. Acting naturally on live TV can be nerve-racking, so if you don't think you can do it, maybe broadcast journalism isn't for you: consider working in print journalism or documentary production instead. Conversely, don't love the camera too much: being on screen day after day can give you authority, but it can also be irritating to the viewer. Use pieces to camera only where you or the editor want that first-hand, walk-me-through touch.

Finally, one of the best ways to understand TV news is to watch a lot of it – so again, you need to be **steeped in TV**. Get to know its strengths, its weaknesses, and its absurdities. Set your video to record all tonight's evening news bulletins, on all the major radio and television channels, including those broadcasting 24-hour news; then tomorrow morning, watch and listen to them all. Look out for how different channels make different decisions about what the stories are, according to the markets they face; but also try to pick out which reports were too bloated, or so short they left you wanting to know more.

Up the career ladder

In TV or radio news, there are two or three ways for your career to progress. First, you can keep reporting for as long as you can: if you love reporting and don't want to get into middle management, this is the way to go. Your goal, on this career route, is both to become a **correspondent** – which means you will be reporting on an individual specialism such as business news or international news – and to join a major broadcaster. If you choose this route, you can do the job as long as editors or viewers can stand the your face: but remember, ageism is rife in the media, so you may one day find yourself ousted by cheaper, less experienced talent. The goal is to make yourself indispensable.

Your second option is to climb the news chain. If you do this, you could become the **editor** of a programme or bulletin – in other words, the person who decides what stories or issues to cover. As an editor, you need all the skills of a TV producer (page 19) plus the ability to manage breaking news, direct presenters and shuffle running orders as you see fit. You will usually spend the eight to 12 hours before your bulletin advising your reporters and correspondents, reviewing packages shortly before they go out, and editing presenters' scripts. To do the job, you need to be a hard-working and experienced news journalist with good leadership and organisation skills. If you excel as an editor, you could go on to be a **series editor** or **executive editor** or join a large broadcaster – or both, in which case your job will be as much about budgets and policy as it is about hard news.

Presenting

Everyone wants to be a TV or radio presenter – and no wonder. As a presenter, you are the key to the success of a programme; the link between the programme-makers and the audience, the expert communicator who puts their face, or a voice, to the show. And as a presenter, you are also incredibly lucky – because it is without doubt one of the most enjoyable, challenging and sought-after jobs in the world.

To do the job well, you need an extraordinary range of skills. You need the confidence to "carry" a programme – be it with the authority of a radio newscaster, the boundless energy of a children's TV presenter, or some mixture of both. You need excellent communication

The radio DJ

Name: **Clare Lloyd**
Current job: **Red Dragon FM Mid-morning show presenter**

What was your first job in broadcasting?
Researcher at BBC TV Centre in London. My first professional presenting job was at Bath FM.

How did you get the job?
I made a demo from an RSL (see radio glossary, page 32) I had been a part of on and off for two years, and sent it out to 27 radio stations around the country. I had four positive replies but no secure offer – until I depped over Easter 2000 in Bath and was then offered a full-time job on the strength of that.

What did the job involve? What was it like?
Presenting the 5.30pm to midnight show for eight months, then the drivetime show for four months! It was very scary to start with, but then great. So, interviews, promoting the station competitions, running a talent competition for new bands in the area – and lots of music. I had to learn the technical equipment too, which was quite daunting to begin with.

What were your educational qualifications at the time? Did you do a course?
No: just A-levels in English lit, English language, then experience followed. I'm not saying this is the right way, but it certainly is a way.

What experience did you have before starting work?
Hospital radio presenting.

How did your career progress after your first job?
I moved to Red Dragon FM, and did overnight shift and weekend shifts. Then I took on the evening slot and now am on mid-mornings. So, very well indeed in an orderly fashion, really!

What are you doing at work this week?
Two competitions. One which is called "birthday bongs", where listeners win money, and a competition with Cif cleaning fluid where a listener wins a cleaner for a day or a year. Also the usual showbiz stuff and a request slot.

What advice would you have for anyone thinking of a career in broadcasting?
Go for it and put all your heart and soul into it. Very competitive! Love it and you will go far.

skills: both the kind you might find useful at a cocktail party (prodigious memory, a bit of sex appeal, the ability to think on your feet or ad-lib, the ability to judge a mood) and the kind you would not (ability to read from a script or autocue, to talk when a producer is shouting in your ear, to know which camera is pointing at you when). Most difficult of all – and this is where the talent really lies – you need to be able to exercise all your skills while looking and sounding as if it is the most natural thing in the world.

If that sounds like you, then good luck; and you will need it, because you are not even halfway there. The number of people with the potential to be a good presenter, sad to say, outstrips the number of presenting jobs; and partly for that reason, almost no presenting jobs are publicly advertised. Some vacancies are filled by resorting to a talent agency; but to get a good talent agent, you need to have presenting experience already, which isn't much use if you're only just starting out. Others are filled by employing people who already work in TV or radio in another capacity: so if you really want to be a

The news anchor

Name: **Jon Snow**
Current job: **presenter, Channel 4 News (ITN)**

What was your first job in TV?
Reporter for ITN, 1976.

How did you get the job?
Nepotism – or that's what I feared, as my cousin Peter already worked there.

What did the job involve? What was it like?
I had done three years in radio, and I didn't know one end of a TV camera from the other. I was asked to do some arts piece for the early evening news: allocated one minute 30 seconds, I came in at four minutes … it was a disaster. There was no training of any sort, no mentoring, and every interest in seeing this arrogant upstart fail!

What were your educational qualifications at the time?
I had no degree – I'd been sent down following an anti-apartheid sit-in. There were no media courses; even if there had been, I wouldn't have been accepted on one.

What experience did you have before starting work?
Radio newscasting and reporting, home and abroad.

How did your career progress after your first job?
Well I'm still with the same company, but on a different channel.

What are you doing at work this week?
Toiling to get a good programme on the air and be a constructive part of it.

What advice would you have for anyone thinking of a career in TV or radio?
Go for it! It's the one profession where you make your own luck … the sky is the limit, and the "s" is not a capital letter.

presenter, then you could do worse than read all the other chapters of this book. Still others are filled by looking through showreels or listening to demo tapes; but while a good showreel is a stepping stone, most producers are bombarded with them from hundreds of people who think the same thing. In all, to get your break, you need to be more than just talented: you need to cover all the options, and be ruthlessly persistent in your pursuit of your goal.

Almost all the advice given in section four of this book – the 10-step plan to getting your broadcasting job – is especially relevant to presenting. Read through it carefully. You will never, of course, get to present a programme without researching it thoroughly (step two); networking is vital too, because the job is all about putting on a public face (step one). Considering a niche is also useful (step eight), because knowledge of a subject – DIY or gardening, in the present

The BBC presenter

Name: **Jeremy Vine**
Current job: **presenter, BBC1 Politics Show and Radio 2's Jeremy Vine Show**

The first thing I had to do, on the first day, was chase a convicted flasher through the city centre to point him out to our photographer.

What were your educational qualifications at the time?
A degree in English literature from Durham University, with, strangely, philosophy bolted on.

What was your first job in journalism/broadcasting?
Trainee reporter, Coventry Evening Telegraph.

How did you get the job?
There was a fire drill during my job interview, and the editor was embarrassed enough to offer me the job as consolation.

What did the job involve? What was it like?
Court cases and football. It was fun, and a constant revelation.

What journalism/ broadcasting experience did you do before starting work?
Lots of student journalism – and Metro Radio, where I played records from two to five in the morning while a student.

How did your career progress after your first job?
I got into the Beeb as a news trainee; and then the editor of the Today programme, Phil Harding, offered me a reporting job after a trial run where I was

attacked with a plank of wood in Carnaby Street by a storekeeper selling Nazi regalia.

What are you doing at work this week?
For Radio 2, having a run in a jeep powered by vegetable oil. For the Politics Show on BBC1, interviewing John Reid on why nobody trusts the government. And going to a leaving do for George Entwistle, who dreamt up the Newsnight van.

What advice would you have for anyone thinking of a career in journalism?
Never take no for an answer. And if you're shot at, duck. That saved my life in the former Yugoslavia.

climate – will help you stand out from the crowd. A short course is handy (step five), not least because it may help you put together a showreel or demo tape at the end of it; and of course that showreel or demo tape (step six) is a critical step in itself.

Experience is, of course, essential, not just because of what you learn, but because of what you can put on your showreel and your CV; but as far as what kind of experience you get is concerned, there is no set route. As a budding radio presenter, you should probably try to DJ on hospital radio or student radio, at the same time as networking and working on your demo tape – although some people just concentrate on getting any radio job, on the basis that it gives them an income and a launchpad to success. As a budding TV presenter, there is student TV; but there is also corporate video, and then any number of the hundreds of smaller multichannel stations that are being launched all the time – shopping channels, for example. Again, some people will find that working up from the bottom as a runner is a good way in.

Never take no for an answer. And if you're shot at, duck

Jeremy Vine

Scriptwriting

Most people have, at some stage, considered devoting their lives to scriptwriting. And no wonder, when the mythology of the job is so seductive. Here is a role, you think, that involves nothing more than a laptop, pen and paper and a brain: surely I can do that? I can get up when I want; spend the morning moping around in search of inspiration, crafting my ideas into brilliant scripts in the afternoon; in the evenings I can send my pitches to the best producers in the business, and wait for the commissions to arrive. What better way can there be to earn a living?

The reality, of course, is that there could hardly be a worse way. First, it is usually only the creative broadcast genres, drama and comedy, that demand specialist scriptwriters; so the demand for your work is inevitably reduced. Second, unless you are at the top of your profession, scriptwriting is hardly ever lucrative – especially in radio, where you will usually start. To learn the craft, moreover, takes a vast investment in time: and time spent learning to write scripts, of course, is time you could be spending earning a living. Only if you cannot imagine yourself doing anything else – if the long hours and financial worries seem a small price to pay for the chance to express yourself on air and on screen – should you even consider it.

That's the health warning. Needless to say, you're going to ignore it and have a go anyway – so here are the tips and skills you need, and the strategies you should use to get ahead if you can.

Skills you need

To be a good scriptwriter, you need to be several kinds of people in one. You need to be creative but also organised; a talented storyteller, but also a disciplined learner; good at research, but also good at knowing when you have researched enough; and, last but not least, good at writing. If you have that little lot, then the only other attribute you need is luck.

You will notice that I listed **creativity** first. In practice, this means you need to be a lateral thinker; a person to whom good ideas suggest themselves all the time. This is not so much so that you can come up with ideas for projects – useful, but not an unusual skill – but so that you can solve the myriad creative problems that a project will inevitably throw up. Scriptwriting is usually a process of trial and error, in which you have to produce 50 or more different ideas for a character or a scene before you find one that works: the better you are at having these ideas, the better you are at writing scripts. As the script develops, moreover, your scenes, conflicts and plots will begin to exist in a fragile equilibrium, in which any minor change disrupts the whole; but as you are writing and revising you will often have to make changes, so you will need 50 more ideas to get the whole

The scriptwriter

Name: **Gillian Richmond**
Current job: **freelance TV/radio scriptwriter, EastEnders core team writer**

What was your first scriptwriting job? What was it like?
My first TV commission was for The Bill, closely followed by a commission for EastEnders. My first radio commission came a month or so earlier when I was asked to write for the Archers. I juggled the three jobs alongside a commission for a new stage play and a part-time job teaching in Hackney. Mostly what I remember from that period was feeling very tired. I also remember the producers and script editors at all three shows being very supportive and patient. I was very lucky.

How did you get the job?
All three shows contacted me via my agent, after I'd had a well-reviewed stage play produced at the Soho Theatre.

What were your educational qualifications at the time?
I had a BA in economics and politics, which was, and remains, completely irrelevant.

This was the 80s. I wasn't aware at the time of there being any screenwriting courses, and wouldn't have thought them appropriate in any case, as I was writing for the stage. I had been involved in writers' workshops at the Soho Theatre. I have subsequently skimmed through a book or two on screenwriting and, I think about 10 years ago, went on a weekend Robert McKee course. Apart from that it's been training on the job.

What experience did you have before starting work?
After leaving university I first worked as an usher at the National Theatre and saw every play several times. I then worked in Wales, Devon and London in Theatre in education, community theatre and community arts, before moving into supply teaching as a way to fund my writing.

How did your career progress after your first job?
Each year has followed a similar pattern of working simultaneously in popular drama while also developing original work – usually to commission. I have written for many popular TV drama series and serials including, in no particular order, Eldorado, Casualty, Maisie Raine, Heartbeat and Silent Witness. I've also had several radio plays produced and, in the early years

before I had children, also continued to write for the theatre.

What are you doing this week?
For a few years now I have been a core writer at EastEnders, and this week I have been working on the second drafts of a pair of episodes which will be shown in the autumn. In addition I have been thinking about how to respond to a request for a series idea from the BBC; contemplating how to develop further a TV script the BBC commissioned and then passed on; and trying not to think about a novel I have bubbling away in a desk drawer.

What advice would you have for anyone thinking of a career in scriptwriting?
Depends what sort of scriptwriting. In popular TV drama, I'd probably say don't write for a show unless you actually like it, and never knowingly patronise your audience. In developing original work I'd say try to find your own distinctive voice. In all cases, I'd advise trying to make good strong creative relationships. Producers and editors usually [not always, but usually] just want to make your work better. Try to accept their notes as assistance not criticism.

shebang functioning once more. Few people have this skill; and if you don't, you will find it hard to succeed.

Creativity, of course, must come with rigorous **organisation**. You *do* have to get up in the morning to be a writer: if you don't, you will find you have run out of money before you have written anything. To be good at storyboarding – that is, creating the complex story structures that make any drama plausible – then either you need a prodigiously algebraic brain, or you need to be able to organise your thoughts clearly using index cards, files, storyboarding software, or a similar system. To create consistent and plausible characters, meanwhile, you need to do an inordinate amount of in-depth research, which also needs to be recorded in an organised way.

Most crucially, you need to be good at **storytelling**. If you are a pub raconteur who is famous for shaggy-dog stories or jokes, then it's true, you do have a head start, because you already have an innate sense of story structure: when to release information and when to withhold it, how to make the whole serve the ending, and so on. For the rest of us, it's a skill we have to learn. It is useful to go on a scriptwriting course: this will teach you the principles of story structure, which should be learned but sometimes ignored. Put crudely, a story may develop from an **inciting incident**, when something happens that causes a character to react; and thanks to this reaction, the character will encounter conflicts or obstacles that raise the stakes further and further, increasing the dramatic tension until the final **climax**, in which the story is resolved and the audience cries. A scriptwriting course will tell you how to divide this story into acts, scenes and at the lowest level "beats", each of which serve to crank up the tension as you go along; it will teach you that throughout the story, both the characters' conscious and unconscious reactions may be used to move the story along; and that other characters may be the subject of a **subplot** which may comment on, or give relief to, the whole. Finally, watch Adaptation, and work out whether the rules matter or not.

Of course, you must learn to **write**. Writing is a different skill from storytelling, although the two are related. A excellent standard of written will help you to write with clarity, so that the audience can get a sense of what each character is thinking. To write good dialogue, you need to have done enough research to get a sense of each character's "voice"; it is helpful to have recorded yourself speaking over the telephone, to get a sense of how people talk in lots of short, broken sentences. Finally, you need to suggest the sounds and images that will complement your writing; though you should not antagonise producers or directors by telling them how to do their jobs.

This brings us the last point: drama and comedy are team businesses, and more often than not you are just the first link in the chain. Especially in TV, your work may be redrafted substantially in order to make it more marketable or to bring it within budget; a director or producer may do this, or they may ask you to do it. Hard as it may seem, you should listen to everybody's opinions, even if you may feel as if the script is torn from your own being.

Ways in

One of the most helpful things to do if you want to get into scriptwriting is to make sure you watch a lot of TV and listen to a lot of radio, in whatever genre you want to work – be it drama or comedy, or both. This, above all, will help you get a sense of whether to work in the business or not; and it will also teach you what kind of scripts tend to get commissions, and what different markets they serve. You will quickly realise, if you didn't know it before, that one of the best ways in is BBC Radio 4, which commissions a lot of original drama; the reason being that radio drama is cheaper to make than TV, so producers who commission you are taking less of a risk.

The next thing to do is to write. Go on a course if this will give you the kick-start you need, but keep writing. If you are not actually writing, then you are not a writer, and will never be until you start. So try and get into a routine. Find a place where there is peace and quiet – the library, maybe, so that you're not always staring at that pile of washing-up – and write for a certain number of hours per day.

What do you write? Anything – but set yourself a goal. Write for a scriptwriting competition, perhaps; write a radio script for BBC Writers' Room; start on that world-beating programme idea you've been dreaming about for years. It doesn't matter what you do at the outset, because unless you a rare talent, you will be on such a steep learning curve that much of what you write is rubbish. Keep writing until you run out of money, give up, or you have something ready to pitch. It can be hard to know when this is, but the answer should be: when you think that any more time spent improving it is a waste of time for you. When this time has come, put the script in a drawer for a couple of weeks and forget all about it. When you come back to it and read it through, you will know – and you can start working on your pitch.

When you are ready, the key thing to remember is marketability. Try to sum up the concept of your script in under 30 words; try to work out who will watch it or listen to it, and why; and try to work out what format it will fill best. Then, work out if you are want to pitch to a programme maker – such as BBC Writers' Room, or an independent production company – or to an agent. (It is always helpful to have an agent if you can, because an agent has better contacts than you and can find you work; that said, they charge up to 15 per cent of your earnings plus VAT.) If you have any contacts who work in comedy or drama, you should use them: unsolicited scripts stand a very low chance of being read with care and attention, and an even lower chance of being successful.

Finally, be flexible. Your first pitch may not come off – but on the back of it, a scriptreader may notice your talent and help you to produce work that gets you that first commission. In which case you will have earned your luck.

The drama developer

Name: **Eleanor Moran**
Current job: **development executive, drama commissioning, BBC**

What was your first job in broadcasting?

A student press attachment in the Channel 4 press office. This lasted for one year, and I then became a properly paid press assistant.

How did you get the job?

I went in on work experience directly after graduating, from Sussex. The job came up, and I applied. I was interviewed along with around six others, and got it.

What did the job involve? What was it like?

I was a junior publicist for arts and music programming. The usual: organising press launches, compiling press cuttings, looking after talent, writing TV billings, placing articles.

What were your educational qualifications at the time?

A first in English from Sussex.

What relevant experience did you have before starting work?

I had temped extensively during my degree, getting loads of useful experience in places like British Screen. It gave me a grounding in the media and also meant I had good office skills.

How did your career progress after your first job?

After nearly 2 years I got a job as an assistant press officer at the BBC. By now I wanted to do something more creative. From there I got an attachement to Dangerfield as a trainee script editor. I then got taken on by United (ITV company) to script-edit series four of Where the Heart Is. I moved to Company TV, where I script-edited Nicholas Nickleby for ITV. I was then head of development at Warner Sisters for 18 months and then got a job as a script editor in independent commissioning, drama, here. In January I was promoted to a development executive role.

What are you doing at work this week?

I am managing the day-to-day running of New Tricks. The first series has been a huge hit. I put together the writing team for the second series. There are now a producer and a script editor in place at the production company, so I am overseeing it from the BBC end. I've been part of a script conference for Fingersmith, which goes into production next month. I have read various scripts as writing samples for New Tricks as well as interviewing a writer for it. I will write script notes for the latest draft of Holmes B, our follow up to Hound of the Baskervilles, also due to shoot

> **Get in to have general chats with as many people as you can**

imminently. I'm going to the theatre, partly to look out for cast. I am working on a project of my own, which I am storylining with a colleague before taking to a writer.

What advice would you have for anyone thinking of a career in TV?

Watch as much as possible, read Broadcast. Gen up as much as you can before seeing anyone (impress them by knowing about them and their organisation). Get in to have general chats with as many people as you can: hopefully they'll keep you in mind if a job comes up. If you want to get into drama, start out trying to get script-reading work. Be very careful of the secretarial route. Running is much more badly paid, but you're less likely to get pigeonholed.

However, if you can get relevant experience in the university holidays, it's absolutely invaluable. Get your office skills up to scratch and sign up with media-specific temping agencies.

The drama producer

Name: **Laura Mackie**
Current job: **head of drama serials, BBC Television**

What was your first job in broadcasting?
I worked as secretary to the art editor at the Radio Times. This included all the usual secretarial duties, but also some picture research and work with photographers and illustrators. It was a great way to get an overall sense of BBC output.

How did you get the job?
I answered an advert in the Evening Standard.

What did the job involve?
It was a very lively department, although the emphasis was obviously on the publishing side of the BBC rather than on programme-making. But it did provide an excellent entry point into the world of the BBC and gave me access to Ariel, the in-house paper, where jobs across the whole of the organisation were advertised.

What were your educational qualifications at the time?
I had a BA in English from London University and had completed a three-month secretarial course.

What experience did you have before starting work?
I'd worked briefly for a scientific publisher.

How did your career progress after your first job?
I moved across to work in radio, first as a production assistant on Stop the Week (offering cheap BBC champagne to Robert Robinson and his guests!), then worked as a researcher on The Food Programme. I took an attachment to television presentation and from there joined the production panel working as a PA across a wide range of programmes from Hi-de-Hi to the Money Programme. My aim was always to work in drama – and eventually I moved across there working on the early days of EastEnders, again as a production assistant, and on other dramas including The Green Man and Making Out. On Making Out I met writer Debbie Horsfield who encouraged my ambition to become a script editor. I script-edited on Casualty, a police series called Out of the Blue and then became a producer, then an executive producer, before moving across to LWT as deputy controller of drama. I came back to the BBC in 2001 and became head of drama serials in May of that year.

What are you doing at work this week?
Meeting writers Dick Clement and Ian La Frenais about another series of Auf Wiedersehen Pet, actor Nat Parker about his role in Inspector Lynley mysteries, watching rushes of next autumn's classic drama, North and South, and our musical drama, Blackpool.

What advice would you have for anyone thinking of a career in broadcasting?
Think about different ways of starting your career – the most obvious routes are sometimes the most over-subscribed, so be prepared to work your way up laterally and by taking unexpected opportunities.

The script editor

The script editor's job is also a fascinating one – part writer, part assistant to both producer and director on the creative side. As a **script editor**, you are responsible for scripts, from the moment manuscripts arrive on your desk to the rehearsal or production stage. You may be involved in commissioning scripts; after that, you will read scripts that are submitted, and work with writers on getting them into shape – not just according to creative requirements, but also for technical, continuity and budget reasons as well. On a long-running serial such as a soap, you will need to have a talent for keeping on top of storylines, and the anticipation to see where continuity problems are going to arise.

Usually, you can start off being a freelance **script reader** for a production company – it doesn't pay that well, but it gets you used to dealing with scripts.

Most editors will have a degree in English or a similarly analytical subject.

> Think about different ways of starting your career – the most obvious routes are sometimes the most over-subscribed
>
> Laura Mackie

The jobs : **Section 2**

Design

Are you interested in how a TV programme or station is made to look the way it does? How the props, the costumes, the sets, the graphics, the make-up and the effects are made to look the way they do? If so, consider a career in TV design.

There are many different ways to progress as a designer, but you need to demonstrate your artistic ability from the start. You will probably have done an undergraduate course, or equivalent, in art or design or a related subject; and you should use this course to create a portfolio of your best design work. Then, as in other parts of TV, you might aim to get experience as a **runner**, usually in an art department of a major broadcaster. As a runner, you will perform all the menial jobs that other artists and designers need – mostly clearing up, helping to lug stuff around, making tea, and so on. Your aim will be to get yourself in position to be offered that first job, freelance or otherwise, in an area that interests you.

Production design

If you are both ambitious and creative, then your long-term aim in TV may be to become a production designer. As a **production designer**, you will be responsible for the look and feel of a production; interpreting the director's vision, you will come up with designs that inform and lift the content of a production – be it a studio show, a drama, or whatever. To become a production designer, you will probably have worked up through one or more different art department roles, and will have built experience working in, or alongside, the following fields:

SET AND PROPS

The set is, of course, a crucial part of the design of any production, be it a studio-based game show or a lavish drama. An entry-level job may be as a **set dresser** or **assistant**, whose job is to keep the sets looking as they are supposed to, working closely with the props team. After that, you may go on to be a **set designer** or **design assistant**, which means you will work closely with the production designer; to do this, you need good knowledge of how lighting and camerawork will affect the result, and you will have to be good at briefing your team to get what you want.

A set designer or assistant designer is in the best position to progress to the role of **art director**, who – in a large production, at any rate – will spend a lot of time briefing artists and managing timetables for the full range of design work.

The **props** team also works to the production designer; most of the job is spent ordering and maintaining the array of objects that the production requires. Organisational skills are essential.

Costume is also a very important part of production design, although there are fewer jobs in the field than there once were. Most costume designers are freelances, brought in to help out on the most lavish productions, especially dramas. As a **costume designer**, you will source, buy, make and maintain costumes, working with both the production designer and the director; the skill is usually to keep within an absurdly small budget as you do. Depending on the size of

The computer graphics boss

Name: **Dave Throssell**
Current job: **head of Mill TV**

What was your first job in broadcasting?
Head of Mill TV. I had spent 20 years in commercials at various places in Soho and New York before running the CGI department at The Mill. Two-and-a-half years ago I set up Mill TV.

How did you get the job?
My first job in the industry was as a 3D CGI artist at the Moving Picture Company in 1982 – yes, there were computers in those days! I was writing software for the military and saw a job in Computing, the IT trade paper, and I got the job.

What did the job involve? What was it like?
I was employed to run their original CGI equipment, which was all home-made, and to write Pascal programs for their "Mirage" machine. I remember having to sit in the edit suite to do programming, and being amazed at the attention to detail for a 30-second ad. It was all about money and schedules, and I suppose it still is.

What were your educational qualifications at the time?
I had a degree in physics which had got me my programming job in the first place, but I learned on the job.

What experience did you have before starting work?
Various summer jobs ranging from breweries to Texas Instruments.

How did your career progress after your first job?
I stayed at MPC for a few years then moved to Rushes to do the same kind of thing. Then on to The Bureau (long gone now) where I ran the CGI department and moved to Softimage software. I then set up in New York for a year, and returned to set up my own company working out of The Mill. Then on to broadcast and running Mill TV.

What are you doing at work this week?
We're finishing a science/history documentary and we're very busy, so I'm helping out with a bit of CG work. I will be having meetings about new projects tomorrow and Friday and will have to work out schedules and budgets for those. On Wednesday I'm off on a recce in the city, and at some point I have to sort out Mill TV accounts and contracts for people.

What advice would you have for anyone thinking of a career in broadcasting?
Do your research into the companies you are approaching so you don't waste your time (and everyone else's) knocking on the wrong doors. And spell people's names properly!

the production, you may have a wardrobe team to work with you; you may start out as a **wardrobe assistant**.

Not even the simplest production could get by without its **hair and make-up artists**. The vast majority are freelances, and almost all are women. The more complex the production, the more interesting the job of a make-up artist becomes; costume drama and special effects are more fun, generally speaking, than spending day after day turning a newsreader orange. As a **make-up designer**, you will manage a team of make-up artists or assistants, usually for a large production; which means you should be calm, unflappable and organised.

Graphic design

Graphic design is usually considered a distinct discipline from production design, although the two do overlap. You will probably work most closely with a producer, as you create credits, on-screen information and other digital effects, often on quite small productions. You should almost certainly have done a graphic design course at undergraduate or postgraduate level, and will start by getting a job as a **graphic design assistant**. With graphic design skills, you could work for a production company or a post-production facility.

If you work for a major broadcaster, you might be lucky enough to create some idents; that is, the sequences between programmes that bear the station logo. Idents are an important way of branding a station, and serve as a kind of history of both TV and graphical techniques; as a result, they retain a kind of retro cult status – among a certain kind of TV obsessive, at any rate.

See also the role of **computer graphics editor**, on page 43, in the chapter on post-production, as a lot of graphics work is done by specialist facilities.

How to get the job

The 10-step plan

Once you have read through the job descriptions in Section 2 and settled on your career path, it is time to work out what you need to do to get into the business as soon as possible. Here are the 10 steps to launching yourself on a career in TV and radio.

1 Build contacts

OK, so the family doesn't have TV in the blood – but that doesn't mean you can't network. Networking is about enlisting *everyone* you know to your cause. And that means everyone – friends, family, work contacts – because everyone might know someone in broadcasting who could be in a position to help you in a career. You don't need to be too pushy; but it's no sin to talk about your ambitions, and to ask people you know if they know someone in the business.

When you find someone who seems promising, call or send them an email, mentioning the person you know in common. Ask them if they can make time for a 10- or 15-minute chat. Most people won't begrudge you this. Try to call at a convenient time. When you get through, don't ask them right out if they can land you a job; chances are they aren't in a position to do so, and will be embarrassed by having to decline. Instead, try to ask them about themselves: how they got into the business, what their working week is like, what advice they can give you. If things are going well, ask them if they take people to do work experience or as a runner (step three). Finally, ask if they know anyone else who can talk to you. Being in the industry already, they should know a lot of people who will be able to tell you about your particular interest or niche. When you're done, make sure they have your details – and drop them a note thanking them for your time.

The reason for all this is that the media – and TV in particular – constitute one of those industries where everyone knows someone who knows someone who needs a job to be done. Sooner or later, an email is going to come round the office of your contacts asking if anyone knows a young person who can be a runner, or do a freelance job that's poorly paid or at an antisocial hour. If you've made the right impression, that's how you get started in a career.

Finally, do keep a contacts book if you can: you never know when you might need a phone number again. Journalists tend to keep one book in hard copy and one on a PC: you should do the same.

2 Research

two

The next step to getting work is the most basic – and the most overlooked. One mantra that job interviewers repeat time and again, in all industries, is: "It's amazing how many people come looking for jobs without knowing the first thing about us." So immerse yourself in whatever medium you want to work in. Immerse yourself in TV, or radio, or both. Focus on the genres you like or companies you particularly want to work for, but not to the exclusion of anything else. We've said it a lot in the pages of this book, but if you don't receive multichannel TV or digital radio, then you should. Non-terrestrial TV was watched by as many viewers as ITV at the end of 2003; can you really expect to get a job if you're ignoring a market of that size, for the sake of the price of a set-top box?

Next, you should get your background knowledge about the industry. The best place to find this is in the trade press – that is, the newspapers about broadcasting itself. There is a list on page 127, but the most useful are usually MediaGuardian, its website MediaGuardian.co.uk; the trade newspapers, particularly Broadcast and Televisual; Ariel, the BBC's in-house paper (which, if you're in London, you can pick up in the foyer of Broadcasting House in Portland Place); and websites such as Digital Spy. Follow the media sections of other newspapers too. Within a few months, you will develop the minimum background knowledge you need.

Next, of course, you need to know where the jobs are. Bear in mind that many jobs will be freelance gigs (see step nine) – but don't ignore MediaGuardian on a Monday (and MediaGuardian.co.uk), which have launched many media types into successful careers. Try the trade press, such as Broadcast – or, if you're a broadcast journalist, Press Gazette. Try the websites of individual employers: many media companies advertise vacancies on their websites. Not all are advertised, though, which is why you need to build your contacts (step two).

Finally, a boring but important point – remember that research is as much about good note-taking as the reading you do. Imagine you have a "chat" with a prospective employer booked in for tomorrow. What was the name of that production company whose work you liked? What could that presenter have done differently? Record your thoughts now, and you won't be struggling to find the information when you need it.

3 Do run, run

Nothing prepares you better for working in the media than being in the media. As a result, working as a runner – often for little or no pay – is an established way to make the contacts you need.

Like anything else, getting a runner's job is mostly about research and networking. First, check the websites of teams that you would consider working for – they may have formal training schemes, or may advertise for runners. The Commercial Radio Companies Association (www.crca.co.uk), for example, contains a frequently updated file of radio work placements; while the BBC has a "work experience hub" (www.bbc.co.uk/jobs/workexperience_hub.shtml). Otherwise, focus again on building your contacts as outlined in step one; meet enough people, asking them if there are work experience opportunities available, and sooner or later you will be offered a stint or two. If all else fails, get a copy of a reference book about TV and radio – the contacts at the back of this book could do for a start – and, using it as a guide, cold-call producers at the six small indies or facilities you would most like to work for. Scary, but effective. The smaller and the more understaffed the company is, the greater your likelihood of success.

Make sure you get the best out of your time as a runner. If you're bitter about having to work for free, don't show it. Adam Cooper has some useful tips on page 18: don't get in the way, try to be as helpful as you can, and remember that a crew can't work on an empty stomach (or, as often as not, without barrels of tea). Whenever you get the chance, ask questions – but not stupid ones, and not when someone is busy doing an important piece of work.

Some people think the way media uses cheap wannabe labour is a bit of a con. True, it does seem rich when a production company paid handsomely by a FTSE-listed broadcaster asks you to work free; if this is the case, make sure you get your expenses paid, but get on with the job. Looking at it in the long term, the money doesn't matter: it's the experience that counts. Take it with both hands.

Don't ignore the other established ways you can get work experience: RSL radio stations, such as hospital radio, spring to mind; and in certain professions, theatre experience can also be useful. These kinds of bodies thrive on unpaid labour from people such as you.

4 Tech skills, tech knowledge

Technology will always be an important part of broadcasting. If you're going for a technical or post-production job, of course, it goes without saying that you should get some basic experience of the skills involved – whether it's doing the lighting at a student theatre, or editing audio at hospital radio station.

But bear in mind that, even if you're not technically minded yourself, it's important to know how technical concerns affect others. As a budding director or a student journalist, you might not know a lot about operating a camera, but you should know the names of all the different camera shots. As a wannabe radio producer, you might not yet know how to operate a mixing desk, but you should have edited audio on a home computer. Broadcasting is all about the team: the better the technical knowledge you have, the better the team works, and the more employable you are.

5 Consider a course

Because of the tech knowledge needed to do most jobs, a TV or radio course can be a very good idea. When choosing a course, try to go for one with a strong practical element. A course is no replacement for actually doing a job – but it can help you make new contacts (step one), get work experience or a runners' job (step three), and build a showreel or demo tape (step six). That said, a place on some high-profile training courses, such as those run by FT2 (Film & Television Freelance Training), can be almost as difficult to get as a half-decent job.

6 Show off your work

It is essential to give a good account of your best work. In TV, especially in presenting, journalism, technical and directing roles, that means creating a showreel; in radio presenting or journalism, it means building a demo; and in artistic and many other jobs, it means building a portfolio. It's your best way of impressing a possible employer, whether or not you have even met.

The best thing about needing a showreel or demo, of course, is that it stops you thinking about the job you want to do, and actually makes you get on and do it. If you're working for a student radio station as a DJ in your spare time (step three), then it's a relatively small step from there to putting a tape together; if you're not, you need to build your experience first. Similarly, if you're a presenter or a picture editor, then any work you do in corporate video will be very useful for a TV showreel. And as we mentioned in step five, a showreel is a valuable product for even a short TV course.

When you come to actually making your tape – or MiniDisc, or CD, or DVD, or whatever – then you'll want to strike a balance between proving your talent (that is, only including work that shows you at your best) and your experience (including work in a wide range of styles). As a newcomer, you should err on the side of brevity; but you can still get a lot into a few minutes if you edit it as tightly as you can. Target it, if possible, to the kind of station you will be sending it to; this may mean making more than one master tape, each giving more prominence to a different type of role.

When you've finished a showreel or demo, make as many copies as you think will last you until you next update it, and a few more besides. Then simply target those companies you would most like to work for, and send them off on spec – with your phone number in a prominent place – saving another batch for the formal and informal contacts you make along the way.

7 Target your CV

The traditional CV is sometimes not needed to get a job in TV or radio, as jobs – especially freelance gigs – are often won informally by word of mouth. For those times you do need a written record of your career, though, you will want to make your CV stand out.

The secret is not just to list your career credits – though they are, of course, vital – but also to show how they equip you for each role you want. So go over your career history to date, work out what is most relevant, and give most space to that. Under each bit of experience you have gained, bullet-point two or three things you did or learned that are especially useful; try to keep these as short as you can. Don't devote too much space to your educational achievements, unless it's a TV or film course; just emphasise those credits and why they matter. List all relevant tech skills prominently. At the bottom, mention a few interests, for a personal touch.

If you are suffering from the "empty CV" syndrome – that is, you haven't got enough career experience to fill a page of A4 – then here is another useful technique. Simply write a concise summary of who you are at the top of the CV, with your most relevant general skills bullet-pointed underneath. Next you write the heading "Experience" and carry on with your usual CV. The approach is good because it humanises you, and makes it clear from the start what stage you're at in your career.

Try not to give employers any excuses to put your application on the "no" pile. Ensure your spelling and grammar are perfect: you might not need to punctuate like Lynne Truss to work as a TV researcher, but getting it wrong on the CV makes you look slapdash. Design should be clean and simple. Use a well-known font such as Times or Arial, at a readable point size.

Finally, include references from people in TV and radio if you can (step one); that way they will still score for you even if they are not actually checked.

8 Consider a niche

If you have a particular interest in and knowledge about a subject – be it arts, books, travel, health or perhaps a region of the country – you should certainly consider making it your niche. This applies to almost any job — presenting, journalism, camera work, location management. Genuine expertise or knowledge about a subject is always bankable. And don't worry about being pigeon holed too early: many broadcasters who start out in niche areas go on to broader things.

9 **Prepare to freelance**

Freelancing will be crucial to your career in TV and radio. At the time of the Skillset census 2003, a quarter of the broadcasting workforce was freelance – and this excludes all those freelances who are not working, so the true proportion is even greater than that. In independent production, about 58 per cent of the workforce was freelance; in commercials, the figure was 89 per cent.

Freelancing means being paid only for the work you do. That might mean being paid only for doing a voice-over for a commercial, or a weekend of operating a boom; as a researcher, it might mean working on a short-term contract for the length of a programme's run. Whichever part of the industry you work in, you might easily go your entire career without getting a permanent job.

Whichever approach you take, you need to be organised and to market yourself. You need to keep a database of contacts, and to keep records of every conversation you have with a prospective employer – even if it was only a casual chat. You should get a set of business cards: broadcasting is one of those professions where everyone seems to have one. Use websites such as Production Base, where freelances can advertise their services. Keep organised files of ideas and opportunities as appropriate, and do plenty of market research as outlined in step one.

If you are offered a job, try to get a contract if you can; many firms will try and keep things informal for the sake of simplicity (they say), but it is in your best interests to protect yourself. Pact, the indies trade association, and Bectu, the broadcasting trade union, have drawn up an agreement covering issues such as employers' contributions to stakeholder pensions; if you work for an indie, get a copy of the agreement to see what your rights are, and make sure your contract mentions the agreement explicitly.

Tax is an issue: if you are working with your own equipment on a project basis, then you should be treated as self-employed, which means you will be paid gross and fill in a tax return. If you work largely in a company's offices, on the other hand, you may be treated as a "casual employee" and taxed at source; you should also be entitled to holiday pay – a valuable perk, though of course few companies actually pay it. Get in touch with the Inland Revenue as soon as you can for advice.

It can help to be a member of a union such as Bectu; 40 per cent of their membership is freelance, so freelances' issues are obviously a major concern to them. The website www.tvfreelances.org.uk, meanwhile, has a database of freelance rates.

Freelancing can be highly stressful and isolating; once you have been doing it for a while, it can also seem like the only way to live your life. If, however, you feel you need a bit more security, then you should try to avoid working in a sector that has a high freelance workforce. See the latest Skillset census (www.skillset.org) for more details.

Prepare for an interview

ten

Not all jobs will need an interview, especially if you're freelancing from gig to gig. But if you get an interview for a big job, congratulations. It means you have the potential to succeed, and will probably be employed in time. Whether it happens this time depends on how you come across.

Remember that interviews, primarily, are about the stories you tell, and how you tell them. You are presenting a version of yourself. So when preparing for interview, look over everything you sent the employer again, to remind yourself what your relevant skills and experience are. Then take time to remember something that happened which backs all that up. If you are applying for a job as a researcher, for example, your CV might mention the runners' job you had in a production company, and you might go on to add that you spent time working in continuity. In the interview, you might be asked to expand on this further. So talk about how you spotted one minor potential problem with the script, and how it made you feel positive that you were able to give something to the team. The implied message here is that you have attention to detail; but also that you are enthusiastic, you take the initiative, and willing to learn – essential skills for any job.

With this technique in mind, you should be able to come up with answers to almost every question you are asked, including the classics. Why do you want the job? How would you cope with difficult people? What would you do if an important contributor suddenly decided not to go on air? As long as you have done all your research (step two) and got enough experience (steps three and four), you should have a story that tells the answer.

After that, it is all about getting the basics right. So dress smartly, even if you will be in T-shirt and jeans when you do the job. Try to moderate your nervous instincts: if you are an extrovert, practise speaking slowly and formally, and thinking before you open your mouth; if an introvert, practise making good eye contact and projecting your voice. Expect the unexpected: you might have an active interviewer who grills you with searching questions, in which case you need to be able to think on your feet; or they might be passive and apparently uninterested in you, in which case you need to take control if you are to have an impact. You might be in a plush meeting room, a tiny office, the company canteen. Be prepared, and you should be able to fight off the nerves.

Finally, it will be your turn to ask the questions. Prepare these in advance, but remember that interviewers will often be rushing to get you out of the room, so you need to interest them too. First, ask about opportunities for career progression: this shows ambition, which is always good. Second, try to ask something about plans for the company, that is relevant to the job you are going to do. Finally, there is money. If salary has not been raised, you should mention that it hasn't been raised yet – an indirect way of asking what it is. Whatever the answer, keep your poker face. You might have to negotiate a pay rise at a later date.

If you don't get the job this time, don't be downhearted – getting an interview is good experience in itself. After a few days, you might call or email to ask what it was that made you fall short by comparison to the candidate that got the job. Chances are it is something you can fix next time.

11 Persevere

eleven

OK, so we said there would be 10 steps. But the 11th is perhaps the most important. In any career, there will be ups and downs – sometimes it will seem as if you are in control of your future, and at other times you will feel stuck in a rut. Just keep persevering and thinking positively. If you can't find work – keep making contacts and building your skills. If you feel stuck, don't be afraid to make new contacts and new skills. It's your life – make the most of it.

TV and Radio contacts

TV Contacts

Office of Communications (Ofcom)
Riverside House
2A Southwark Bridge Road
London SE1 9HA
020 7981 3000
www.ofcom.gov.uk

Ofcom Media Office
020 7981 3033
mediaoffice@ofcom.org.uk

BBC

MAIN BBC ADDRESSES

Television Centre
Wood Lane, London
W12 7RJ

BBC White City
201 Wood Lane, London
W12 7TS

Broadcasting House
Portland Place, London
W1A 1AA

www.bbc.co.uk
020 8743 8000

BBC Television

Television Centre
020 8743 8000
General enquiries:
info@bbc.co.uk
www.bbc.co.uk/television
Director of television: Jana Bennett

General press enquiries
press.office@bbc.co.uk
www.bbc.co.uk/pressoffice

Media TV enquiries
020 8576 9900
publicity.frontdesk@bbc.co.uk
www.bbc.co.uk/pressoffice

BBC channels

BBC One
Television Centre
020 8743 8000
www.bbc.co.uk/bbcone
*Controller: Lorraine Heggessey;
controller of daytime: Alison
Sharman
(daytime.proposals@bbc.co.uk)*

BBC Two
Television Centre
020 8743 8000
www.bbc.co.uk/bbctwo
*Controller: Roly Keating; controller
of daytime: Alison Sharman*

BBC Three
Television Centre
020 8743 8000
www.bbc.co.uk/bbcthree
Controller: Stuart Murphy

BBC Four
Television Centre
020 8576 3193
www.bbc.co.uk/bbcfour
Controller: Janice Hadlow

CBBC
Television Centre
020 8743 8000
www.bbc.co.uk/cbbc
Controller: Dorothy Prior

CBeebies
Television Centre
020 8743 8000
www.bbc.co.uk/cbeebies
Controller: Dorothy Prior

BBC America
7475 Wisconsin Avenue,
11th Floor
Bethesda,
USA MD 20814
00 1 301 347 2222
bbcamerica@bbc.co.uk
www.bbcamerica.com
*Programme executive:
Alison Fredericks*

BBC Canada
121 Bloor Street East,
Suite 200
Toronto, Ontario,
Canada
M4W 3M5
00 416 934 7800
feedback@bbccanada.com
www.bbccanada.com

BBC Food
PO Box 5054,
London
W12 0ZY
020 8433 2221
bbcfood@bbc.co.uk
www.bbcfood.com
Editor: David Weiland

BBC News 24
Television Centre
020 8743 8000
bbcnews24@bbc.co.uk
www.bbc.co.uk/bbcnews24
Editorial director: Mark Popescu

BBC Parliament
4 Millbank, London SW1P 3JA
020 7973 6216
parliament@bbc.co.uk
www.bbc.co.uk/bbcparliament

BBC Prime
PO Box 5054, London
W12 0ZY
020 8433 2221
bbcprime@bbc.co.uk
www.bbcprime.com
Editor: David Weiland

BBC World
Television Centre
020 8576 2308
bbcworld@bbc.co.uk
www.bbcworld.com
Editorial director: Sian Kevill

BBC nations and regions

Director of nations and regions
Pat Loughrey
Controller of English regions
Andy Griffee
Network development, nations and regions
Colin Cameron, room 3187
BBC Scotland, 0141 338 2424

BBC Scotland
Broadcasting House
Queen Margaret Drive
Glasgow
G12 8DG
0141 339 8844
www.bbc.co.uk/scotland
Controller: Ken MacQuarrie

BBC Wales
Broadcasting House
Llandaff,
Cardiff
CF5 2YQ
029 2032 2000
www.bbc.co.uk/wales
Controller: Menna Richards

BBC Northern Ireland
Broadcasting House
Ormeau Avenue,
Belfast
BT2 8HQ
028 9033 8000
www.bbc.co.uk/northernireland
Controller: Anna Carragher

BBC East
The Forum,
Millennium Plain
Norwich
NR2 1BH
01603 619 331
look.east@bbc.co.uk
www.bbc.co.uk/england/lookeast
*Head of regional and local
programmes: Tim Bishop*

BBC East Midlands
London Road, Nottingham
NG2 4UU
0115 955 0500
emt@bbc.co.uk
www.bbc.co.uk/england
/eastmidlandstoday
*Head of regional and local
programmes: Alison Ford*

BBC London
35c Marylebone High Street
London W1U 4QA
020 7224 2424
yourlondon@bbc.co.uk
www.bbc.co.uk/london
*Head of regional and local
programmes: Michael MacFarlane*

BBC North
Broadcasting Centre
Woodhouse Lane,
Leeds LS2 9PX
0113 244 1188
look.north@bbc.co.uk
www.bbc.co.uk/england
/looknorthyorkslincs
*Head of regional and local
programmes: Colin Philpott*

BBC North East and Cumbria
Broadcasting Centre,
Barrack Road
Newcastle upon Tyne
NE99 2NE
0191 232 1313
look.north.northeast.cumbria@
bbc.co.uk
www.bbc.co.uk/england
/looknorthnecumbria
*Head of regional and local
programmes: Wendy Pilmer*

BBC North West
New Broadcasting House
Oxford Road, Manchester
M60 1SJ
0161 200 2020
nwt@bbc.co.uk
www.bbc.co.uk/manchester
*Head of regional and local
programmes: Martin Brooks*

BBC South
Broadcasting House,
Havelock Road
Southampton SO14 7PU
02380 226201
south.today@bbc.co.uk
www.bbc.co.uk/england/
southtoday
*Head of regional and local
programmes: Eve Turner*

BBC South East
The Great Hall,
Mount Pleasant Road
Tunbridge Wells TN1 1QQ
01892 670000
southeasttoday@bbc.co.uk
www.bbc.co.uk/england
/southeasttoday
*Head of regional and local
programmes: Laura Ellis*

BBC South West
Broadcasting House, Seymour
Road
Mannamead, Plymouth PL3 5BD
01752 229201
spotlight@bbc.co.uk
www.bbc.co.uk/england/spotlight
*Head of regional and local
programmes: John Lilley*

BBC West
Broadcasting House
Whiteladies Road,
Bristol BS8 2LR
0117 973 2211
pointswest@bbc.co.uk
www.bbc.co.uk/england/
pointswest
*Head of regional and local
programmes: Andrew Wilson*

BBC West Midlands
The Mailbox, Birmingham B1 1XL
0121 567 6767
midlands.today@bbc.co.uk
www.bbc.co.uk/birmingham
*Head of regional and local
programmes: David Holdsworth*

BBC News
Television Centre
020 8743 8000
http://news.bbc.co.uk
Director of BBC News
Helen Boaden
Deputy director of BBC News
Mark Damazer
Head of communications
Janie Ironside Wood

BBC Television News
Room 1502, Television Centre
020 8624 9043
*Head of television news: Roger
Mosey; deputy: Rachael Attwell*

BBC Newsgathering
020 8743 8000
*Head of newsgathering: Adrian Van
Klaveren*

Current affairs
*Head of current affairs:
Peter Horrocks*

Political programmes unit

BBC Westminster, 4 Millbank
London SW1P 3JA
020 7973 6000
*Head of political programmes:
Fran Unsworth;
political editor: Andrew Marr*

BBC News Online

Television Centre
http://news.bbc.co.uk
Head of new media: Richard Deverell

BBC EDITORS & CORRESPONDENTS

*Home editor: Mark Easton
Political editor: Andrew Marr
Business editor: Jeff Randall
World affairs editor: John Simpson
Diplomatic editor: Brian
Hanrahan*

Home and abroad

*Home affairs: Margaret Gilmore;
education: Mike Baker; health:
Karen Allen; social affairs: Daniel
Sandford; royal: Nicholas Witchell,
Peter Hunt; political: Laura
Trevelyan; defence: Paul Adams;
security: Frank Gardner; rural
affairs: Tom Heap; diplomatic:
Bridget Kendall, James Robbins;
environment and science: David
Shukman; media: Torin Douglas;
technology (BBC News Online):
Alfred Hermida, Mark Ward*

Special correspondents

*Jeremy Bowen, Fergal Keane,
Gavin Hewitt;
TV news: Ben Brown;
BBC News 24: Philippa Thomas*

World

World affairs

Peter Biles

Europe

*Europe: Tim Franks, Chris Morris,
Stephen Sackur; Paris: Allan Little,
Caroline Wyatt; Berlin: Ray
Furlong; Rome: David Willey;
Greece: Richard Galpin; Moscow:
Damian Grammaticas; south
Europe: Brian Barron; central
Europe: Nick Thorpe*

Middle East

*Orla Guerin, James Reynolds, Paul
Wood; Turkey: Jonny Dymond*

Americas

*Washington: Nick Bryant, Matt
Frei, Jon Leyne, Clive Myrie, Ian
Pannell, Justin Webb; California:
David Willis; Mexico and central
America: Claire Marshall; South
America: Elliott Gotkine*

Other

*Africa: Hilary Andersson;
east Africa: Andrew Harding;
south Asia: Adam Mynott;
south-east Asia: Kylie Morris;
central Asia: Monica Whitlock;
world media: Sebastian Usher; also
Dominic Hughes, Jill McGivering,
Rageh Omaar, Matthew Price*

FLAGSHIP NEWS AND POLITICS PROGRAMMES

Breakfast

Room 1605, News Centre
Television Centre
020 8624 9700
breakfasttv@bbc.co.uk
*Editor: Richard Porter;
presenters: Dermot Murnaghan,
Natasha Kaplinsky*

Newsnight

Television Centre
020 8624 9800
*Editor: George Entwhistle;
presenters: Jeremy Paxman,
Kirsty Wark, Gavin Esler*

Panorama

Room 1118, BBC White City
020 8752 7152
panorama@bbc.co.uk
*Editor: Mike Robinson;
deputy editors: Andrew Bell and
Sam Collyns*

Politics Show

4 Millbank, London SW1P 3JQ
020 7973 6199
politicsshow@bbc.co.uk
Presenter: Jeremy Vine

Question Time

Mentorn, 43 Whitfield Street
London W1T 4HA
020 7258 6800
Presenter: David Dimbleby

Six O'Clock News

Television Centre
020 8624 9996
*Presenters: George Alagiah,
Sophie Raworth*

Ten O'Clock News

Television Centre
020 8624 9999
*Editor: Kevin Bakhurst; presenters:
Huw Edwards, Fiona Bruce*

Factual and learning

Director of factual and learning

John Willis 020 8752 6501
Controller, factual TV
Glenwyn Benson 020 8743 8000

PROGRAMMES

Arena

Room 2168, BBC White City
020 8752 5172
Series editor: Anthony Wall

Everyman

Room 5048, BBC Manchester
Broadcasting House,
Oxford Road
Manchester M60 1SJ
0161 244 3321
ruth.pitt@bbc.co.uk
Creative director: Ruth Pitt

Horizon

Room 4523, BBC White City
020 8752 6134
horizon@bbc.co.uk
Editor: Matthew Barrett

Imagine

Arts Department, 2nd Floor
BBC White City
020 8752 4092
ian.macmillan@bbc.co.uk
Series Producer: Ian Macmillan

Money programme

Room 4116, BBC White City
020 8752 7400
Executive editor: Clive Edwards

One Life

Room 5503, BBC White City
020 8752 6608
todd.austin@bbc.co.uk
Commissioning editor: Todd Austin

Panorama

Room 1118, BBC White City
020 8752 7152
Editor: Mike Robinson

Storyville

Room 201, 1 Mortimer Street
London W1T 3JA
020 7765 5211
storyville@bbc.co.uk
Commissioning editor: Nick Fraser

This World

Room 1362, BBC White City
020 8752 7500
thisworld@bbc.co.uk
Editor: Karen O'Connor

Timewatch

Room 3150, BBC White City
020 8752 7079
Editor: John Farren

FACTUAL & LEARNING CONTACTS

Arts
2nd Floor, BBC White City
020 8752 4092
claire.lewis.02@bbc.co.uk
Executive producer: Claire Lewis;
commissioner, arts and culture:
Franny Moyle
Arts (Wales)
Room 4001, BBC Wales
029 2032 2943
paul.islwyn.thomas@bbc.co.uk
Head of arts, Wales:
Paul Islwyn Thomas
Classical music
Room EG09, Television Centre
020 8895 6541
Head of TV, classical music and
performance: Peter Maniura
Music (Wales)
Room E4113, BBC Wales
029 2032 2111
davidm.jackson@bbc.co.uk
Head of music, Wales:
David Jackson

Current affairs
Room 1172, BBC White City
020 8752 7005
Head of current affairs:
Peter Horrocks

Documentaries and contemporary factual
Room 3559, BBC White City
020 8752 5766
genfact.proposals@bbc.co.uk
Head of documentaries: Alan
Hayling; acting commissioner:
Tom Archer; development
executives: Nicky Colton &
Sara Brailsford
Factual (Northern Ireland)
2nd Floor, BBC Northern Ireland
028 9033 8207
Head of factual and learning,
NI: Bruce Batten; editor, network
factual, NI: Eamon Hardy,
020 8576 7045
Head of factual network production,
NI: Fiona Campbell, 020 8752 6074
Factual (Scotland)
Room 3178, BBC Scotland
0141 338 3646
andrea.miller.01@bbc.co.uk
Head of factual programmes,
Scotland: Andrea Miller
Factual (Wales)
Room 4020, BBC Wales
029 2032 2976
Head of factual programmes, Wales:
Adrian Davies

Education
Room 3416, BBC White City
020 8752 5241
Executive editor: Karen Johnson
Education (Northern Ireland)
Education Unit, First Floor
BBC Northern Ireland
028 9033 8445
Head of factual and learning,
NI: Bruce Batten; editor, learning,
NI: Kieran Hegarty
Education (Scotland)
Room 230, BBC Scotland
0141 338 1507
Editor, education, Scotland:
Moira Scott
Education (Wales)
Room E3106, BBC Wales
029 2032 2834
Head of education and learning,
Wales: Dr Eleri Wyn Lewis

Lifeskills TV
Room 2308, BBC White City
020 8752 4574
Head of Lifeskills TV: Seetha Kumar

Specialist factual, current affairs and arts
Room 2156, BBC White City
020 8752 6810
specfact.proposals@bbc.co.uk
Head of independent
commissioning: Adam Kemp;
commissioner, specialist factual:
Emma Swain; senior
commissioning executives:
Krishan Arora, Lucy Hetherington;
executive editor: Jacquie Hughes

Drama and entertainment

Director of drama, entertainment and CBBC
Alan Yentob   020 8743 8000

DRAMA & ENTERTAINMENT CONTACTS

Comedy
Room 4045, Television Centre
020 8743 8000
Head of comedy commissioning:
Mark Freeland; head of comedy
entertainment: Jon Plowman
Comedy and entertainment
(Scotland)
Room 3167, BBC Scotland
0141 338 2370
Head of comedy and entertainment,
Scotland: Mike Bolland

Daytime
Room 3560
BBC White City
020 8752 6225
Senior commissioning executive,
daytime: Dominic Vallely
Daytime entertainment
Room 6070, Television Centre
020 8576 9960
Commissioning executive, daytime
entertainment: Gilly Hall

Drama
Room D333, Centre House
56 Wood Lane,
London W12 7SB
020 8576 4935
Controller, commissioning, drama:
Jane Tranter; head of drama
serials: Laura Mackie; controller of
continuing drama series: Mal
Young; head of drama
commissioning: Gareth Neame
Drama (Northern Ireland)
BBC Northern Ireland
020 8576 1664
Head of drama, NI: Patrick Spence
Drama (Scotland)
Room 2170, BBC Scotland
0141 338 2517
Head of television drama, Scotland:
Barbara McKissack
Drama (Wales)
Room E2106, BBC Wales
029 2032 2935
Head of drama, Wales:
Julie Gardner

Entertainment
Room 6070, Television Centre
020 8225 6992
Controller, entertainment,
commissioning: Jane Lush

Entertainment (Northern Ireland)
Room 229, BBC Northern Ireland
028 9033 8375
mike.edgar@bbc.co.uk
Head of entertainment, events and
sport, NI: Mike Edgar

CBBC
Room E1012, Television Centre
020 8576 1280
Controller of CBBC: Dorothy Prior

Acquisitions
Room 360 DB, Television Centre
020 8576 1105
Head of acquisitions and
co-productions:
Theresa Plummer Andrews

CBBC Creates
Room E1200, Television Centre
020 8576 1040
Development executive, CBBC Creates: Amanda Gabbitas

CBBC Scotland
Room 2104, BBC Scotland
0141 338 2012
Head of Scotland: Donalda MacKinnon

Drama
Room E817, Television Centre
020 8576 8245
Head of drama: Elaine Sperber

Entertainment
Room E701, Television Centre
020 8225 9269
Head of entertainment: Anne Gilchrist

News and factual
Room E111, Television Centre
020 8576 3118
Head of news and factual: Roy Milani

Pre-school
Room N105, Neptune House
BBC Elstree, Clarendon Road,
Borehamwood, Herts WD6 1JF
020 8228 7072
Head of pre-school: Clare Elstow

Sport

Director of sport
Peter Salmon

Finance controller
Richard Jones 020 8225 6173

Live sport and highlights
Room 5060, Television Centre
020 8225 8400
andrew.thompson.01@bbc.co.uk

Head of new media, sports news and development
Andrew Thompson

Ceefax
Television Centre 020 8225 7022

Programme acquisition

Controller, programme acquisition
George McGhee 020 8743 8000

New media and technology

BBC Bush House
Strand, London WC2B 4PH
020 8743 8000
Director of new media and technology: Ashley Highfield
bbc.co.uk
*Controller, internet: Tony Ageh
Emerging platforms
Controller: Angel Gambino
BBCi (interactive TV)
Controller, 24/7 interactive
television: Rahul Chakkara; head,
interactive TV programming:
Emma Somerville
BBC Kingwood Warren (R&D)
Acting head: Ian Childs*

BBC Films

1 Mortimer Street, London
W1T 3JA
020 7765 0251
*Head of BBC Films: David
Thompson; executive producer &
head of development: Tracy Scoffield*
020 7765 0475

Business services

BBC International Unit
020 8576 1963
international.unit@bbc.co.uk
www.bbc.co.uk/international
*Manager: Peter James
Supplies TV facilities to overseas
broadcasters transmitting from UK*

BBC Monitoring
Marketing Unit, Caversham Park
Reading RG4 8TZ
0118 948 6289
csu@mon.bbc.co.uk
www.bbcmonitoringonline.com
and www.monitor.bbc.co.uk
Monitors world media

BBC Research Central
Broadcasting House
020 7557 2452
research-central@bbc.co.uk
www.bbcresearchcentral.com
*Senior researchers: Helen Turner,
Huw Martin, Guy Watkins, Angie
Francis, Kyla Thorogood, Richard
Jeffery, Jacqueline Faulkner,
Michael Paige
Information, footage,
pronunciation, radio and photo
research services*

BBC Training and Development
35 Marylebone High Street
London W1U 4PX
0870 122 0216
training@bbc.co.uk
www.bbctraining.co.uk
Press contact:
Louise Findlay-Wilson
01993 823011
louise@energypr.co.uk
*Training solutions in programme-
making, broadcasting and new
media*
Elstree
Clarendon Road, Borehamwood
Herts WD6 1JF
Wood Norton Training Centre
Evesham, Worcestershire
WR11 4YB

BBC Ventures Group
020 7765 2938
bbcventuresgroup@bbc.co.uk
*Commercial director: David
Moody; head of press and PR:
Alison Jeremy
Wholly owned commercial
subsidiary, comprising BBC Vecta,
BBC Broadcast, BBC Resources and
BBC Technology
BBC Broadcast*
Television Centre
020 8225 6666
bbcbroadcast@bbc.co.uk
www.bbcbroadcast.com
*Managing director: Pam Masters
Offers range of play-out and
channel management services
across multiple media platforms;
planning to move in 2004 to:
Media Village, BBC White City, 201
Wood Lane, London
BBC Resources*
0870 010 0883
bbcresources@bbc.co.uk
www.bbcresources.com
*Managing director: Mike Southgate
Production facilities*

BBC Costumes and Wigs
Victoria Road, London W3 6UL
020 8576 1761
costume@bbc.co.uk;
wigs@bbc.co.uk
www.bbcresources.com

BBC Outside Broadcasts
Kendal Avenue, London W3 0RP
020 8993 9333
ob@bbc.co.uk
www.bbcresources.com

BBC Post-Production
Television Centre
020 8225 7702
postproduction@bbc.co.uk
www.bbcresources.com

Bristol
Broadcasting House
White Ladies Road
Bristol BS8 2LR
0117 974 6666
postproduction@bbc.co.uk
www.bbcresources.com
Birmingham
BBC Pebble Mill
Birmingham B5 7QQ
0121 432 8621
postproduction@bbc.co.uk
www.bbcresources.com

BBC Studios
Television Centre
020 8576 7666
tvstudio.sales@bbc.co.uk
www.bbcresources.com

BBC Technology
3rd Floor, Brock House
19 Langham Street,
London W1 1AA
020 7765 4748
bbctechnology-sales@bbc.co.uk
www.bbctechnology.com
*Managing director: Ann Wilson
Offers solutions in media, broadcast
and interactive applications to the
BBC and other companies*

BBC Vecta
The Studio, 1 Mortimer Street
London W1T 3JA
020 7765 0850
amanda.harris@bbc.co.uk
www.bbcvecta.com
*Managing director: Mark
Popkiewicz; communications
manager: Amanda Harris
Represents BBC in commercial
exploitation of rights; works with
BBC Research and Development to
bring developments to market*

BBC Worldwide
Woodlands, 80 Wood Lane
London W12 0TT
020 8433 2000
www.bbcworldwide.com
*Managing director: Peter Phippen
Commercial arm: businesses
include distribution, TV channels,
magazines, books, videos, spoken
word, music, DVDs, licensed
products, CD-ROMs, English
language teaching, videos for
education and training, interactive
telephony, co-production, library
footage sales, magazine
subscription exhibitions, live
events, film and media monitoring*

Advisory bodies

**Broadcasting Council for
Scotland**
The Secretary,
Broadcasting House
Queen Margaret Drive
Glasgow G12 8DG
0141 339 8844

Broadcasting Council for Wales
The Secretary,
Broadcasting House
Llandaff, Cardiff CF5 2YQ
029 2032 2000

**Broadcasting Council for
Northern Ireland**
Head of Public Affairs and
Secretary,
Broadcasting House,
Ormeau Avenue
Belfast BT2 8HQ
028 9033 8000

**Central Religious Advisory
Committee**
The Secretary,
Broadcasting House
London W1A 1AA
020 7580 4468

English National Forum
Head of Press and Public Affairs,
English Regions
BBC Broadcasting Centre
Pebble Mill Road
Birmingham B5 7QQ
0121 432 8888

**Governors' World Service
Consultative Group**
BBC World Service,
Bush House
Strand, London WC2B 4PH
020 7240 3456

BBC governors

Chairman of governors:
Michael Grade
Vice-chairman:
Anthony Salz
Governors:
Deborah Bull
Dame Ruth Deech
Dermot Gleeson
Professor Merfyn Jones
Professor Fabian Monds
Dame Pauline Neville-Jones
Angela Sarkis
Sir Robert Smith (until end 2004)
Ranjit Sondhi
Richard Tait

TV and radio contacts : **Section 4**

89

ITV Network

200 Grays Inn Road
London WC1X 8HF
020 7843 8000
*Controls commissioning and
scheduling across entire ITV network,
including non-ITV plc regions*

NETWORK CONTROLLERS

Acquisitions
Jeremy Boulton 020 7843 8120
Arts, current affairs and religion
Steve Anderson 020 7843 8110
Children's and youth
Steven Andrew 020 7843 8132
Comedy
Sioned Wiliam 020 7843 8093
Drama
Nick Elliot 020 7843 8202
Head of network drama:
Jenny Reeks 020 7843 8211
Entertainment
Claudia Rosencrantz
020 7843 8105
Factual
Bridget Boseley 020 7843 8297
Head of continuing series
Corrine Hollingworth
020 7843 8211
Sport
Brian Barwick 020 7843 8113
ITV 50th Anniversary
Liam Hamilton 020 7843 8107

ITV channels

ITV1
020 7843 8000
www.itv.com/itv1
ITV2
020 7843 8000
www.itv.com/itv2
Channel editor: Zai Bennett,
020 7843 8129; controller of
commissioned programmes:
Daniella Neumann, 020 7843 8101
ITV News
200 Grays Inn Road
London WC1X 8XZ
020 7833 3000
press: itvplanning@itn.co.uk
www.itv.com/news
Editor-in-chief: David Mannion

ITV plc

London Television Centre
Upper Ground,
London
SE1 9LT
Chief executive: Charles Allen;
chairman: Sir Peter Burt
Controls 11 of the 15 ITV franchises
ITV plc board
Chief executive: **Charles Allen**
Chairman: **Sir Peter Burt**
Deputy chairman:
Sir George Russell
Directors:
Henry Staunton
David Chance
James Crosby
John McGrath
Sir Brian Pitman
Etienne de Villiers

ITV PLC DIVISIONS

ITV News Group
020 7396 6000
*Chief executive: Clive Jones
Includes ITV1's national and
international news output, and
regional news for ITV plc
franchises; plus ITV plc's 40% stake
in ITN*
ITV Broadcasting
020 7843 8000
*Chief executive: Mick Desmond;
head of programmes: Nigel Pickard
Runs ITV plc's 11 regional ITV1
franchises; runs ITV2;
runs sales house*
ITV sales
200 Grays Inn Road
London WC1X 8XZ
020 7396 6000
*Managing director: Graham Duff;
director of ITV sales: Gary Digby;
director of sales operations: Jill
Kerslake; director of knowledge
management: Andy Bagnall*
Granada
020 7620 1620
*Chief executive: Simon Shaps
Production arm
Press office 020 7843 8218/8219*

ITV News
ITN, 200 Grays Inn Road
London WC1X 8XZ
020 7833 3000
*Editor-in-chief: David Mannion;
editor: Deborah Turness; deputy
editor: Jonathan Munro;
managing editor: Robin Elias;
head of ITV News channel:
Dominic Crossley-Holland
Key presenters: Sir Trevor
McDonald; Mary Nightingale;
Katie Derham; Mark Austin;
Nicholas Owen; Alastair Stewart*
Editors and correspondents
*UK editor: Tom Bradby
Political editor: Nick Robinson
Consumer affairs editor: Chris Choi
International news editor: Bill Neely
Business and economics editor:
Caroline Kerr
Science editor: Lawrence McGinty
Sports editor: Tim Ewart
Senior correspondent: James Mates*
Home and abroad
*News correspondents: Shiulie
Ghosh, Joyce Ohajah, Mark
Webster, Helen Wright; news
reporters: Catherine Jacob,
Philip Reay-Smith, Romilly
Weeks; political: Angus Walker,
Libby Wiener; north of England:
Tim Rogers; south of England:
Adrian Britton; Wales and west
of England: Geraint Vincent;
Scotland: Martin Geissler;
medical: Sue Saville; crime:
Dan Rivers; media and arts:
Nina Nannar; sport: Felicity Barr*
World
*International news: Andrea
Catherwood; Europe: Juliet
Bremner; Washington: Robert
Moore; Middle East: Julian
Manyon; Africa: Neil Connery;
Asia: John Irvine
Press officer: Saskia Wirth
020 7430 4825
saskia.wirth@itn.co.uk
Press releases to:
itvplanning@itn.co.uk*

ITV regions

ITV Anglia
Anglia House,
Norwich NR1 3JG
01603 615151
firstname.lastname@itv.com
www.angliatv.com
*Managing director: Graham
Creelman; controller of
programmes: Neil Thompson;
head of regional affairs: Jim
Woodrow; press officer: Lisa
Munghan-Gray*
News at Anglia
0870 240 6003
news@angliatv.com
Controller of news: Guy Adams
Cambridge regional office
ITV Anglia
26 Newmarket Road
Cambridge CB5 8DT
01223 467076
Chelmsford regional office
64–68 New London Road
Chelmsford CM2 0YU
01245 357676
Ipswich regional office
Hubbard House
Ipswich IP1 2QA
01473 226157
Luton regional office
16 Park Street
Luton LU1 2DP
01582 729666
Northampton regional office
77b Abington Street
Northampton NN1 2BH
01604 624343
Peterborough regional office
6 Bretton Green
Peterborough PE3 8DY
01733 269440

ITV Border
The Television Centre
Durranhill,
Carlisle CA1 3NT
01228 525101
www.border-tv.com
*Managing director: Paddy Merrall;
production controller:
Neil Robinson;
head of news: Ian Proniewicz;
press officer: Louise Maving*

ITV Central
Gas Street, Birmingham B1 2JT
0121 643 9898
firstname.lastname@itv.com
www2.itv.com/central
*Managing director: Ian Squires;
controller of news and operations:
Laurie Upshon; head of regional
programming: Duncan Rycroft;
press officer: Christopher Strange;
editor Central News West: Dan Barton*
Central News East
Carlton Studios, Lenton Lane
Nottingham NG7 2NA
0115 986 3322
*News editor: Mike Blair
Studios marked for closure;
operation to move to
Birmingham office*
Central News South
9 Windrush Court
Abingdon Business Park
Abingdon
Oxford OX14 1SA
01235 554123
News editor: Ian Rumsey

ITV Granada
Quay Street,
Manchester M60 9EA
0161 832 7211
firstname.lastname@itv.com
www.granadatv.com
*Managing director: Susan
Woodward; controller of
programmes: Kieron Collins;
executive producer regional
programmes: Eamonn O'Neal;
controller of regional affairs: Jane
Luca; news editor: Cerys Griffiths*
Blackburn regional news centre
Daisyfield Business Centre
Appleby Street
Blackburn BB1 3BL
01254 690099
Chester regional news centre
Bridgegate House, 5 Bridge Place
Lower Bridge Street
Chester CH1 1SA
01244 313966
Lancaster regional news centre
White Cross, Lancaster LA1 4XQ
01524 60688

ITV London
London Television Centre
Upper Grounds,
London SE1 9LT
020 7620 1620
firstname.lastname@itv.com
www2.itv.com/london
*Managing director: Christy
Swords; controller of regional
programming: Emma Barker; head
of regional affairs: Helen Andrews*

London News Network
200 Gray's Inn Road
London WC1X 8HF
020 7430 4000
firstname.lastname@itvlondon.com
www.itvlondon.co.uk
*Planning editor: Arti Lukha; head
of news: Stuart Thomas; news
editors: Brendan McGowan and
Robin Campbell*

ITV Meridian
Television Centre,
Southampton
Hampshire SO14 0PZ
023 8022 2555
news@meridiantv.com
firstname.lastname@
granadamedia.com
www.meridiantv.co.uk
*Managing director; Lindsay
Charlton; controller of
programmes: Mark Southgate;
head of regional affairs: Alison
Pope; head of news: Guy Phillips*
Maidstone news office
ITV Meridian,
Westpoint
New Hythe,
Kent ME20 6XX
01622 882244
Newbury news office
ITV Meridian,
Strawberry Hill House
Strawberry Hill, Newbury
Berkshire RG14 1NG
01635 552266

Tyne Tees Television
City Road
Newcastle Upon Tyne NE1 2AL
0191 261 0181
news@tynetees.tv;
firstname.lastname@itv.com
www.tynetees.tv
*Managing director and controller of
programmes: Graeme Thompson;
head of regional affairs and press
contact: Norma Hope; head of news:
Graham Marples*
*Tees Valley & North Yorkshire
news office*
Tyne Tees Television
Belasis Hall Technology Park
Billingham, Teesside TS23 4EG
Newsroom: 01642 566999
newstoday@tynetees.tv
Senior editor: Bill Campbell

TV and radio contacts : **Section 4**

91

ITV Wales

The Television Centre
Culverhouse Cross
Cardiff CF5 6XJ
029 2059 0590
info@itvwales.com;
news@itvwales.com;
firstname.lastname@itvwales.com
www.itvwales.com
*Acting managing director and
controller of programmes: Elis
Owen; head of regional affairs
and press contact: Mansel Jones;
head of news: John G Williams*
Carmarthen news office
ITV Wales
Top Floor, 19–20 Lammas Street
Carmarthen SA31 3AL
01267 236809
*West Wales correspondent:
Giles Smith*
Colwyn Bay news office
ITV Wales
Celtic Business Centre,
Plas Eirias, Heritage Gate,
Abergele Road
Colwyn Bay LL29 8BW
01492 513888
colwyn@itvwales.com
*North Wales correspondents:
Carole Green and Ian Lang*
Newtown news office
ITV Wales, St David's House
Newtown SY16 1RB
01686 623381
*Mid-Wales correspondent:
Rob Shelley*
Wrexham news office
ITV Wales, Crown Buildings
31 Chester Street
Wrexham 01978 261462
*North Wales correspondent:
Paul Mewies*
ITV West
Television Centre, Bath Road
Bristol BS4 3HG
0117 972 2722
reception@itv.com;
firstname.lastname@itv.com
www.itv1west.com
*Managing director: Mark Haskell;
controller of programmes: Jane
McCloskey; head of regional
affairs: James Garrett*
Newsdesk
0117 972 2151/2152
itvwestnews@itv.com
Head of news: Steve Egginton
Press office
0117 972 2214
*Head of press and community
relations: Richard Lister*

ITV Westcountry
Langage Science Park
Western Wood Way
Plymouth PL7 5BQ
01752 333333
firstname.lastname@itv.com
www.westcountry.co.uk
*Managing director: Mark Haskell;
director of programmes: Jane
McCloskey; controller – business
affairs: Peter Gregory; controller –
technical operations: Mark
Chaplin; press contact: Rebecca
Turner*
Main newsdesk
01752 333329
news@westcountry.co.uk
Controller of news: Phil Carrodus
Barnstaple news office
ITV Westcountry, 1 Summerland
Terrace, Barnstaple EX32 8JL
01271 324244
Exeter news office
ITV Westcountry,
St Luke's Campus
Magdalene Road,
Exeter EX4 4WT
01392 499400
Penzance News Office
ITV Westcountry,
Parade Chambers
10 Parade Street
Penzance TR18 4BU
01736 331483
Taunton news office
ITV Westcountry,
Foundry Cottage
Riverside Place, St James Street
Taunton TA1 1JH
01823 322335
Truro news office
ITV Westcountry,
Courtleigh House
Lemon Street, Truro TR1 2PN
01872 262244
Weymouth news office
ITV Westcountry, 8 King Street
Weymouth DT4 7BP
01305 760860

ITV Yorkshire

The Television Centre,
Kirkstall Road
Leeds, West Yorkshire LS3 1JS
0113 243 8283
firstname.lastname@itv.com
www.yorkshiretv.com
*Managing director: David Croft,
0113 222 7184; controller of
regional programmes: Clare
Morrow, 0113 222 8724; head of
regional affairs: Sallie Ryle, 0113
222 7118*

*Calendar (ITV Yorkshire
News programme)*
0845 121 1000
calendar@yorkshiretv.com
*Head of news: Will Venters,
0113 222 8822*
Grimsby office
Immage Studios, Margaret Street
Immingham, Grimsby DN40 1LE
01469 510661
Hull office
23 Brook Street, Hull HU2 8PM
01482 324488
Lincoln office
88 Bailgate, Lincoln LN1 3AR
01522 530738
Sheffield office
23 Charter Square
Sheffield S1 3EJ
0114 272 7772
York office
York St John's College
Lord Mayors Walk
York YO31 7EX
01904 610066
Press office
0113 222 7129
Press officer: Jo Gough

Grampian TV

Television Centre
Craigshaw Business Park
West Tullos,
Aberdeen AB12 3QH
01224 848848
firstname.lastname@smg.plc.uk
www.grampiantv.co.uk
*Managing director and controller
of regional programmes:
Derrick Thomson;
head of news: Henry Eagles*

Scottish TV

200 Renfield Street,
Glasgow G2 3PR
0141 300 3000
firstname.lastname@smg.plc.uk
www.scottishtv.co.uk
*Managing director and controller of
regional programmes: Bobby Hain*
Press office
0141 300 3670
Press officer: Kirsten Elsby
Newsdesk
0141 300 3360
Head of news: Paul McKinney

Channel Television
Television Centre,
La Pouquelaye
St Helier,
Jersey
JE1 3ZD
01534 816816
news room: 01534 816688
broadcast@channeltv.co.uk
www.channeltv.co.uk
Managing director: Michael Lucas;
director of programmes:
Karen Rankine
(karen.rankine@channeltv.co.uk);
director of special projects:
Gordon de Ste Croix
(gordon@channeltv.co.uk);
director of resources and
transmission: Kevin Banner
Guernsey office
Television House,
Bulwer Avenue
St Sampson,
Guernsey
GY2 4LA
01481 241888
broadcast.gsy@channeltv.co.uk
London office
Unit 16A,
3rd Floor,
Enterprise House
59–65 Upper Ground
London SE1 9PQ
020 7633 9902

UTV
Ormeau Road,
Belfast
BT7 1EB
028 9032 8122
firstinitiallastname@utvplc.com
www.u.tv
Group chief executive: John
McCann; director of television:
Alan Bremner; head of press and
PR: Orla McKibbin; head of news:
Rob Morrison

Channel 4

124 Horseferry Road
London SW1P 2TX
020 7396 4444
Chief executive
Andy Duncan
Managing director
David Scott 020 7306 6590;
assistant: Lee Bassett
020 7306 8637
Commercial director
Andy Barnes 020 7306 8200;
assistant: Dee Caldwell
020 7306 8201
Director of television
Kevin Lygo 020 7306 6907;
assistant: Helen Pickett
020 7306 3771
Managing director, 4 Ventures
Rob Woodward 020 7306 3777;
assistant: Olga Boff
020 7306 3740

PRESS

Head of press & publicity:
Matt Baker 020 7306 8666;
assistant: Pip Lowe 020 7306 8523

COMMISSIONING

Director of television
Kevin Lygo 020 7306 3775
Comedy
Head of comedy & comedy films:
Caroline Leddy 020 7306 8718
Assistant:: Cathy Mason
020 7306 8066
Daytime and features
Commissioning editor,
daytime: Adam MacDonald
020 7306 8033;
Editor, daytime and features:
Mark Downie 020 7306 5150
Documentaries
Head: Peter Dale 020 7306 8314
assistant: Emily Renshaw-Smith
020 7306 8676
Commissioning editors:
Hilary Bell 020 7306 5173;
Danny Cohen (Cutting Edge)
020 7306 6912; deputy: Sam
Bickley 020 7306 1044;
assistant editor: Katie Speight
020 7306 8727
Editor, independent film and video:
Jess Search 020 7306 8312
Drama
Head: John Yorke 020 7306 6970
assistant: Beverley Booker
020 7306 364; deputy:
Lucy Richer 020 7306 6970

Editors: Camilla Campbell (series)
020 7306 3783; Hannah Weaver
(events) 020 7306 5536; assistant
editor: Liz Pilling 020 7306 8621
E4
Head, programming, E4 & digital:
Murray Boland 020 7306 8671;
assistant: Sasha Phillips
020 7306 8672)
Commissioning editor: Deborah
O'Connor 020 7306 3649;
head of scheduling: David Booth
020 7306 6582;
planner: Shireen Tayabali
020 7306 5591
Entertainment
Head: Andrew Newman
020 7306 6342
Commissioning editor: Katie Taylor
020 7306 8679; deputy:
Ruby Kuraishe 020 7306 6950
Factual entertainment
Head: Julian Bellamy
020 7306 6436; assistant:
Claudia Emery 020 7306 5537
Editors: Sharon Powers
020 7306 5379; Nav Raman
020 7306 8746; Andrew
Mackenzie 020 7306 3680;
Debbie Searle (cross-platform
development) 020 7306 2656
Features
Head: Sue Murphy
020 7306 8616; assistant:
Daniella Eversby 020 7306 5192
Commissioning editor:
Emma Westcott 020 7306 8476;
executive producer:
Philippa Ransford 020 7306 8424
Music, youth & T4
Head: Jules Oldroyd
020 7306 8229
Editor: Neil McCallum
020 7306 8588; assistant editor:
Cath Lovesey 020 7306 5622
Nations and regions
Director: Stuart Cosgrove
0141 568 7105;
assistant: Debbie Walker
News and current affairs
Head: Dorothy Byrne
020 7306 8588;
assistant: Louise Platel
020 7306 8132
Editors: Kevin Sutcliffe
(investigations) 020 7306 1068;
Mark Rubens 020 7306 8771

TV and radio contacts : Section 4

93

Science and education

Head: Simon Andreae
020 7306 8289; assistant:
Katie Vogel 020 7306 8431)
Editor, education: Simon Dickson
020 7306 3799; commissioning
editor, 4Learning, schools and
youth: Deborah Ward
020 7306 8499; deputy CE:
Bridget Bakokodie
020 7306 6043; reader: Clare
Boyd 020 7306 3781

Specialist factual

Head TBA; assistant: Ebona
Eastmond-Henry 020 7306 8745
History: head Hamish Mykura
020 7306 1036; (Assistant editor:
Edwina Waddy 020 7306 8303)
editor Ralph Lee 020 7306 3863.
Religion: Aaqil Ahmed 020 7306
8065. Arts & performance: Jan
Younghusband 020 7306 5153.

Sport

Head: David Kerr: 020 7306 6581
Deputy commissioning editor:
Deborah Poulton 020 7306 8501
Commissioning support
Managing editor: Janey Walker
020 7306 8623; assistant:
Melissa Hameed 020 7306 8282;
manager, commissioning &
suppliers: Helen Robertson
020 7306 6433; manager, talent
development: Charlotte Black
020 7306 5505; editorial
manager, cultural diversity:
Mary Fitzpatrick 020 7306 6454;
disability advisor: Alison Walsh
020 7306 8125

Programme acquisition

June Drumgoole 020 7306 8050;
assistant: Sarah Lloyd
020 7306 8733

BROADCASTING

Controller: Rosemary Newell
020 7306 8620;
head of schedules: Jules Oldroyd
020 7306 8229; deputy scheduler:
John Williams 020 7306 8257;
planner: Lynne Jarrett 020 7306
8231; senior planner: Lucy Rogers
020 7306 8536; finance planning:
Steve Harding 020 7306 8511,
Ray Banks 020 7306 6965, Gayle
Higginbotham 020 7306 5362,
Paul Matias 020 7306 8042

Agency sales: Matt Shreeve
020 7306 8240; airtime
management: Merlin Inkley
020 7306 8254; channel
operations: Steve White 020 7306
8403; commercial affairs:
Sara Geater 020 7306 8619;
client & strategic sales:
Mike Parker 020 7306 8242;
corporate development:
Michael Hodgson 020 7306 5356;
finance: Sue Ford 020 7306 8234;
marketing: Bill Griffin 020 7306
6583; sales, marketing & research:
Hugh Johnson 020 7306 8633;
research & insight:
Claire Grimmond 020 7306 8779;
sponsorship: David Charlesworth
020 7306 8043; strategy: Jonathan
Thompson 020 7306 8799

4Ventures

124 Facilities
Tony Chamberlain 020 7306 8110
4Channels
Dan Brooke 020 7306 6497;
assistant: Wendy Foster
020 7306 6448
4Creative
Richard Burdett 020 7306 8110;
assistant: Clare Wells
020 7306 1005
4Learning
Heather Rabbatts 020 7306 5125;
assistant: Louise Ann Cotter
020 7306 5541
4Rights (C4I)
Paul Sowerbutts 020 7306 6459;
assistant: Karol Roker
020 7306 6905
4Rights (consumer products)
Mike Morris 020 7306 5364;
assistant: Kristell Farr
020 7306 5510
4Ventures
Anmar Kawash 020 7306 5350;
assistant: Clare Brown
020 7306 6461
E4
Murray Boland 020 7306 8671;
assistant: Sasha Phillips
020 7306 8672
Film Four channel
Tom Sykes 020 7306 6442;
assistant: Jolene Yeo
020 7306 3691
Interactive
Andy Taylor 020 7306 3651

Media projects
Graeme Mason 020 7306 3796;
assistant: Rebecca Turner
020 7306 6588

Channel 4 News

ITN, 200 Grays Inn Road
London WC1X 8XZ
020 7833 3000
www.channel4.com/news
*Editor: Jim Gray; deputy editor:
Martin Fewell; managing editor:
Gay Flashman*

Newsdesk 020 7430 4601

Press 020 7430 4220
Fiona.Railton@itn.co.uk
*Press & publicity manager:
Fiona Railton*

Presenters
Anchor: Jon Snow; noon anchor:
Krishnan Guru-Murthy, Sue
Turton, Samira Ahmed
Senior home news editor
Evette Edwards
Political editor
Elinor Goodman
Senior foreign news editor
Deborah Rayner
International editor
Lindsey Hilsum
Commissioning editor, independent productions
Fiona Campbell
Correspondents
Chief correspondent: Alex
Thomson; home affairs: Simon
Israel; political: Gary Gibbon;
social affairs: Victoria Macdonald;
science: Tom Clarke;
science/defence: Julian Rush;
economics: Liam Halligan;
arts: Nicholas Glass; Midlands:
Carl Dinnen; Scotland:
Sarah Smith; foreign affairs:
Jonathan Miller; Washington:
Jonathan Rugman; Asia:
Ian Williams; reporters:
Katie Razzall, Stephen Smith,
Darshna Soni; sport: Sue Turton

Five

22 Long Acre, London
WC2E 9LY
020 7550 5555
firstname.lastname@five.tv
www.five.tv
*Director of programmes: Dan
Chambers, 020 7550 5673 (PA
Sarah Jackson, 020 7550 5522);
controller of broadcast services:
David Burge, 020 7691 6260;
head of marketing: Simon
Downing, 020 7550 5531; brand
manager: Jo Fuller, 020 7550 5528
Five, address as above;
Tel: 020 7550 5551; head of sales:
Nick Milligan; email:
nick.milligan@five.tv*
Press office 020 7550 5558
*Head of press & corporate affairs:
Paul Leather 020 7550 5541;
deputy head of press: Tracey
O'Connor 020 7550 5553;
marketing & publicity executive:
Louise Bowers 020 7550 5662;
entertainment publicist:
Nick Dear 020 7550 5634; drama
serials: Marie Louise Pumfrey
020 7550 5538; factual and
features: Louise Plank 020 7550
5659; acquisitions & youth:
Tamara Bishopp 020 7550 5539*

GENRES

Arts Controller: Kim Peat
020 7421 7107
Children Controller of children's
programmes: Nick Wilson
Drama Temporary controller of
drama: Jane Harris;
Daytime Controller: Kim Peat
020 7421 7107
Factual entertainment
Controller: Steve Gowans;
deputy controller: Liam
Humphreys 020 7550 5628;
deputy commissioning editor:
Ian Dunkley 020 7550 5659
Features & entertainment
Controller: Ben Frow
020 7421 7118

History Controller: Alex
Sutherland
News & current affairs Senior
programme controller: Chris
Shaw 020 7421 7122; deputy
controller of news, current affairs
and documentaries: Ian Russell
020 7550 5529
Religion Controller: Kim Peat
020 7421 7107
Science Controller: Justine
Kershaw 020 7421 7112
Sport Controller: Robert Charles
020 7421 7185
Youth & music Controller:
Sham Sandhu 020 7421 7184
Other departments
Acquisitions Director: Jeff Ford
020 7421 7166
Interactive Controller: Sham
Sandhu 020 7421 7184;
producer: Steven Bonner
020 7550 5663
Scheduling and planning
Director: Susanna Dinnage
020 7550 5588

---

five news

Until 2005: ITN
200 Grays Inn Road
London WC1X 8XZ
020 7833 3000
www.itn.co.uk/fivenews
*Editor: Gary Rogers; political
editor: Andy Bell; presenters:
Kirsty Young, Charlie Stayt,
Rob Butler, Katie Ledger;
defence and foreign affairs
correspondent: James Bays;
consumer: Charlotte Hume; north
of England: Ben Scotchbrook;
senior reporters: Ben Ando, Mark
Jordan; reporters: Colin Campbell,
Keith Doyle, Catherine Jones*
From January 2005: Sky News
(see page 96)

ITN

200 Grays Inn Road
London WC1X 8XZ
020 7833 3000
www.itn.co.uk
*Chief executive: Mark Wood;
director of corporate affairs: Sophie
Cohen; managing director,
multimedia content: Nicholas
Wheeler; head of production, ITN
Factual: Marilyn Bennett; head of
ITN factual: Philip Dampier;
managing director, ITN Archive:
Alwyn Lindsay*

RTÉ

Radio Telefís Éireann
New Library Building, Donnybrook
Dublin 4, Ireland
00 353 1 208 3111
info@rte.ie
www.rte.ie
*Irish national broadcaster.
Communications manager, TV:
Kathriona Edwards*
Press and information:
00 353 1 208 3434
firstname.lastname@rte.ie
*Press contacts: acquisitions and
drama: Sharon Brady;
entertainment: Dympna Clerkin;
factual: Dervla Keating; Fair City
(soap): Tara O'Brian; music,
sport and young people: Richie
Ryan; news and current affairs:
Carolyn Fisher*

KEY GOVERNMENT CONTACTS FOR DIGITAL TV

Department for Culture, Media and Sport
2–4 Cockspur Street
London SW1Y 5DH
020 7211 6000
enquiries@culture.gov.uk;
broadcasting@culture.gov.uk
www.culture.gov.uk/broadcasting
Culture secretary: Tessa Jowell
Press: *Mark Devane; 020 7211 6267;*
Mark.devane@culture.gsi.gov.uk
digitaltelevision@culture.gov.uk
www.digitaltelevision.gov.uk

Department for Trade and Industry
1 Victoria Street,
London SW1H 0ET
020 7215 5000
dti.enquiries@dti.gsi.gov.uk
www.dti.gov.uk/industries
/broadcasting
Head of broadcasting policy and
director of digital television project:
Jane Humphreys; deputy project
manager, digital television: David
Fuhr; broadcasting policy advisor:
John Franck; head of broadcasting
technology: Ian Dixon
Press: *Nic Fearon; 020 7215 5952;*
nic.fearon@dti.gsi.gov.uk
digitaltelevision@culture.gov.uk
www.digitaltelevision.gov.uk

BSkyB

British Sky Broadcasting
Grant Way, Isleworth
TW7 5QD
0870 240 3000
www.sky.com
Chief executive: James Murdoch;
chief operating officer: Richard
Freudenstein: managing director,
sales, marketing & interactive:
Jon Florsheim; managing director,
Sky Sports: Vic Wakeling; director
of corporate communications:
Julian Eccles
Press office 0870 240 3000
Director of publicity: Adrian Lee;
head of programme publicity:
Richard Turner; Sky One: Stephen
Browning; Sky Movies: Phil
Evans; Sky News: Stella Tooth; Sky
Sports: Chris Haynes; consumer
PR: Gabby Bennett

SKY CHANNELS

Sky Networks
Managing director, Sky Networks:
Dawn Airey; deputy managing
director, Sky Networks/director of
film channels & acquisitions:
Sophie Turner-Laing; director of
commercial affairs: Delia Bushell
All Sky channels bar sport

Sky One, Sky One Mix
www.skyone.co.uk
Controller: James Baker

Sky Box Office
www.skymovies.com
Director of film channels &
acquisitions: Sophie Turner-Laing

Sky Cinema 1 & 2
www.skymovies.com
Director of film channels &
acquisitions: Sophie Turner-Laing

Sky Movies 1 & 2
www.skymovies.com
Director of film channels &
acquisitions: Sophie Turner-Laing

Sky Sports 1, 2 & 3; Extra; News
www.skysports.com
Managing director, Sky Sports: Vic
Wakeling

Sky Travel, Travel Extra, Shop
www.skytravel.co.uk
General manager, Sky Travel:
Barbara Gibbon

Sky Vegas Live, Sky Bet
www.skyvegaslive.com
Managing director, Sky Bet: Nick
Rust

The Amp
www.theamp.tv
Head of music: Jo Wallace

Scuzz
www.scuzz.tv
Head of music: Jo Wallace

Flaunt
www.flaunt.tv
Head of music: Jo Wallace

Sky Active
www.sky.com/skyactive
Managing director, Sky Interactive:
Ian Shepherd
Interactive

Sky Business
www.sky.com/business
Commercial marketing director:
Iain Holden
Sales to non-domestic clients

Sky Ventures
www.sky.com/ventures
Head of Sky Ventures & commercial
management: Matthew Imi
Joint venture channels and services

Sky News
www.skynews.co.uk
Head of Sky News: Nick Pollard
Key presenters
Afternoon: Kay Burley, Mark
Longhurst; Live at Five: Anna
Botting, Jeremy Thompson
Correspondents
Political: Adam Boulton, Jon Craig,
Jenny Percival, Peter Spencer, Glen
O'Glaza; business: Michael Wilson,
Heather Scott, Juliet Errington, Alex
Crawford; crime: Martin Brunt;
health: Nicola Hill, Thomas Moore;
foreign: Richard Bestic, Colin
Brazier, Keith Graves, Emma Hurd,
Laurence Lee, Tim Marshall, Stuart
Ramsay, Dominic Waghorn,
Andrew Wilson; entertainment:
Georgie Arnold, Neil Sean, Matt
Smith; royal: Geoff Meade; other:
David Bowden, David Chater,
Michelle Clifford, Lisa Holland,
Peter Sharp; also regional bureaux
and 25 other reporters

Cable

NTL UK
NTL House
Bartley Wood Business Park
Bartley Way, Hook
Hampshire RG27 9UP
01256 752000
www.ntl.com
Managing director, NTL Home:
Aizad Hussain; managing director,
NTL Business: Tom Bennie
Press: 01256 752000
Contact: Justine Parrish

NTL Broadcast
Crawley Court, Winchester
Hampshire SO21 2QA
01962 823434
www.ntlbroadcast.com
Managing director: Peter Douglas
Press: 01962 822582
Contact: Bruce Randall

Telewest Communications
Export House
Cawsey Way
Woking, Surrey GU21 6QX
01483 750900
www.telewest.co.uk
Acting chief executive: Barry Elson
Press: 020 7299 5888
Contact: Jane Hardman

Cablecom Investments
The Coach House
Bill Hill Park
Wokingham
Berks RG40 5QT
0118 979 2076
customer@cablecom.co.uk
www.cablecom.co.uk
*Managing director: Charles
Tompkins*

WightCable
56 Love Lane
Cowes
Isle of Wight PO31 7EU
01983 242424
enquiries@wightcable.com
www.wightcable.com
Managing director: Duncan Kerr
WightCable North
3 Chalmers Place
Riverside Business Park
Irvine
North Ayrshire KA11 5DH
01294 230000
enquiries@wightcablenorth.com
www.wightcablenorth.com
Press: 01294 231145
pr@wightcablenorth.com
Contact: Emma Dawson

Video Networks
205 Holland Park Avenue
London W11 4XB
020 7348 4000
info@videonetworks.com
www.videonetworks.com
Chairman and CEO: Roger Lynch
Press: 020 7348 4110
Contact: Nick Southall

Digital terrestrial

Freeview
Broadcast Centre, (BC3 D5)
201 Wood Lane,
London W12 7TP
0870 880 9980
www.freeview.co.uk
General manager: Lib Charlesworth
*Free-to-view digital terrestrial
service, owned by Crown Castle, BBC
and BSkyB*
Press: 020 7229 4400
Contact: Nick Clark
nick.clark@nelsonbostock.com

Crown Castle UK
Warwick Technology Park
Gallows Hill, Heathcote Lane
Warwick CV34 6TN
01926 416000
MarketingUK@crowncastle.com
www.crowncastle.com
Managing director: Peter Abery
*Digital terrestrial transmitter
operator; part-owner of Freeview*
Press: 01926 416870
Contact: Stephen Arnold

Top-Up TV
PO Box 208, Twickenham
TW1 2YF
0870 054 5354
enquiries@topuptv.com
www.topuptv.com
Chairman: David Chance
*Offers top-up pay channels for
Freeview viewers*

TV channels

Adventure One
Grant Way, Isleworth TW7 5QD
020 7705 3000
natgeoweb@bskyb.com
www.nationalgeographic.co.uk
*General manager:
Simon Bohrsmann*

African and Caribbean TV
28F Lawrence Road
London N15 4EG
020 8809 7700
info@actv.org.uk
www.actv.org.uk
*Programme controller:
Rose McDonald*

The Amp
Grant Way, Isleworth TW7 5QD
0870 240 3000
www.theamp.tv
Head of music: Jo Wallace

Artsworld
Great West House (15th floor)
Great West Road, Brentford
Middlesex TW8 9DF
020 7805 2404
Press:
judith.holmes@artsworld.com
www.artsworld.com
*Programme controller:
Alison Martin*

AsiaNet
Studio complex,
Puliyarakonam PO
Trivandrum 695 573
India
00 91 471 237 8407
webmaster@asianetglobal.com
www.asianetglobal.com

attheraces
11–13 Charlotte Street
London W17 1RH
020 7705 3000
team@attheraces.co.uk
www.attheraces.co.uk
*Managing director: Sir Iain Hogg;
head of betting: David Stewart*

B4U
Transputec House
19 Heather Park Drive
Wembley HA0 1SS
020 8795 7171
Press: sajnit@b4unetwork.com
www.b4utv.com
Programme controller: Anita Roy

B4U Music
Transputec House
19 Heather Park Drive
Wembley HA0 1SS
020 8795 7171
Press: sajnit@b4unetwork.com
www.b4utv.com
Programme controller: Anita Roy

BBC America
7475 Wisconsin Avenue
11th Floor
Bethesda, USA MD 20814
00 1 301 347 2222
bbcamerica@bbc.co.uk
Press: press.office@bbc.co.uk
www.bbcamerica.com
*Programme executive: Alison
Fredericks*

BBC Canada
121 Bloor Street East, Suite 200
Toronto, Ontario,
Canada M4W 3M5
00 416 934 7800
feedback@bbccanada.com
Press: press.office@bbc.co.uk
www.bbccanada.com

BBC Food
PO Box 5054, London W12 0ZY
020 8433 2221
bbcfood@bbc.co.uk
Press: press.office@bbc.co.uk
www.bbcfood.com
Editor: David Weiland

BBC Four
Television Centre, Wood Lane
London W12 7RJ
020 8576 3193
Press: press.office@bbc.co.uk
www.bbc.co.uk/bbcfour
Controller: Janice Hadlow

BBC News 24
Television Centre, Wood Lane
London W12 7RJ
020 8743 8000
bbcnews24@bbc.co.uk
Press: press.office@bbc.co.uk
www.bbc.co.uk/bbcnews24
Editoral director: Mark Popescu

97

BBC One
Television Centre, Wood Lane
London W12 7RJ
020 8743 8000
Press: press.office@bbc.co.uk
www.bbc.co.uk/bbcone
Controller: Lorraine Heggessey;
controller of daytime:
Alison Sharman
(daytime.proposals@bbc.co.uk)

BBC Parliament
4 Millbank, London SW1P 3JA
020 7973 6216
parliament@bbc.co.uk
Press: press.office@bbc.co.uk
www.bbc.co.uk/bbcparliament

BBC Prime
PO Box 5054, London W12 0ZY
020 8433 2221
bbcprime@bbc.co.uk
Press: press.office@bbc.co.uk
www.bbcprime.com
Editor: David Weiland

BBC Three
Television Centre, Wood Lane
London W12 7RJ
020 8743 8000
bbcthreefeedback@bbc.co.uk
Press: press.office@bbc.co.uk
www.bbc.co.uk/bbcthree
Controller: Stuart Murphy

BBC Two
Television Centre, Wood Lane
London W12 7RJ
020 8743 8000
Press: press.office@bbc.co.uk
www.bbc.co.uk/bbctwo
Controller: Roly Keating

BBC World
Television Centre, Wood Lane
London W12 7RJ
020 8576 2308
bbcworld@bbc.co.uk
Press: press.office@bbc.co.uk
www.bbcworld.com
Editorial director: Sian Kevill

Biography Channel
Grant Way, Isleworth TW7 5QD
0870 240 3000
Press: biographychannelpress@
bskyb.com
www.thebiographychannel.co.uk
Channel director: Richard Melman

Bloomberg Television
City Gate House
39–45 Finsbury Square
London EC2A 1PQ
020 7330 7797
Press: dwachtel@bloomberg.net
www.bloomberg.com/tv
Executive editor, broadcast:
Ken Cohn

Boomerang
Turner House
16 Great Marlborough Street
London W1F 7HS
020 7693 1000
Press: lucy.amos@turner.com
www.cartoonnetwork.co.uk
Press website:
www.europe.turnerinfo.com
Channel manager: Dan Balaam

The Box
Mappin House
4 Winsley Street
London W1W 8HF
020 7182 8000
Press:
maureen.corish@emap.com
www.emap.com
Programme director: Dave Young;
director of music: Simon Sadler

Bravo
160 Great Portland Street
London W1W 5QA
020 7299 5000
Press: jakki_lewis@flextech.co.uk
www.bravo.co.uk
Programme controller: Richard
Woolfe

British Eurosport
55 Drury Lane, London
WC2B 5SQ
020 7468 7777
Press: swalker@eurosport.com
www.eurosport.co.uk
Programming director:
Pierre Jean Sebert

Cartoon Network
Turner House
16 Great Marlborough Street
London W1F 7HS
020 7693 1000
Press: lucy.amos@turner.com
www.cartoonnetwork.co.uk
Press website:
www.europe.turnerinfo.com
Channel manager: Don Gardiner

CBBC
Television Centre, Wood Lane
London W12 7RJ
020 8743 8000
Press: press.office@bbc.co.uk
www.bbc.co.uk/cbbc
Controller: Dorothy Prior

CBeebies
Television Centre, Wood Lane
London W12 7RJ
020 8743 8000
Press: press.office@bbc.co.uk
www.bbc.co.uk/cbeebies
Controller: Dorothy Prior

Challenge
160 Great Portland Street
London W1W 5QA
020 7299 5000
Press: jakki_lewis@flextech.co.uk
www.challenge.co.uk
Programme controller:
Jonathan Webb

Chelsea TV
Stamford Bridge, Fulham Road
London SW6 1HS
020 7915 1980
chelseatv@chelseafc.com
www.chelseafc.com
Managing director: Chris Tate

Chinese Channel
Teddington Studios, Broom Road
Teddington TW11 9NT
020 8614 8364
newseditor@chinese-
channel.co.uk
www.chinese-channel.co.uk
Head of programming:
Desmond Ng

CNBC Europe
10 Fleet Place, London
EC4M 7QS
020 7653 9300
Press: cblenkinsop@
cnbceurope.com
www.cnbceurope.com
Programme controller:
Harry Fuller

CNN
Turner House
16 Great Marlborough Street
London W1F 7HS
020 7693 1000;
Press: 020 7693 0942
Press: chris.dwyer@turner.com
http://edition.cnn.com
International managing editor for
EMEA: Nick Wrenn

The Community Channel
3–7 Euston Centre,
Regent's Place
London NW1 3JG
020 7874 7626
Press: helenad@
communitychannel.org
www.communitychannel.org
Channel controller: Jane Mote

Discovery Animal Planet
160 Great Portland Street
London W1W 5QA
020 7462 3600
Press: becky_weathers@
discovery-europe.com
www.discoverychannel.co.uk
Channel director: Eliza Burrows

Discovery Channel
160 Great Portland Street
London W1W 5QA
020 7462 3600
Press: lee_hobbs@
discovery-europe.com
www.discoverychannel.co.uk
Channel director: Katy Thorogood

Discovery Civilisation
160 Great Portland Street
London W1W 5QA
020 7462 3600
Press: jo_march@
discovery-europe.com
www.discoverychannel.co.uk
Channel director: Katy Thorogood

Discovery Health
160 Great Portland Street
London W1W 5QA
020 7462 3600
Press: libby_rowley@
discovery-europe.com
www.discoverychannel.co.uk
Channel director: Clare Laycock

Discovery Home and Leisure
160 Great Portland Street
London W1W 5QA
020 7462 3600
Press: claire_phillips@
discovery-europe.com
www.discoverychannel.co.uk
Channel director: Paul Welling

Discovery Kids
160 Great Portland Street
London W1W 5QA
020 7462 3600
Press: libby_rowley@
discovery-europe.com
www.discoverychannel.co.uk
Channel director: Clare Laycock

Discovery Science
160 Great Portland Street
London W1W 5QA
020 7462 3600
Press: jo_march@
discovery-europe.com
www.discoverychannel.co.uk
Channel director: Katy Thorogood

Discovery Travel and Adventure
160 Great Portland Street
London W1W 5QA
020 7462 3600
Press: claire_phillips@
discovery-europe.com
www.discoverychannel.co.uk
Channel director: Paul Welling

Discovery Wings
160 Great Portland Street
London W1W 5QA
020 7462 3600
Press: jo_march@
discovery-europe.com
www.discoverychannel.co.uk
Channel director: Katy Thorogood

Disney Channel
Chiswick Park, Building 12
566 Chiswick High Road
London W4 5AN
020 8636 2000
Press:
rachel.babington@disney.com
www.disneychannel.co.uk
*Director of programming and
acquisitions: James Neal*

E4
124 Horseferry Road
London SW1P 2TX
020 7396 4444
Press: mbeake@channel4.co.uk
www.channel4.com/e4
*Head of programming:
Murray Boland*

Eurosport International
55 Drury Lane,
London WC2B 5SQ
020 7468 7777
Press: swalker@eurosport.com
www.eurosport.com
*Programming director:
Pierre Jean Sebert*

Eurosportnews
55 Drury Lane, London
WC2B 5SQ
020 7468 7777
Press: swalker@eurosport.com
www.eurosport.co.uk
*Programming director:
Pierre Jean Sebert*

Extreme Sports Channel
The Media Centre
19 Bolsover Street
London W1W 5NA
020 7886 0770
Press: zoe@
extremesportschannel.com
www.extreme.com
*Head of acquisitions: Andy
Warkman*

Fantasy Channel
Suite 14, Burlington House
St Saviours Road, St Helier
Jersey JE2 4LA
01534 703700
admin@nasnet.je
Programme controller: Peter Farell

Filmfour
124 Horseferry Road
London SW1P 2TX
020 7396 4444
Press: spinder@channel4.co.uk
www.filmfour.com
Head of film: Tessa Ross

Flaunt
Grant Way, Isleworth TW7 5QD
0870 240 3000
www.flaunt.tv
Head of music: Jo Wallace

FTN
160 Great Portland Street
London W1W 5QA
020 7299 5000
Press: judy_wells@flextech.co.uk;
jessica_alder@flextech.co.uk
www.ftn.tv
*Programme controller:
Richard Woolfe*

God TV
Crown House, Borough Road
Sunderland SR1 1HW
0191 568 0800
info@god.tv
www.GOD.tv
Network controller: Wendy Alec

Granada Men and Motors
Franciscan Court, 16 Hatfields
London SE1 8DJ
020 7578 4040
Press:
malcolm.packer@gsb.co.uk
www.menandmotors.co.uk
*Director of programming:
Gary Shoefield*

Hallmark
234a Kings Road
London SW3 5UA
020 7368 9100
info@hallmarkchannel.co.uk
Press: janemuirhead@
hallmarkchannel.com
www.hallmarkchannel.co.uk
*Director of acquisitions:
Rosy Hill-Davies*

History Channel
Grant Way, Isleworth TW7 5QD
0870 240 3000
Press: historychannelpress@
bskyb.com
www.thehistorychannel.co.uk
Channel director: Richard Melman

Hits Channel
Mappin House, 4 Winsley Street
London W1W 8HF
020 7182 8000
Press:
maureen.corish@emap.com
www.emapadvertising.com
*Programme director: Dave Young;
director of music: Simon Sadler*

ITV1
200 Grays Inn Road
London WC1X 8XZ
020 7843 8000
www.itv.com/itv1
*Director of programmes: Nigel
Pickard; director of programme
strategy: David Bergg*

ITV2
200 Grays Inn Road
London WC1X 8XZ
020 7843 8000
www.itv.com/itv2
Channel editor: Zai Bennett
020 7843 8129; controller of
commissioned programmes:
Daniella Neumann 020 7843 8101

ITV News
200 Grays Inn Road
London WC1X 8XZ
020 7833 3000
Press: itvplanning@itn.co.uk
www.itv.com/news
Editor-in-chief: David Mannion

Kerrang TV
Mappin House, 4 Winsley Street
London W1W 8HF
020 7182 8000
Press:
maureen.corish@emap.com
www.emapadvertising.com
Programme director: Dave Young;
director of music: Simon Sadler

Kiss TV
Mappin House, 4 Winsley Street
London W1W 8HF
020 7182 8000
Press:
maureen.corish@emap.com
www.emapadvertising.com
Programme director: Dave Young;
director of music: Simon Sadler

Living
160 Great Portland Street
London W1W 5QA
020 7299 5000
Press: judy_wells@flextech.co.uk;
jessica_alder@flextech.co.uk
www.livingtv.co.uk
Programme controller: Richard
Woolfe

Magic TV
Mappin House, 4 Winsley Street
London W1W 8HF
020 7182 8000
Press:
maureen.corish@emap.com
www.emapadvertising.com
Programme director: Dave Young;
director of music: Simon Sadler

MTV Base
MTV, Hawley Crescent
London NW1 8TT
020 7284 7777
Press:
parker.eleanor@mtvne.com
www.mtv.co.uk
Head of development (for
programme commissions):
Chris Sice

MTV Dance
MTV, Hawley Crescent
London NW1 8TT
020 7284 7777
Press:
parker.eleanor@mtvne.com
www.mtv.co.uk
Head of development (for
programme commissions):
Chris Sice

MTV UK & Ireland
MTV, Hawley Crescent
London NW1 8TT
020 7284 7777
Press:
parker.eleanor@mtvne.com
www.mtv.co.uk
Head of development (for
programme commissions):
Chris Sice

MTV2
MTV, Hawley Crescent
London NW1 8TT
020 7284 7777
Press:
parker.eleanor@mtvne.com
www.mtv.co.uk
Head of development (for
programme commissions):
Chris Sice

Music Choice Europe
Fleet House
57–61 Clerkenwell Road
London EC1M 5AR
020 7014 8700
Press:
djones@musicchoice.co.uk
www.musicchoice.co.uk
Head of music and PR: Dylan Jones

MUTV
4th Floor
274 Deansgate
Manchester M3 4JB
0161 834 1111
mutv@mutv.com
www.manutd.com/mutv
Editor-in-chief: Bob Farrer

Nation 217
6&7 Princes Court
Wapping Lane
London E1W 2DA
020 7942 7942
william.van.rest@nation217.tv
www.nation217.tv
Head: William van Rest

National Geographic Channel
Grant Way, Isleworth TW7 5QD
020 7705 3000
natgeoweb@bskyb.com
www.nationalgeographic.co.uk
General manager:
Simon Bohrsmann

Nick Jr
Nickelodeon House
15-18 Rathbone Place
London W1T 1HU
020 7462 1000
www.nickjr.co.uk
Director of programming:
Howard Litton

Nickelodeon
Nickelodeon House
15–18 Rathbone Place
London W1T 1HU
020 7462 1000
www.nick.co.uk
Director of programming:
Howard Litton

Nicktoons TV
Nickelodeon House
15–18 Rathbone Place
London W1T 1HU
020 7462 1000
www.nick.co.uk/toons
Director of programming:
Howard Litton

Paramount Comedy
UK House, 4th Floor
180 Oxford Street
London W1D 1DS
020 7478 5300
Press:
zoe.diver@paramountcomedy.com
www.paramountcomedy.co.uk
Director of programming:
Heather Jones

Plus
Franciscan Court
16 Hatfields
London SE1 8DJ
020 7578 4040
Press:
malcolm.packer@gsb.co.uk
www.plustv.co.uk
Director of programming:
Gary Shoefield

Q TV
Mappin House
4 Winsley Street
London W1W 8HF
020 7182 8000
Press:
maureen.corish@emap.com
www.emapadvertising.com
Programme director: Dave Young;
director of music: Simon Sadler

QVC
Marco Polo Hous
346 Queenstown Road
Chelsea Bridge
London SW8 4NQ
020 7705 5600
Press: 020 7886 8440
www.qvcuk.com
Planning manager: Susan Hellyar

Revelation TV
117a Cleveland Street
London W1T 6PX
020 7631 4446
howard@revelationtv.com
leslie@revelationtv.com
www.revelationtv.com
Head of programming:
Howard Conder

Sci-Fi
5–7 Mandeville Place
London W1U 3AR
020 7535 3500
press 020 7535 3591
www.uk.scifi.com
Head of programming &
acquisitions: Monica Iglesias

Scuzz
Grant Way, Isleworth TW7 5QD
0870 240 3000
www.scuzz.tv
Head of music: Jo Wallace

Setanta Sport Europe
52 The Haymarket, St James's
London SW1Y 4RP
020 7930 8926
setantauk@setanta.com
www.setanta.com
Joint managing director:
Leonard Ryan

Sky Bet
Grant Way, Isleworth TW7 5QD
0870 240 3000
www.skybet.com;
www.skybetvegas.com
Head of programme publicity:
Richard Turner –
richard.turner@bskyb.com

Sky Box Office
Grant Way, Isleworth TW7 5QD
0870 240 3000
www.skymovies.com
Director: Sophie Turner-Laing

Sky Cinema 1 & 2
Grant Way, Isleworth TW7 5QD
0870 240 3000
www.skymovies.com
Director: Sophie Turner-Laing

Sky Movies 1
Grant Way, Isleworth TW7 5QD
0870 240 3000
www.skymovies.com
Director: Sophie Turner-Laing

Sky Movies 2
Grant Way, Isleworth TW7 5QD
0870 240 3000
www.skymovies.com
Director: Sophie Turner-Laing

Sky News
Grant Way, Isleworth TW7 5QD
0870 240 3000
www.skynews.co.uk
Head of Sky News: Nick Pollard

Sky One
Grant Way, Isleworth TW7 5QD
0870 240 3000
www.skyone.co.uk
Controller: James Baker

Sky One Mix
Grant Way, Isleworth TW7 5QD
0870 240 3000
www.skyone.co.uk
Controller: James Baker

Sky Sports 1, 2 & 3
Grant Way, Isleworth TW7 5QD
0870 240 3000
www.skysports.com
Managing director: Vic Wakeling

Sky Sports Extra
Grant Way, Isleworth TW7 5QD
0870 240 3000
www.skysports.com
Managing director: Vic Wakeling

Sky Sports News
Grant Way, Isleworth TW7 5QD
0870 240 3000
www.skysports.com
Managing director: Vic Wakeling

Sky Travel
Grant Way, Isleworth TW7 5QD
0870 240 3000
www.skytravel.co.uk
General manager: Barbara Gibbon

Sky Travel Extra
Grant Way, Isleworth TW7 5QD
0870 240 3000
www.skytravel.co.uk
General manager: Barbara Gibbon

Sky Travel Shop
Grant Way, Isleworth TW7 5QD
0870 240 3000
www.skytravel.co.uk
General manager: Barbara Gibbon

Sky Vegas Live
Grant Waym Isleworth TW7 5QD
0870 240 3000
www.skyvegaslive.com

Smash Hits Channel
Mappin House, 4 Winsley Street
London W1W 8HF
020 7182 8000
Press:
maureen.corish@emap.com
www.emapadvertising.com
Programme director: Dave Young;
director of music: Simon Sadler

Sony Entertainment TV Asia
34 Foubert's Place
London W1V 2BH
020 7534 7575
Press: ash_jaswal@spe.sony.com
www.setasia.tv
Head of UK and Europe:
Nilam Panchal

Star TV
Great West House
Great West Road, Brentford
Middlesex TW8 9DF
020 7805 2326
Press: rinku.devgun@bskyb.com
www.uk.startv.com
UK marketing executive:
Rinku Devgun

SUBtv
4th Floor
140 Buckingham Palace Road
London SW1W 9SA
020 7881 2540
info@jvtv.net
www.jvtv.net
Commercial manager: Joy Golden;
creative director: Jon Kingdon

TMF (available on Freeview)
MTV, Hawley Crescent
London NW1 8TT
020 7284 7777
Press:
hershon.mandy@mtvne.com
www.vh1.co.uk
Acting general manager (for
programme commissions):
Steve Shannon

Toonami
Turner House
16 Great Marlborough Street
London W1F 7HS
020 7693 1000
Press: lucy.amos@turner.com
www.cartoonnetwork.co.uk;
Press:
www.europe.turnerinfo.com
Channel manager: Paul Cackett

Travel Channel
66 Newman Street
London W1T 3EQ
020 7636 5401
Press: petra@travelchannel.co.uk
www.travelchannel.co.uk
Head of programming:
Angela Taylor

Trouble
160 Great Portland Street
London W1W 5QA
020 7299 5000
Press: jakki_lewis@flextech.co.uk
www.trouble.co.uk
Programme controller:
Jonathan Webb

Turner Classic Movies
Turner House
16 Great Marlborough Street
London W1F 7HS
020 7693 1000
Press: ann.rosen@turner.com
www.tcmonline.co.uk
Press website:
www.europe.turnerinfo.com
Channel manager: Alan Musa

UKTV Bright Ideas
UKTV, 2nd Floor,
Flextech Building
160 Great Portland Street
London W1W 5QA
020 7299 6200
Press: dorita.hollins@uktv.co.uk
www.uktv.co.uk
Head of lifestyle: Nick Thorogood

UKTV Documentary
UKTV, 2nd Floor,
Flextech Building
160 Great Portland Street
London W1W 5QA
020 7299 6200
Press: rebecca.hook@uktv.co.uk
www.uktv.co.uk
Head of factual: Charlotte Ashton

UKTV Drama
UKTV, 2nd Floor,
Flextech Building
160 Great Portland Street
London W1W 5QA
020 7299 6200
Press: carolyn.ball@uktv.co.uk
www.uktv.co.uk
Head of entertainment: Matt Tombs

UKTV Food
UKTV, 2nd Floor,
Flextech Building
160 Great Portland Street
London W1W 5QA
020 7299 6200
Press: dorita.hollins@uktv.co.uk
www.uktvfood.co.uk
Head of lifestyle: Nick Thorogood

UKTV G2
UKTV, 2nd Floor,
Flextech Building
160 Great Portland Street
London W1W 5QA
020 7299 6200
Press: carolyn.ball@uktv.co.uk
www.uktv.co.uk
Head of entertainment: Matt Tombs

UKTV Gold
UKTV, 2nd Floor,
Flextech Building
160 Great Portland Street
London W1W 5QA
020 7299 6200
Press: carolyn.ball@uktv.co.uk
www.uktv.co.uk
Head of entertainment: Matt Tombs

UKTV History
UKTV, 2nd Floor,
Flextech Building
160 Great Portland Street
London W1W 5QA
020 7299 6200
Press: rebecca.hook@uktv.co.uk
www.uktv.co.uk
Head of factual: Charlotte Ashton

UKTV People
UKTV, 2nd Floor,
Flextech Building
160 Great Portland Street
London W1W 5QA
020 7299 6200
Press: rebecca.hook@uktv.co.uk
www.uktv.co.uk
Head of factual: Charlotte Ashton

UKTV Style
UKTV, 2nd Floor,
Flextech Building
160 Great Portland Street
London W1W 5QA
020 7299 6200
Press: dorita.hollins@uktv.co.uk
www.uktvstyle.co.uk
Head of lifestyle: Nick Thorogood

VH1
MTV, Hawley Crescent
London NW1 8TT
020 7284 7777
Press:
hershon.mandy@mtvne.com
www.vh1.co.uk
*Acting general manager (for
programme commissions):
Steve Shannon*

VH1 Classic
MTV, Hawley Crescent
London NW1 8TT
020 7284 7777
Press:
hershon.mandy@mtvne.com
www.vh1.co.uk
*Acting general manager (for
programme commissions):
Steve Shannon*

VH2
MTV, Hawley Crescent
London NW1 8TT
020 7284 7777
Press:
hershon.mandy@mtvne.com
www.vh1.co.uk
*Acting general manager (for
programme commissions):
Steve Shannon*

Zee TV
64 Newman Street
London W1T 3ES
020 7637 4502
media@zeenetwork.com
www.zeetelevision.com
*Programmes manager:
Pranab Kapadia*

Data services

Teletext
Building 10
Chiswick Park
566 Chiswick High Road
London W4 5TS
0870 731 3000
editor@teletext.co.uk
www.teletext.co.uk
*Has a licence to use spare capacity
within the Channel 3 (ITV) signal*

Data Broadcasting International
Allen House
Station Road
Egham
Surrey TW20 9NT
01784 471515
sales@databroadcast.co.uk
www.databroadcast.co.uk

6TV Southampton
023 8023 2400
feedback@southamptontv.co.uk
www.southamptontv.co.uk

Abacus TV
01508 570970
sales@abacustv.co.uk
www.abacustv.co.uk

BFBS Forces Radio and TV
01494 878290
sarah.dornford-may@ssvc.com
www.ssvc.com

Bloomsbury Television (BTV)
020 7387 3827
btv@ucl.ac.uk
www.homepages.ucl.ac.uk
/~uczxbts

BVTV
01582 581753
info@bvtv.co.uk
www.bvtv.co.uk

C4TV
c4tv@cant.ac.uk
www.c4online.co.uk

Caledonia Television
01463 790310
george.cocker@tvaye.co.uk
www.tvaye.co.uk

Capital TV (Wales)
02920 488500
capitaltv@newsnet.co.uk
www.newsnet.co.uk

Channel M
0161 475 4855
info@channelm.co.uk
www.channelm.co.uk

EBS New Media
01462 895999
ben@newmedia.co.uk
www.ebs.newmedia.com

Glasgow University Student Television (GUST)
0141 341 6216
gust@src.gla.ac.uk
www.src.gla.ac.uk/gust

Glasgow's Own Television Channel Limited
0141 331 0077
rockettvf@aol.com

Leeds University Union TV (LUUTV)
0113 3801423
nick.smith@luutv.co.uk
www.luutv.co.uk

Loughborough Students Union TV (LSUTV)
01509 635045
manager@lsutv.co.uk
www.lsutv.co.uk

Middlesex Broadcasting Corporation (MATV Channel 6)
0116 253 2288
info@matv.co.uk
www.matv.co.uk

Nerve TV
01202 595765
sucptomms@bournemouth.ac.uk
www.subu.org.uk/nerve

Nexus UTV
01603 456161
sunexus@uea.ac.uk
www.uea.ac.uk/~sunexus

North West Television Services (Channel 9 – Coleraine, Limavady, Londonderry/Derry)
028 7131 4400
info@c9tv.tv
www.c9tv.tv

Northern Visions
028 9024 5495
info@northernvisions.org
www.northernvisions.org

Oxford Broadcasting Limited (Six TV)
01865 557000
admin@oxfordchnnel.com
www.oxfordchannel.com

Red TV
01223 722722
tim@dawemedia.co.uk
www.redtv.co.uk

Solent TV (Isle of Wight)
01983 522344
info@solent.tv
www.solent.tv

STOIC Student Television of Imperial College
020 7594 8104
james@stoictv.com
www.stoictv.com

Thistle Television
01698 833773
andrew.everitt@thistletv.com
www.thistletv.com

TV Portsmouth
023 8023 2400
enquiries@portsmouthtv.co.uk
www.portsmouthtv.co.uk

XTV
01392 263598
gareth@xtv.org.uk
www.xtv.org.uk

YCTV - Youth Culture Television
020 8964 4646
stuartr@yctv.org
www.yctv.org

York University St John Student Television (YSTV)
01904 624624
station.director@ystv.york.ac.uk
www.ystv.york.ac.uk

TV and radio contacts : Section 4

Independent production companies

Key companies

ALL3MEDIA
87–91 Newman Street
London W1T 3EY
020 7907 0177
www.allthreemedia.com
Chief executive: Steve Morrison; chief operating officer: Jules Burns; creative director: David Liddiment
Formerly Chrysalis TV
Assembly TV
Riverside Studios
Crisp Road, London W6 9RL
020 8237 1075
judithmurrell@
riversidestudios.co.uk
www.allthreemedia.com
Chief executive:
William Burdett-Coutts
• *Black Books; Jo Brand's Hot Potatoes; In Exile*
Bentley Productions
Pinewood Studios
Pinewood Road
Iver, Bucks SL0 0NH
01753 656594
www.allthreemedia.com
Managing director:
Brian True-May
• *Midsomer Murders; Ultimate Force*
Cactus TV
373 Kennington Road
London SE11 4PS
020 7091 4900
touch.us@cactustv.co.uk
www.cactustv.co.uk
Managing directors: Simon Ross, Amanda Ross
• *Richard & Judy*
Lion Television
Lion House
26 Paddenswick Road
London W6 0UB
020 8846 2000
mail@liontv.co.uk
www.liontv.co.uk
Scotland: 0141 331 0450
New York: +001 212 206 8633
LA: +001 310 566 7940
Managing directors: Richard Bradley, Nick Catliff, Shahana Meer, Jeremy Mills; director of production: Patsy Blades; executive producers: Bill Locke, Hilary Rosen
• *Bad Behaviour; Days That Shook the World; Britain's Finest; Castles; Royal Deaths and Diseases; Passport to the Sun*

North One TV
Maywood House
46–52 Pentonville Road
London N1 9HF
020 7502 6000
annelise.unitt@northonetv.com
www.allthreemedia.com
Managing director: Neil Duncanson; chief executive: John Wohlgemuth; head of production, entertainment: Pip Haddow; production logistics manager: Robert Gough
• *Formula One; World Rally; The Top Ten series; Speed Sunday; Fifth Gear*

Celador Productions
39 Long Acre
London WC2 9LG
020 7845 6999
tvhits@celador.co.uk
www.celador.co.uk
Managing directors: Paul Smith, Danielle Lux; head of entertainment: Colman Hutchinson; head of production: Heather Hampson; development executives, comedy: Vanessa Haynes, Humphrey Barclay; marketing manager: Michael Seres
• *You Are What You Eat; It's Been A Bad Week; Who Wants To Be a Millionaire?; Winning Lines; Britain's Brainiest*

Diverse
Gorleston Street
London W14 8XS
020 7603 4567
reception@diverse.tv
www.diverse.tv
Head of post-production: Paul Bates; director of programmes: Narinder Minhas; creative director: Roy Ackerman; head of production: Janet Smyth; bookings: Fay Searl
• *Operatunity; The Plot to Kill Hitler; The House of War; The Real George V; The Truth About Gay Animals*

Endemol UK
Shepherds Building Centre,
Clarecroft Way, Shepherds Bush
London W14 0EE
0870 333 1700
info@endemoluk.com
www.endemoluk.com
Chief executive: Tom Barnicoat; managing director: Nikki Cheetham; director of production: Clare Pickering; heads of production: Petrina Good, Richard Thomson
• *Big Brother; Fame Academy; Orange British Academy Film Awards; Ground Force; Changing Rooms; Restoration; The Salon 2; The Games*

Hat Trick Productions
10 Livonia Street, London
W1F 8AF
020 7434 2451
info@hattrick.com
www.hattrick.com
Managing directors: Denise O'Donoghue, Jimmy Mulville; head of production: Laura Djanogle
• *Have I Got News For You; Bodies; Bromwell High; Room 101; The Kumars at No. 42; Father Ted; Jeffrey Archer - The Truth; Underworld; Drop The Dead Donkey*

IWC Media
St George's Studio
93-97 St George's Road
Glasgow G3 6JA
0141 353 3222
info@iwcmedia.co.uk
www.iwcmedia.co.uk
London: 020 7684 1661
Chairman: Alan Clements; managing director: Sue Oriel; creative directors: Zad Rogers, Hamish Barbour; head of documentaries: Charlotte Moore; news editor: Kirsty Walk; head of factual: Adam Barker
• *Ultimate Cars; 18th Street; Other Side; Location, Location, Location; The Planman; Changemakers; Hunt for Jill Dando's Killer*

Princess Productions
Whiteley's Centre
151 Queensway
London W2 4SB
020 7985 1985
reception@princess.tv.com
www.princess.tv.com
Managing director: Sebastian Scott;
head of production: Sarah
Buckenham
• Ruby Does the Business; Back to
Reality; Bump 'n' Grind; Ri:se;
The Wright Stuff

Prospect Pictures
Wandsworth Plain
London SW18 1ET
020 7636 1234
rhys@prospect-uk.com
www.prospect-uk.com
Wales 029 2055 1177
Capital studios, London:
020 8877 1234
Directors: Rhys John, Tony
McAvoy; managing director:
Barry Lynth; head of production:
Louise Doffman
• Saturday Kitchen; Good Food
Live; Under One Roof; Straight
Dates by Gay Mates; A-list Diet
with Food Doctor

Ragdoll (UK)
Timothy's Bridge Road
Stratford Upon Avon CV37 9NQ
01789 404100
pinewood@ragdoll.co.uk
www.ragdoll.co.uk
USA: +001 212 966 4477
Director of production: Sue James
• Open a Door; Rosie and Jim; Tots
TV; Brum; Teletubbies; Teletubbies
Everywhere; Boohbah

RDF Media
The Gloucester Building
Kensington Village, Avonmore
Road
London W14 8RF
020 7013 4000
contactus@rdfmedia.com
www.rdfmedia.com
LA: +001 818 817 5200
Head of production: Jane Wilson;
production executive: Jo Crawley;
press and marketing executive:
Alice Robertson; senior producer:
David Wise; executive producers:
Jenny Crowther, Martin Davidson,
Jill Robinson
• Faking It 4; Wife Swap & Celebrity
Wife Swap; Scrapheap Challenge 5;
Century of the Self; Holiday
Showdown

September Films
Glen House, 22 Glenthorne Road
London W6 0NG
020 8563 9393
september@septemberfilms.com
www.septemberfilms.com
USA: +001 323 960 8085
Chief executive: Marcus Plantin;
director of production: Elaine Day;
director of factual and digital
channels: Sam Brick; head of
drama and film development:
Nadine Mellor
• Holiday Homes Nightmares;
Clubbing on the Frontline; The
Bottom Line; New Tycoons; Secrets
and Lies; Instant Wedding;
Making It

Talkback Thames Productions
20–21 Newman Street
London W1T 1PG
020 7861 8000
reception@talkbackthames.tv
www.talkbackthames.tv
Chief executive: Peter Fincham;
executive editor: Daisy Goodwin
• Family Affairs; Bo' Selecta!; I'm
Alan Partridge; Smack the Pony;
Jamie's Kitchen; Property Ladder;
Perfect Strangers

The Television Corporation
30 Sackville Street
London W1S 3DY
020 7478 7300
tvcorp@tvcorp.co.uk
www.tvcorp.co.uk
Mentorn London: 020 7258 6800;
Oxford Mentorn: 01865 318 450;
Glasgow Mentorn:
0141 204 6600
Director of programmes: George
Carey; managing director,
Mentorn: Charles Thompson; head
of programmes, Mentorn Scotland:
Jane Rogerson; head of Mentorn
Midlands: Eamonn Matthews;
head of communications: Mark Ogle
• Robot Wars; Britain's Worst
Driver; Botham's Ashes; Gillette
World Sport; Hitler's Legacy;
Club Culture; Question Time;
The Real Monty

Tiger Aspect Productions
7 Soho Street
London W1D 3DQ
020 7434 6700
general@tigeraspect.co.uk
www.tigeraspect.co.uk
Managing director: Andrew Zein;
executive producer, entertainment:
Anastasia Mouzas; head of factual:
Paul Sommers; head of comedy:
Clive Tulloh; head of history and
features: Charles Brand
Comedy, drama, entertainment,
factual and animation.
• Teachers; Murphy's Law; Fat
Friends; Streetmate; Gimme
Gimme Gimme

TWI (Trans World International)
Pier House
Strand on the Green
London W4 3NN
020 8233 5000
kmullins@imgworld.com
www.imgworld.com
Managing director: Andrew
Hampel; head of production:
Graham Fry
• Japan's War (in colour series);
Wimbledon; The Olympics;
Premier League; PGA European
Tour; Colour of War

Twofour Productions
Quay West Studios
Old Newnham
Plymouth PL7 5BH
01752 333900
enq@twofour.co.uk
www.twofour.co.uk
Managing director: Charles Wace;
director of business
communications: Charles Mills;
director of broadcast programming:
Jill Lourie; director of production:
Shireen Ward; director of broadcast
development: Melanie Leach
• G Girls; Gardens Through Time;
Dead Famous; The City Gardener;
Ideal Home Show

Wall To Wall
8–9 Spring Place
Kentish Town
London NW5 3ER
020 7485 7424
mail@walltowall.co.uk
www.walltowall.co.uk
Head of production: Helena Ely
• Life Beyond the Box: Norman
Stanley Fletcher; New Tricks;
The Regency House Party

Zenith Entertainment
43–45 Dorset Street
London W1U 7NA
020 7224 2440
general@zenith-
entertainment.co.uk
www.zenith-entertainment.co.uk
Managing director of production;
Ivan Rendall
• *Byker Grove, 2000 Acres of Sky,*
CD:UK; RE-Covered; Headliners;
Garden Rivals, Room Rivals;
Brian's Boyfriends; Murder
Most Foul

Other production companies
----

12 Yard Productions
020 7432 2929
contact@12yard.com
www.12yard.com
Managing director: David Young
• *Dog Eat Dog; Weakest Link; In It*
To Win It; Without Prejudice?;
Double Cross; EggHeads; Here
Comes The Sun; Three's A Crowd

1A Productions
01360 620855
langshot@nildram.co.uk
Managing director; Norman Stone
• *Tales From the Madhouse;*
Man Dancin'

3BM Television
020 7251 2512
3bmtv@3bmtv.co.uk
www.3bmtv.co.uk
Managing director: Daniel Korn
• *War Lords; Children of Abraham;*
Zero Hour: Ten Days to D-Day

The 400 Company
020 8746 1400
info@the400.co.uk
www.the400.co.uk
Managing director: Mark Sloper
• *The Real TT Heroes; Full Throttle*
Famous

A Works TV
0118 934 2380
adrian@aworks.tv
www.aworks.tv
• *Sergeant Stripes (BBC)*

Absolutely Productions
020 7930 3113
info@absolutely-uk.com
www.absolutely-uk.com
Managing director: Miles Bullough
• *Barry Welsh; Pub Quiz; Stressed*
Eric; Trigger Happy TV

Acacia Productions
020 8341 9392
projects@acaciaproductions.co.uk
www.acaciaproductions.co.uk
Managing director:
J Edward Milner
• *Documentary and news,*
environment, current affairs and
human rights

Accomplice Television
00 353 1 660 3235
office@accomplice-tv.com
www.iftn.ie
Managing director: David Collins
• *Bachelors Walk Series 1, 2, 3*

Addictive Television
020 7700 0333
mail@addictive.com
www.addictive.com
Head of production: Nik Clarke;
Graham Daniels
• *Spaced Out; Transambient; Night*
Shift; The Web Review,
Mixmasters (ITV1); Visual Stings
(Magnetic Channel)

Aimimage Production Company
020 7482 4340
atif@aimimage.com
www.aimimage.com
Managing director: Ahmad Zadeh
• *Terra Circa; Balls to Basra;*
The Family Portrait

Alibi Productions
020 7845 0400
rogerholmes@alibifilms.co.uk
www.alibifilms.co.uk
Chief executive officer:
Roger Holmes
• *Sir Gadabout; The Safe House;*
Goodbye Mr Steadman

Angel Eye Film and Television
020 7437 0082
office@angeleye.co.uk
www.angeleye.co.uk
Managing director:
Richard Osborne
• *Beginners Luck; Estate Agents;*
Lady Macbeth; The Last Chances

Antelope
01243 370806
mick.csaky@antelope.co.uk
www.antelope.co.uk
31 Willow Road, London
NW3 1TL
Chief executive and creative
director: Mike Csaky
• *Docs: Mozart in Turkey; Rebel*
Music: The Bob Marley Story;
Geiko Girl; Africa Live; Epic
Journey; 13-part series about Kyoto

APT Films
020 7284 1695
admin@aptfilms.com
www.aptfilms.com
Managing director: Jonny Persey
• *Wondrous Oblivion (feature);*
Solomon and Gaenor (Oscar
nomination, best foreign film);
The Chosen Ones; Solo One; When I
Lived in Modern Times

At It Productions
020 8964 2122
enquiries@atitproductions.com
www.atitproductions.com
Managing director: Martin
Cunning, Chris Fouracre
• *T4; LA Pool Party; Sun Sea and*
Silicone; Perfect Getaway;
Chancers; Popworld; 25 Years of
Smash Hits

Atlantic Productions
020 7371 3200
info@atlanticproductions.tv
www.atlanticproductions.tv
Managing director: Anthony Geffen
• *Spartans; The Queen of Sheba;*
Nefertiti Resurrected; Mystery of the
Tibetan Mummy; The Real Jules
Verne; Tutankhamen: a murder
mystery

Big Bear Films
020 7229 5982
office@bigbearfilms.co.uk
www.bigbearfilms.co.uk
Managing directors: John Stroud,
Marcus Mortimer
• *My Hero (BBC1); Strange (with*
BBC1); Agatha Raisin; Hairy
Bikers Cookbook

Big Heart Media
020 7608 0352
info@bigheartmedia.com
www.bigheartmedia.com
Managing director: Colin Izod
• *Grid Club/music Studio; Spin 'n*
Groove; Street Corner Symphony;
Rewind; Cape Farewell

Big Umbrella Media
01225 817500
production@
bigumbrellamedia.co.uk
www.bigumbrellamedia.co.uk
Third Floor, 37 Foley Street
London W1W 7TN
020 7631 2050
Managing director: Martin Head
• *Living with the New Cross Fire;*
Sir Frank Whittle: The Man who
Shrank the World

Big Wave Productions
01243 532531
info@bigwavetv.com
www.bigwavetv.com
Managing director: Sarah Cunliffe
• *Bug Attack; Death on the Amazon; Secret Weapons*

Black Coral Productions
020 8520 2881
bcp@coralmedia.co.uk
www.m4media.net
Managing director: Lazell Daley
• *Killing Time; Phil's Job; Which Witch is Which*

Blackwatch Productions
0141 222 2640
info@blackwatchtv.com
www.blackwatchtv.com
Managing director: Nicola Black
• *Boys with Breasts; Snorting Coke with the BBC; Designer Vagina*

Blakeway Productions
020 8743 2040
admin@blakeway.co.uk
www.blakeway.co.uk
Managing director:
Denys Blakeway
• *Empire: how Britain made the modern world; Strike: When Britain Went to War; American Colossus; Prince William; Winston's War; The Major Years*

Blast! Films
020 7267 4260
blast@blastfilms.co.uk
www.blastfilms.co.uk
Managing director:
Edmund Coulthard
• *Principles of Lust; The Death of Klinghoffer; Tales from Pleasure Beach*

Blue Egg Television/Blue Egg Studios
0870 765 0007
info@blueegg.tv
www.blueegg.tv
Managing director: Jill Scott
• *James Bond: Die Another Day; San Antonio, Orange Commercial*

Brechin Productions
020 8876 4333
clive@brechin.com
www.brechin.com
Managing director: Clive Doïg
• *See it, Saw it; Turnabout; Eureka*

Brian Waddell Productions
028 9042 7646
strand@bwpltv.co.uk
www.bwpltv.co.uk
Managing director: Brian Waddell
• *The Craig Doyle Show; Carhunt; Chasing Time In... (13-part travel series, National Geographic); Ulster Fly; Boffins (6 × 30'); Life After*

Brighter Pictures
020 8222 4100
info@brighter.co.uk
www.brighter.co.uk
Managing director: Gavin Hay
• *Take the Mike; Bombay Blush; Diet Another Day*

Brighter Pictures Scotland
0141 572 0861
scotland@brighter.co.uk
www.brighter.co.uk
Managing director: Gavin Hay
• *Get a New Life (BBC2); Tabloid Tales (BBC1), Nick Nairn; Dinner Ladies (BBC Scotland)*

Brighton TV
01273 224260
info@brighton.tv
www.brighton.tv
Managing director: David Pounds
• *Tales of the Living Dead; Big Boutique*

Brook Lapping Productions
020 7428 3100
info@brooklapping.com
www.brooklapping.com
Managing director: Brian Lapping
• *I met Osama Bin Laden; The fall of Milosevic; Avenging Terror; Before the Booker; I Met Adolf Eichmann*

Cactus TV
202 7091 4900
touch.us@cactustv.co.uk
www.cactustv.co.uk
Managing directors: Amanda Ross, Simon Ross
• *The Spirit of Diana, The Debate; Songs of Bond; Cliff Richard, The Hits I Missed; Richard & Judy; British Soap Awards*

Caledonia, Sterne And Wyld
0141 564 9100
info@caledonia-tv.com
www.caledonia-tv.com
Managing director:
Seona Robertson
• *Sun Worshippers; King Jamie and the Angel; The Real Tartan Army II*

Carnival (Films and Theatre)
020 8968 0968
info@carnival-films.co.uk
www.carnival-films.co.uk
Managing director: Brian Eastman
• *Shadowlands; Firelight; Bugs; As If; Poirot; Rosemary and Thyme*

Channel X
020 7428 3999
info@channelx.co.uk
www.channelx.co.uk
Managing director: Alan Marke
• *Reeves & Mortimer; Date That; Popetown*

Cicada Films
020 7266 4646
cicada@cicadafilms.com
www.cicadafilms.com
Managing director:
Frances Berrigan
• *Ancient inventions; NYPD Animal Squad; Fat Fiancees; The Abyss; Beyond Pompeii; Bikini*

Circle Multimedia
01243 601482/01628 509501
circlemultimedia@hotmail.com
www.circlemultimedia.com
Director: Jenny Burgess
• *Wire in the Blood; Alchemist's Cat (feature film); Afterlife (feature film); Conqueror (feature film), The Cloak (TV-DVD)*

Clearcut Communications
0161 427 3052
info@clearcut.freeserve.co.uk
Managing director:
Robin Anderson
• *Sex and the Village; On the Edge (Granada); Sense of Place (BBC1); Shanghai'd (BBC2); Proof Positive (pilot for Discovery America)*

Clerkenwell Films
020 7608 2726
andy@clerkenwellfilms.com
Managing director:
Murray Ferguson
• *Quite Ugly One Morning; Dr Jekyll and Mr Hyde (Universal TV); Inspector Rebus, Parlabane (ITV1)*

Collinwood O'Hare Entertainment
020 8993 3666
info@crownstreet.co.uk
www.collingwoodohare.com
Managing director:
Christopher O'Hare
• *Animal Stories, Eddy and the Bear, The King's Beard, Yoko! Jakamoko! Toto!*

COLOUR Television
0141 222 2442
mail@colour-tv.com
www.colour-tv.com
- *EX-S; Edinburgh Nights; Love Bites; Fully Booked; Dali and the Doctor; Silicone Soul*

The Comedy Unit
0141 305 6666
comedyunit@comedyunit.co.uk
www.comedyunit.co.uk
Managing directors: Colin Gilbert, April Chamberlain
- *Still Game; The Karen Dunbar Show; Offside; Yo! Diary!; Taxi for Cowan Spanish Special; New Year specials: Chewin' The Fat; Only An Excuse?*

Company Pictures
020 7380 3900
enquiries@companypictures.co.uk
www.companypictures.co.uk
Managing directors: Charlie Pattinson, George Faber
- *Life and Death of Peter Sellers; Shameless; Forty; White Teeth; Anna Karenina*

Cosgrove Hall Films
0161 882 2500
animation@chf.co.uk
www.chf.co.uk
Managing director; Lee Marriott
- *Andy Pandy; Bill & Ben; Postman Pat; Enjie Benji; Dangermouse*

CTVC
020 8950 4426
ctvc@ctvc.co.uk
www.ctvc.co.uk
Head of programmes: Ray Bruce
- *Imber, Britain's Lost Village; Tonight; Shariah TV; Victim 001; Bethlehem Year Zero; John Meets Paul; A Mediterranean Journey; Understanding Islam*

Dai4Films
07976 819611
info@dai4films.com
www.dai4films.com
Managing director: Neil Davies
- *The Montserrat Volcano; Islands in the Sun; Working Machines; Double or Nothing; Raw Spice; Dirty Streets*

Dan Films
020 7916 4771
enquiries@danfilms.com
www.danfilms.com
Director: Julie Baines
- *Creep; Sons of the Wind; The Republic of Love*

Darlow Smithson Productions
020 7482 7027
mail@darlowsmithson.com
www.darlowsmithson.com
Managing director: John Smithson
- *Touching the Void; We Built the City; Dragons World*

Darrall Macqueen
020 7407 2322
info@darrallmacqueen.com
www.darrallmacqueen.com
Managing directors: Maddy Darrall, Billy Macqueen
- *The Crust; Play the Game; Smile series 1,2,3 (BBC2); U Get Me series 1,2,3 (CBBC)*

Dazed Film and TV
020 7549 6840
info.film&tv@dazegroup.com
www.dazedfilmtv.com
Managing director: Laura Hastings-Smith
- *Perfect; Stop for a Minute; Untold Beauty, (BBC3)*

DLT Entertainment UK
020 7631 1184
jbartlett@dltentertainment.co.uk
www.dltentertainment.com
Managing director: John Bartlett
- *As Time Goes By; Love on a Branch Line; My Family, (BBC1); Meet My Folks, (BBC1)*

DNA Films
020 7292 8700
info@dnafilms.com
www.dnafilms.com
Managing director: Andrew MacDonald
- *28 Days Later*

Double Exposure
020 7490 2499
reception@doublex.com
www.doublex.com
Managing director: Andrew Bethell
- *The House; Culloden; Pleasure Beach*

Eagle and Eagle
020 8995 1884
producer@eagletv.co.uk
www.eagletv.co.uk
Producer: Robert Eagle
- *The Nuclear Boy Scout (C4); Robo Sapiens (Discovery/TLC); Big Questions (C4 Learning)*

Eagle Films
01372 844484
enquiries@eaglefilms.co.uk
www.eaglefilms.co.uk
Producer: Katrina Moss
- *Bitter Honey; The Sins of the Father; It Started with a Kiss; The Road to Somewhere*

Ecosse Films
020 7371 0290
webmail@ecossefilms.com
www.ecossefilms.com
Managing director: Douglas Rae
- *Amnesia; Like Father Like Son; Monarch of the Glen; The Ambassador; Mrs Brown; Charlotte Gray*

Educational Broadcasting Services Trust
020 7613 5082
enquiries@ebst.co.uk
www.ebst.co.uk
Chief executive: Dr Jim Stevenson
- *Looking at Learning; Maths for Engineers; Maths tutor – Algebra*

Electric Sky
01273 224240
info@electricsky.com
www.electricsky.com
Managing director: David Pounds
- *Myths of Mankind; Iraq – in the Shadow of the Palms; First Human Clone*

The Elstree Production Company
01932 572680
enquiries@elsprod.com
www.elsprod.com
Producer: Greg Smith
- *Agnes Brown; George Orwell's Animal Farm; David Copperfield*

Extreme Production
028 9080 9050
dmalone@extremeproduction.com
www.extremeproduction.com
Managing director: David Malone
- *Macintyre's Millions; Clash of the Celtic Giants; Ballykissanything; Country Practice*

FACE Television
01256 350022
paula@facetv.co.uk
www.facetv.co.uk
Managing director: Paul Friend
- *Wildlife SOS series 1,2; Lifeboat Rescue; World Wildlife Photographer*

Faction Films
020 7690 4446
faction@factionfilms.co.uk
www.factionfilms.co.uk
Managing directors: David Fox, Sylvia Stevens, Peter Day
- *Aphrodite's Drop; Murder in the Family; Love for Sale (BBC); Resistencia; Cinematic Orchestra (C4); Sonic Revolution (C4/Levi's); Point Annihilation (surf drama)*

The Farnham Film Company
01252 710313
info@farnfilm.com
www.farnfilm.com
Managing director: Ian Lewis
• *Dance with the Devil; Intergalactic*
Kevin; Mona the Vampire; The
Druid's Tune

Festival Film and TV
020 8297 9999
info@festivalfilm.com
Managing director: Ray Marshall
• *Feature films: Man Dancin';*
The Colour

Film and Music Entertainment
020 7636 9292
info@fame.uk.com
www.fame.uk.com
Managing director: Mike Downey
• *Guy X; Deathwatch; The Enemy*

Fireside Favourites
020 7439 6110
info@firesidefavourites.co.uk
www.firesidefavourites.co.uk
Managing director: Gavin Claxton
• *House of Rock; Infamous Five,*
series 1 and 2

Flame Television
020 7713 6868
contact@flametv.co.uk
www.theflamegroup.co.uk
Managing director: Roger Bolton
• *Discovery Health 2 bulletins; Cage*
Combat (Carlton); Crime Team
(C4); Square Planet (Discovery
Europe); Roadies 2 (UK
Horizons); Ann Summers
Uncovered (Carlton); Dim Crims
(Five); Jane Goldman Investigates
(Living TV); Wild Prince (C4)

Flashback Television
020 7490 8996
mailbox@flashbacktv.co.uk or
bristol@flashbacktv.co.uk
www.flashbacktv.co.uk
1–2 Fitzroy Terrace
Lower Redland Road, Bristol
BS6 6TF 0117 973 8755
Managing director:
Taylor Downing
• *D-Day: The lost evidence; Regency*
Feast; The badness of King George
IV; Nigella Bites; Speed Machines;
Battlestations

Flick features
020 7855 3697
info@flickfeatures.com
www.flickfeatures.co.uk
Director: John Deery
• *Hell4Leather; Feature films:*
Conspiracy of Silence; Pictures of
Anna (in development)

Flying Elephant Films
020 8230 6920
info@flyingelephant.co.uk
www.flyingelephant.co.uk
Managing director: Preeyf Nair
• *A Story That Begins at the End;*
A Different Life; You Know What
I'm Saying

Focus Productions
0117 904 6292
martinweitz@
focusproductions.co.uk;
maddern@focusproductions.co.uk
www.focusproductions.co.uk
PO Box 173
Stratford-upon-Avon CV37 7ZA
01789 298948
Managing director: Martin Weitz
• *Pharaoh's Holy Treasure (BBC2);*
This Sceptred Isle, The Jewish
Journey (BBC R4). Winner Sony
Gold Award. Projects 2003:
Witness on Saint-making (C4);
The Godfather of the Blues (BBC4)

Footstep Productions
020 7836 9990
info@footstep-productions.com
www.footstepproductions.com
Managing director:
Collette Thomson
• *Worktalk; Voces Espanolas*

Free@Last TV
020 7242 4333
barry@freeatlasttv.co.uk
www.freeatlasttv.co.uk
Executive producer: Barry Ryan
• *The Spiderman Story; Making Of*
Jackass The Movie; Rock 'n' Roll
Myths; Blackadder@20;
Adored:The Stone Roses Story;
Mobo Unsung; Dr Who@40

Fresh One Productions
020 7359 1000
andrew@freshone.tv
Managing director: Andrew Conran
• *Jamie's School Dinners;*
Oliver's Twist; Jamie's Kitchen

Fulcrum TV
020 7939 3160
info@fulcrumtv.com
www.fulcrumtv.com
Managing directors:
Christopher Hird, Richard Belfield
• *The State of Texas; The Christmas*
Truce; The Utimate Psychic
Challenge; Belonging; The Man
from the Met

Genesis Media Group
029 2066 6007
alan@genesis-media.co.uk
www.genesis-media.co.uk
Producer and programme director:
Alan Torjussen
• *Peter Warlock; Ceiri and his*
Music; Love Talk; Leila Megane;
corporate & govt projects plus
travel, arts, music and docs for TV

Ginger Television
020 7663 2300
production@ginger.tv
www.ginger.tv
Managing director:
Elisabeth Partyka
• *Czech Mates; High School Projects*
USA; Extreme lives – My Right
Foot; Don't Drop the Coffin (ITV);
Timewatch – The Secrets of Enzo
Ferrari (BBC2)

Glasshead
020 8740 0024
media@glasshead.co.uk
www.glasshead.co.uk
Managing director:
Lambros Atteshlis
• *Blue Dragon; Watch Magic*
Grandad; Real Science

Green Bay Media
029 2064 2370
john-geriant@green-bay.tv
www.green-bay.tv
Managing director: Phil George,
John Geraint
• *An Archbishop Like This; A Bloody*
Good Friday; Do Not Go Gentle

Green Umbrella Ltd
0117 973 1729
postmaster@umbrella.co.uk
www.umbrella.co.uk
Managing director: Nigel Ashcroft
• *Journey to the Centre of the Earth;*
Escape from Berlin; Galileo's
Daughter

Greenlit Productions
020 7287 3545
info@greenlit.co.uk
www.greenlit.co.uk
Managing director: Jill Green
• *Foyle's War; The Swap; Menace;*
Trust

Greenpoint Films
020 7240 7066
info@greenpointfilms.com
www.greenpointfilms.co.uk
Managing directors:
Patrick Cassavetti, Ann Scott,
Simon Relph
• *Only Human; Hideous Kinky;*
The Land Girls

Grosvenor Park Productions
020 7529 2500
chris.chrisafis@grosvenorpark.com
www.grosvenorpark.com
Managing director: Daniel Taylor
• *Reign of Fire; Being Julia; Colour*
  Me Kubrick; Count of Monte Cristo;
  Spider

Gruber Films
0870 366 9313
office@gruberfilms.com
www.gruberfilms.com
Managing director:
Richard Holmes
• *Shooting Fish; Waking Ned; The*
  Abduction Club

Hand Pict Productions
0131 346 1111
ask@handpict.com
www.handpict.com
Director: George Cathro
• *Adoption Stories; East Coast Boy,*
  West Coast Man; Numero Una

Hanrahan Media
01789 450182
info@hanrahanmedia.com
www.hanrahanmedia.tv
Managing director: Will Hanrahan
• *Your Stars; Renovation Creation;*
  Star Lives (ITV); World's Biggest
  Ghost Hunt; Most Haunted Live
  (LivingTV); Men's Health (Bravo)

Hasan Shah Films
020 7722 2419
hsfilms@blueyonder.co.uk
Managing director: Hasan Shah
• *Short: Art Of The Critic. Feature in*
  development 2003: A Little Scary

Hopscotch Films
0141 334 5576
info@hopscotchfilms.co.uk
www.hopscotchfilms.co.uk
Managing directors:
Charlotte Wontner, Clara Glynn,
John Archer
• *Writing Scotland; Detox or Die;*
  Last Train to Beechwood

Hot Shot Films
028 9031 3332
info@hotshotfilms.com
www.hotshotfilms.com
Managing directors: Brendan J.
Byrne, Jimmy McAleavey
• *Living History; Blind Vision;*
  Street Detectives; So You Thought
  You Knew the Plantation; Heroes

Hotbed Media
0121 248 3900
mail@hotbedmedia.co.uk
Managing director: Johannah Dyer
• *Under the Hammer; Songs of*
  Praise; Real Brassed Off; 100
  Worst Britons; Everything Must
  Go; 100 Worst Pop Records; Star
  Portraits with Rolf Harris

Hourglass Productions
020 8540 8786
productions@hourglass.co.uk
www.hourglass.co.uk
Managing director: Martin Chilcott
• *Energy for Nature; DNA and*
  Rocket Science, Living Donation

HRTV
020 7494 3011
mail@hrtv-online.com
www.hrtv-online.com
Managing director: Jerry Hibbert
• *Tractor Tom; Stressed Eric series II*

Hyphen Films
020 7734 0632
nmk@hyphenfilms.com
Managing director: N.M. Kabir
• *Spotlights and Saris; Bollywood*
  Dancing; Bollywood Women –
  Intros; Bismillah of Benaras;
  Bollywood Celebrities; Bollywood
  2004

Icon Films
0117 924 8535
info@iconfilms.co.uk
www.iconfilms.co.uk
Managing director:
Laura Marshall
• *Belgrano; King Cobra; Einstein's*
  Brain

Illumina Digital
020 8600 9300
info@illumina.co.uk
www.illumina.co.uk
Managing director: Andrew Chitty
• *DFES; National Theatre; Culture;*
  Net Cymru

Illuminations Films
020 7288 8400
griff@illumin.co.uk
www.illumin.co.uk
Managing director: Keith Griffiths
• *The Piano Tuner of Earthquakes;*
  London Orbital; Little Otik

Images Of War
020 7267 9198
derek@dircon.co.uk
www.warfootage.com
Managing director: Derek Blades
• *Mass for Peace; Invasion; D-Day;*
  Footage for Hitler's Britain; 300
  hours of war-related material

Imago Productions
01603 727600
mail@imagoproductions.tv
www.imagoproductions.tv
Managing director: Vivica Parsons
• *Grudge Match; Perfect Man; The*
  Coach; Sporty Facts; Bryan's Olde
  and Bitter

Independent Image
01883 654867
info@indimage.com
www.indimage.com
Managing director: David
Wickham
• *Chefs in the City; Cannabis*
  from the Chemist; Interpol's
  Most Wanted

Infinite Pictures
01752 830000
info@infinitepictures.com
www.infinitepictures.com
Managing director: David Nottage
• *Boy's Toys; Civvie to Sailor;*
  Centre Stage

Infonation
020 7370 1082
mail@infonation.org.uk
www.infonation.org.uk
Managing director: Ron Blythe
• *Under One Umbrella; Protected*
  Meal Times; Challenge UK

Intelfax
020 7928 2727
billskirrow@intelfax.co.uk
www.intelfax.co.uk
Managing director: Bill Skirrow
• *Subtitles for: 21st Century War;*
  A Band Called Treacle

**Intermedia Film and Video
(Nottingham)**
0115 955 6909
info@intermedianotts.co.uk
www.intermedianotts.co.uk
Managing director: Ceris Morris
• *One For The Road; Slot Art;*
  Shifting Units; The Entertainer;
  DV Shorts; First Cut

**International Media Productions
(IMP)**
020 8690 9674
improductions@tiscali.co.uk
www.improductions.co.uk
Producer/director: Paul Moody
• *Arriva; Tiny Lives; A Beacon for*
  Culture

ITN factual
020 7430 4511
itn.factual@itn.co.uk
www.itn.co.uk
Head of ITN Factual:
Philip Armstrong
• *Hunt for The Hood/Bismarck;*
Leonardo's Dream Machines;
Sars – Global Killer; Are Your Kids
on Drugs?
IWC Media
0141 429 1750
info@iwcmedia.co.uk
www.warkclements.com
Managing director: Sue Oriel
• *Relocation, Relocation, Relocation;*
Location, Location, Location;
Jeopardy; The First World War
(C4)
Jay Media
01270 884453
media@jaymedia.co.uk
www.jaymedia.co.uk
Managing director: Nigel Jay
• *Skill City; Manchester Evening*
News; Preston City Council
The Jim Henson Company
020 7428 4000
fanmail@henson.com
www.henson.com
Managing director: Pete Coogan
• *Muppet series; Aliens in the*
Family; Bear in the Big Blue House
Keo Films
020 7490 3580
keo@keofilms.com
www.keofilms.com
Managing director: Andrew Palmer
• *River Cottage Diner; Surviving*
Extremes; 10 Years Younger
The Kilroy Television Company
020 7893 7900
info@kilroy.co.uk
Head of production:
Graham Walters
• *Panorama; Now You're Talking!;*
The Kilroy Programme
Landmark Films
01865 297220
info@landmarkfilms.com
www.landmarkfilms.com
Managing director: Nick O'Dwyer
• *Extraordinary Illness; Beauty*
School; Real Life Swap

Landseer Productions
020 7485 7333
mail@landseerfilms.com
www.landseerfilms.com
Managing director and producer:
Derek Bailey
• *Resurrecting St Luke's; South*
Bank Show – Johnnie Ray; The
Magic Mountain
Leopard Films
0870 420 4232
mail@leopardfilms.com
www.leopardfilms.com
Managing director: James Burstall
• *Car Booty; Cash in the Attic;*
Money Spinners; Elvis Mob
Liberty Bell Productions
0191 222 1200
info@libertybell.tv
www.libertybell.tv
Managing directors: Stuart Prebble,
Andrea Wonfor; head of features:
Judith Holder
• *Grumpy Old Men; Victoria Wood's*
Big Fat Documentary; Stella's
Story; For the Benefit of Mr Parris
Libra Television
0161 236 5599
hq@libratelevision.com
www.libratelevision.com
Managing directors: Madeline
Wiltshire, Louise Lynch
• *Gross; Citizen Power; How to be a*
Bully; Copycat Kids; History
Busters
Little Bird
00 353 1 613 1710
info@littlebird.ie
www.littlebird.ie
Co Chairmen: James Mitchell,
Jonathan Cavendish
• *Bridget Jones 2 – The Edge of*
Reason; Trauma; Churchill the
Hollywood Years; In my Father's
Den
Loose Moose
020 7287 3821
info@loosemoose.net
www.loosemoose.net
Managing director:
Glenn Holberton
• *Pepperoni; Chips Ahoy!; Brisk Iced*
Tea
Lupus Films
020 7419 0997
info@lupusfilms.net
www.lupusfilms.net
Managing directors:
Camilla Deakin, Ruth Fielding
• *Little Wolf's Book of Badness (C4);*
Wilde Stories; Little Wolf's
Adventure Academy; Mia, Cool
Hunter

M Power Media
0117 923 7333
enquiries@mpowermedia.uk.com
www.mpowermedia.uk.com
Managing director: Stef Brammar
• *Bristol City Council; Oxfam; Wells*
Cathedral School
Macmillan Media
0870 350 2150
info@macmillanmedia.co.uk
www.macmillanmedia.co.uk
Managing director:
Michael Macmillan
• *Corporate video*
Malachite
01790 763538
info@malachite.co.uk
www.malachite.co.uk
Managing director:
Charles Mapleston
• *Fiore; Children of the Mafia;*
Organic Farm
Maverick Television
0121 771 1812
mail@mavericktv.co.uk
www.mavericktv.co.uk
Chairman: Johnnie Turpie
• *Ten Years Younger; Celebrity*
Disfigurement
Maya Vision International
020 7836 1113
info@mayavisionint.com
www.mayavisionint.com
Producer and director:
Rebecca Dobbs
• *Great Mysteries (working title);*
Hitler's Search for the Holy Grail;
Conquistadors; In Search of
Shakespeare; Two Moons (feature)
Mentorn
020 7258 6800
mentorn@mentorn.co.uk
www.mentorn.co.uk
Managing director:
Charles Thompson
• *Robot Wars; Techno Games;*
Britain's Worst Driver
Mint Productions
028 9024 0555
info@mint.ie
www.mint.ie
Belfast 028 9024 0555
Dublin 00 353 1 491 3333
Managing director: Steve Carson
• *Abu Hamza; Two Day Coup; De*
Lorean; Workers Strike; Crash;
Emmet; All the Queen's Men; Who
Kidnapped Shergar?

Monkey
020 7749 3110
info@monkeykingdom.com
www.monkeykingdom.com
Managing director: Dom Loehnis
• *What Sadie Did Next; Swag; He's Starsky I'm Hutch*

Multi Media Arts
0161 374 5566
info@mmarts.com
www.mmarts.com
Managing director:
Michael Spencer
• *Powerhouse; The Blizzard of Odd; Reality Bites*

Mute Marmalade
020 7449 2552
info@mutemarmalade.com
www.mutemarmalade.com
Managing director:
Jonathan Bentata
• *Black Soles; The Runner; Making Mistakes*

Mykindofshow.com
020 7739 0234
mail@mykindofshow.com
www.mykindofshow.com
Managing director:
Kirsten De Keyser
• *Follow That Tomato; Borscht, Blackbread and Champagne; Bin Sins; Six Degrees of Penetration; Tuscany To Go; Home Health Show*

Nexus Productions
020 7749 7500
info@nexusproductions.com
www.nexusproductions.com
Managing director: Chris O'Reilly
• *Catch Me if You Can; Goldfrapp; Erasure; Nike; T- Mobile; Aiwa; Monkey Dust*

October Films
020 7284 6868
info@octoberfilms.co.uk
www.octoberfilms.co.uk
Managing director: Tom Roberts
• *Suicide Bombers; Rugby World Cup – England's Story; Access to Evil*

Open Mind Productions
020 7437 0624
enquiries@openmind.co.uk
www.openmind.co.uk
Managing director: Roland Tongue
• *Paz; The Shiny Show; The Number Crew*

ORTV
020 8614 7200
info@ortv.co.uk
www.ortv.co.uk
Managing director:
Nicholas Claxton
• *John McCarthy – Out of the Shadows; Heart of the Lioness; Saddam's Iraq*

Oxford Film And Television
020 7483 3637
email@oftv.co.uk
www.oftv.co.uk
Creative director:Nicholas Kent
• *Philip Larkin: Love and Death in Hull; Lionheart: the Crusade; Second Generation (all C4); Superfly; Terry Jones' Medieval Tales; National Trust (BBC)*

Paladin Invision
020 7371 2123
pitv@pitv.com
www.pitv.com
Managing directors: William Cran, Clive Syddall
• *Commanding Heights; Do You Speak American?*

Pathe Pictures
020 7323 5151
orlaghcollins@pathe-uk.com
www.pathe.com
Managing director:
Francois Ivernel
• *Natural History; Girl With a Pearl Earring; Millions*

Pepper's Ghost Productions
020 8546 4900
enquiries@peppersghost.com
www.peppersghost.com
Managing director: Paul Michael
• *Tiny Planets; Policecat Fuzz; Bus Stop; Kingfisher Tailor*

Pesky
020 7430 0200
hodge@pesky.com
www.pesky.com
Directors: David Hodgson, Clare Underwood
• *Stress Maniacs (C4 pilot); Amazing Adrenalini Brothers; Thingamijig; I Could Murder A Curry*

Pilot Film and TV Productions
020 8960 2721
info@pilotguides.com
www.pilotguides.com
Director: John Pilot
• *Globe Trekker; Pilot Guides; Planet Food; Ian Wright Live*

Pioneer Productions
020 8748 0888
pioneer@pioneertv.com
www.pioneertv.com
Managing director: Stuart Carter
• *Naked Science; Danger Man; Tycoon Toys*

Planet 24 Productions
020 7612 0671
alice@planet24.co.uk
www.planet24.com
Managing director: Ed Forsdick
• *Mechanick; How to Pull... ; Big Breakfast*

Planet Wild
0161 233 3090
office@planetwild.co.uk
www.planetwild.co.uk
Managing director: Paula Trafford
• *Cilla in Black and White; George Best's Story; Pushy Parents*

Presentable
029 2057 5729
all@presentable.co.uk
www.presentable.co.uk
Managing director: Megan Stewart
• *Celebrity Poker Club; Late Night Poker; Conversations with Ronan Williams*

The Press Association
020 7963 7474
broadcasting.info@pa.press.net
www.pabroadcasting.com
Managing director:
Sean Curtis-Ward
• *A network of reporters, camera crews and editing facilities across the UK and Ireland*

Principal Films
020 7928 9287
films@principalmedia.com
www.principalmedia.com
Managing director: Richard Sattin
• *Concorde – A Love Story; Mountains and Man; Maidens of the Lost Ark*

Prism Entertainment
020 8969 1212
info@prism-e.com
www.prismentertainment.co.uk
Managing directors: Mike Crosby, Amelia Johnson
• *The Stables; FAQ series 3; Beat the Cyborgs*

Raw Charm
029 2064 1511
enquiries@rawcharm.tv
www.rawcharm.tv
Managing director: Pam Hunt
• *War Stories; Grave Detectives; Simon Weston's War Heroes*

Real Life Media Productions
0113 237 1005
info@reallife.co.uk
www.reallife.co.uk
Managing director: Ali Rashid
• *Mum, I'm a Muslim; Baby Baby;*
Britain's Most Dangerous Prisoner

Red Fig
020 7944 0500
info@redfig.com
www.redfig.com
Marketing/PR: Heidi Scrimgeour
• *I'm A Celebrity... Get Me Out Of*
Here!; Popstars: The Rivals; Wild In
Your Garden; The Big Conversation;
Heaven and Earth; Asylum Day;
Darkhouse; Justin Timberlake
Karaoke Line

Red Green and Blue Company
020 8746 0616
max@rgbco.com
www.rgbco.com
Production office:
1 Underwood Row
London N1 7LZ
020 7490 1788
Directors:Max Whitby, Cathy Collis
• *DNA Interactive*

Red Kite Animations
0131 554 0060
info@redkite-animation.com
www.redkite-animation.com
Managing director: Ken Anderson
• *The Secret World of Benjamin*
Bear; The Loch Ness Kelpie; Wilf
the Witch's Dog

Red Production Company
0161 827 2530
info@redlimited.co.uk
www.redproductioncompany.com
Managing director:
Andrew Critchley
• *Blue Blood; Jane Hall Big Bad Bus*
Ride; Mine All Mine

Reef Television
020 7836 8595
mail@reeftv.com
www.reef.tv
Managing director:
Richard Farmbrough
• *Sun Sea & Bargain Spotting; Put*
Your Money Where Your House Is;
Model Gardens

Reel Life Television
020 7713 1585
enquiries@reel-life-tv.co.uk
www.reel-life-tv.co.uk
Managing directors: Chris Raine,
Celine Smith
• *Songs of Praise; Moving On Up;*
Focus on Fear; Job Bank;
Singled Out

Renting Eyeballs Entertainment
020 7437 4417
malcolm.rasala@
rentingeyeballs.com
www.rentingeyeballs.com
Managing director: Mark Maco
• *Commercials, promos, brand*
television, motion pictures

Resource Base
023 8023 6806
post@resource-base.co.uk
www.resource-base.co.uk
Managing director: Karen
Gilchrist, Hilary Durman
• *VEE-TV; Without You; World of*
Difference (C4); Lion Mountain;
Who Cares? (BBC)

Richmond Films and Television
020 8327 0430
PO Box 33154
London NW3 4AZ
mail@richmondfilms.com
Managing director: Sandra Hastie
• *In Two Minds; Privates; Wave*
Lengths

Ricochet Films
020 7251 6966
mail@ricochet.co.uk
www.ricochet.co.uk
Managing director: Nick Powell
• *Who Rules the Roost; Fight Box;*
Living in the Sun

Ronin Entertainment
020 7734 3884
mail@ronintv.com
www.ronintv.com
Managing directors: Richard
Hearsey, Robin Greene
• *The Impressionable Jon Culshaw;*
Fort Boyard; It's a Knockout

RS Productions
0191 224 4301
info@rsproductions.co.uk
www.rsproductions.co.uk
Managing director: Mark Lavender
• *Frozen; Elephants and Angels;*
Laughter When We're Dead;
Thereby Hangs a Tale

Sally Head Productions
020 8607 8730
admin@shpl.demon.co.uk
Managing director: Sally Head
• *Forefathers; Plastic Man; Tipping*
The Velvet; The Cry; Mayor of
Casterbridge; The Return

Samson Films
00 353 1 667 0533
info@samsonfilms.com
www.samsonfilms.com
Managing director: David Collins
• *Co-producer: Blind Flight;*
Honeymooners; Abduction Club;
Most Fertile Man in Ireland.
Feature development: Mir Friends;
Immortal; Havoc

Scream Films
020 8995 8255
info@screamfilms.com
www.screamfilms.com
Managing director: Susie Dark
• *Famous and Frightened; Dell*
Winton's Wedding; Terror Alert

Screenhouse Productions
0113 266 8881
info@screenhouse.co.uk
www.screenhouse.co.uk
Chief executive: Barbara Govan
• *Star Date; Science Shack; Snapshot*

Seventh Art Productions
01273 777678
info@seventh-art.com
www.seventh-art.com
Managing director: Phil Grabsky
• *Tim Marlow on .... Edward*
Hopper; Easter in Art; Pelé –
World Cup Hero; Great Artists II;
The Boy Who Plays on the
Buddhas of Bamiyan

Shed Productions
020 8215 3387
shed@shedproductions.com
www.shedproductions.com
Managing director:
Eileen Gallagher
• *Footballers Wives; Bad Girls*

Shine
020 7313 8000
info@shinelimited.com
www.shinelimited.com
Managing director: Elizabeth
Murdoch
• *Dispatches; Fit to Eat; Take That*

SMG TV Productions
0141 300 3000
elizabeth.partyka@smg.plc.uk
www.smgtv.co.uk
Director: Surinder Gautama
• *Taggart; Club Reps: The Workers;*
Good Bye Mr Chips; Medics of the
Glen; Squeak!; How 2

Smith And Watson Productions
01803 863033
info@smithandwatson.com
www.smithandwatson.com
Managing director: Nick Smith
• *Building a Dream; Bill Wyman's*
Blues; A Story of Peter Rabbit and
Beatrix Potter

Smoking Dogs Films
020 7249 6644
info@smokingdogsfilms.com
www.smokingdogsfilms.com
Managing director: David Lawson
• *Urban Soul – Making of Modern*
R&B; The Wonderful World of
Louis Armstrong; Goldie – When
Satin Returns

So Television
020 7960 2000
info@sotelevision.co.uk
www.sotelevision.co.uk
Director: Jon Magnusson
• *Comedy Lab; v Graham Norton*
(Channel 4)

Specific Films
020 7580 7476
info@specificfilms.com
Managing director:
Michael Hamlyn
• *Last Seduction II; Paws; Mr*
Reliable; Priscilla, Queen of
the Desert

Spire Films
01865 371979
mail@spirefilms.co.uk
Managing director: David Wilcox
• *Delia Smith; Romans*

Sunset + Vine
020 7478 7300
reception@sunsetvine.co.uk
www.sunsetvine.co.uk
Leeds 0113 284 2495
Managing director: John Leach
• *Cricket; Gillette World Sport;*
Gumball Rally

Sunstone Films
020 7431 0535
sunstonefilms@aol.com
www.sunstonefilms.co.uk
• *Before Columbus; Lords of the*
Maya; Warhorse; Gladiators: The
Brutal Truth

Talent Television
020 7421 7800
entertainment@talenttv.com
www.talenttv.com
Creative director: John Kaye Cooper
• *Inside Clyde; Best of Friends;*
Casino, Casino

Telemagination
020 7434 1551
mail@tmation.co.uk
www.telemagination.co.uk
Head of studio: Beth Parker
• *Pongwiffy; Little Ghosts;*
Something Else; Metalheads;
Cramp Twins; Heidi (theatrical
release)

Television Junction
0121 248 4466
info@televisionjunction.co.uk
www.televisionjunction.co.uk
Managing directors: Paul Davies,
Yvonne Davies
• *Double Act; Seeing Science; Think*
About It

Tell-Tale Productions
020 8324 2308
info@tell-tale.co.uk
www.tell-tale.co.uk
Managing director: Karl Woolley
• *Tweenies; Boo*

Tern Television
0224 211123
www.terntv.com
73 Crown Street
Aberdeen AB11 6EX
0141 243 5658
Managing directors: David
Strachan, Gwyneth Hardy
• *Chancers; Fraserburgh; 2003*
Reloaded; Mapman

Tigress Productions
020 7434 4411
general@tigressproductions.co.uk;
general@tigressbristol.co.uk
www.tigressproductions.co.uk
2 St Paul's Road, Clifton
Bristol BS8 1LT
0117 933 5600
Managing director:
Jeremy Bradshaw
• *Snakemaster; The Jeff Corwin*
Experience; Dolphin Murders;
The Science of Combat

Tinopolis
01554 880880
info@tinopolis.com
www.tinopolis.com
Managing director: Ron Jones
• *P'nawn Da; Wedi 7; Le Rygbi*

Torpedo
029 2076 6117
info@torpedoltd.co.uk
www.torpedoltd.co.uk
Chairman: Mark Jones
• *Fishlock's Sea Stories; Jigsaw;*
Horatio's Holiday

Touch Productions
01747 828030
enquiries@touchproductions.co.uk
www.touchproductions.co.uk
Managing director:
Malcolm Brinkworth
• *Feeding Martin (Meridian); Beasts*
of the Roman Games (C4); Life of a
Ten Pound Note (BBC); The
Missing Chink (C4); Party
Maestro (BBC)

TransAtlantic Films
020 8735 0505
mail@transatlanticfilms.com
www.transatlanticfilms.com
Cabalva, Whitney-On-Wye
Hereford HR3 6EX
01497 831800
Managing director:
Corisande Albert
• *Amazing Animal Adaptors;*
Extreme Body Parts; Science
of Love

Turn On Television
0161 247 7700
mail@turnontv.co.uk
www.turnontv.co.uk
Managing director: Angela Smith
• *Viva La Diva; Bangkok Bound;*
Special Delivery

TV6
020 7610 0266
mail@tv6.co.uk
www.tv6.co.uk
Managing director: Richard Reisz
• *Horizon: Percy Pilcher's Flying*
Machines (BBC); Horizon: King
Solomon's Stone (BBC); Landscape
Mysteries (BBC); Hidden Egypt
(Nat Geo); Into the Great Pyramid
(live, Fox Network)

Unique Communications Group
020 7605 1200
ucg@uniquegroup.co.uk;
info@uniquecomms.com
www.uniquecomms.com
Managing director: Noel Edmonds
• *British Comedy Awards 2003*
(ITV); Stars Behind Bars (Five);
Harley Street (Living TV); I'm the
Answer (ITV)

Vera Productions
020 7436 6116
cree@vera.co.uk
Managing director: Elaine Morris
• *The Big Impression (BBC1);*
Between Iraq and A Hard Place (C4);
Bremner Bird and Fortune (C4)

Vivum Intelligent Media
020 7729 2749
nick@vivum.net
www.vivum.net
Managing director: Nick Rosen
- *2003 (BBC Radio 3, 4 Channel 4)*
  World Trade Centre series (PBS);
  documentary in Russia (BBC4);
  high-brow factual content

Wag TV
020 7688 1711
post@wagtv.com
www.wagtv.com
Managing director: Martin Durkin
- *Inter Sex; Divine Designs; Dave*
  Courtney's Underworld; The
  Great Scientist

Wild Dream Films
01273 236168
mail@wild-dream.com
www.wild-dream.com
Managing director: Stuart Clarke
- *Map Makers; Ancient Discoveries*
  series 1, 2

Wild Rover Productions
028 9050 0980
enquiries@wild-rover.com
www.wild-rover.com
Managing director: Philip Morrow
- *Just For Laughs; A Day In The*
  Westlife of Shane; Would You Pass
  the Eleven Plus?

Wilton Films
020 7749 7282
info@wiltonfilms.com
cvs@wiltonfilms.com
www.wiltonfilms.com
Managing director: Paul Mitchell
- *Hotspots; Chechnya; The*
  Alternative Rock 'n' Roll Years;
  Lords of the Spin

Windfall Films
020 7251 7676
enquiries@windfallfilms.com
www.windfallfilms.com
Managing director: David Dugan
- *D-Day: The Ultimate Conflict; The*
  Great Escape Revealed; Men of
  Iron

World Of Wonder
020 7428 3444
wow@worldofwonder.co.uk
www.worldofwonder.net
Chief executive: Fenton Bailey
- *Matt's Old Masters; Housebusters;*
  The Art Show – Spoils of War

World Wide Pictures
020 7434 1121
info@worldwidegroup.ltd.uk
www.worldwidegroup.ltd.uk
Managing directors:
Richard King, Ray Townsend,
Chris Courtenay-Taylor
- *Bad Girls; videos for the Office of*
  the Deputy Prime Minister

World's End Productions
020 7751 9880
info@wordsendproductions.com
www.worldsendproductions.com
Managing directors: Jim Philips,
Jerry Drew
- *Shoot Me; Going Down to South*
  Park; Dead Casual; Live at
  Johnny's; Fighting Talk.
  Co-production with Celador:
  Johnny & Denise

Zeal Television
020 8780 4600
www.zealtv.net
Chief executive: Peter Christiansen
- *Building the Dream; Come and*
  Have a Go if You Think You're
  Smart Enough; Resistance;
  Demolition; Super Human;
  Sushi TV

Zeppotron
0870 333 1700
contact@zeppotron.com
www.zeppotron.com
Creative directors: Neil Webster,
Ben Caudell, Charlie Brooker
- *People's Book of Records; Playing*
  Tricks; The Cowboy Trap

Zig Zag Productions
020 7353 7799
production@zigzag.uk.com
www.zigzagproductions.tv
Managing director: Danny Fenton
- *Fashanu's Football Challenge;*
  Inside the Mind of Frank Bruno;
  Three Lions; DIY Births; Celebrity
  Gladiators

TV and film studios

3 Mills Studios
Three Mill Lane
London E3 3DU
020 7363 3336
info@3mills.com
www.3mills.com
Managing director: Daniel Dark

3 Sixty Media
Quay Street
Manchester M60 9EA
0161 827 2020
enquiry@3sixtymedia.com
www.3sixtymedia.com
Head of studios: Paul Bennett

Ardmore Studios
Herbert Road, Bray
Co Wicklow, Ireland
00 353 1 286 2971
film@ardmore.ie
www.ardmore.ie
Managing director: Kevin Moriarty

BBC Elstree Centre
Clarendon Road, Borehamwood
Herts WD6 1JF
020 8228 7102
www.bbc.co.uk
Senior facility manager: Sue Spree

BBC TV Centre Studios
BBC TV Centre
Wood Lane, Shepherds Bush
London W12 7RJ
020 8743 8000
bbcresources@bbc.co.uk
www.bbcresources.co.uk
Principal facilities manager:
Gary Collins

Black Island Studios
9–11 Alliance Road,
Acton
London W3 0RA
020 8956 5600
blackisland@compuserve.com
www.blackislandstudios.net
Managing director: Steve Guidici

Box Studios
15 Mandela Street
London NW1 0DU
020 7388 0020
mail@boxstudios.co.uk
www.boxstudios.co.uk
Directors: Philip Bier,
Chris Gascoigne

Bray Studios
Down Place, Windsor Road
Water Oakley, Windsor
Berks SL4 5UG
01628 622111
B.earl@tiscali.co.uk
Studio manager: Beryl Earl

Broadley Studios
Broadley House
48 Broadley Terrace
London NW1 6LG
020 7258 0324
markfrench@broadleystudios.com
www.broadleystudios.com
Managing director: Mark French

Canalot Production Studios
222 Kensal Road
London W10 6BN
020 8960 8580
andrea.kolokasi@
  workspacegroup.co.uk
www.workspacegroup.co.uk
Studio manager: Andrea Kolokasi

Capital Studios
13 Wandsworth Plain
London SW18 1ET
020 8877 1234
louise.prior@prospect-uk.com
www.capitalstudios.co.uk
Studio manager: Bobbi Johnstone

Central Studios
Location House, 5 Dove Lane
Bristol BS2 9HP
0117 955 4777
info@centralstudios.co.uk
www.centralstudios.co.uk
Studio manager: Dave Garbe

Corinthian Television Facilities
Chiswick Park, Building 12
566 Chiswick High Road
London W4 5AN
020 8100 1000
charlotte.alves@ctv.co.uk
www.ctv.co.uk
Studio manager: Shelley Wallis

CTS and Lansdowne Recording
Lansdowne House
Lansdowne Road
London W11 3LP
020 7727 0041
info@cts-lansdowne.co.uk
www.cts-lansdowne.co.uk
Studio manager: Chris Dibble

Depot Studios
29–31 Brewery Road
London N7 9QH
020 7609 1366
info@thedepotstudios.com
www.thedepotstudios.com
Studio manager: Helen Hilton

Desisti Lighting (UK)
15 Old Market Street
Thetford, Norfolk IP24 2EQ
01842 752909
desisti@globalnet.co.uk
www.desisti.co.uk
Director: John Reay-Young

Dukes Island Studios
2 Dukes Road, Acton
London W3 0SL
020 8956 5600
info@islandstudios.net
www.islandstudios.net
Studio manager: Steve Guidici

Ealing Studios
Ealing Green, London W5 5EP
020 8567 6655
info@ealingstudios.com
www.ealingstudios.com
Studio manager: Jeremy Pelzer

East Side Studios
40A River Road, Barking
Essex IG11 0DW
020 8507 7572
info@eastsidestudios.com
www.eastsidestudios.com
Studio manager: Simon Price

**Elstree Film and Television
Studios**
Shenley Road, Borehamwood
Herts WD6 1JG
020 8953 1600
info@elstreefilmtv.com
www.elstreefilmtv.com
Directors: Julie Wicks, Neville Reid

Enfys
Unit 31 Portanmoor Road
East Moors, Cardiff
South Glamorgan, Wales
CF2 5HB
029 2049 9988
mail@enfys.tv
www.enfys.tv
*Studio manager:
Sarah-Jane Salmon*

Fountain TV Studios
128 Wembley Park Drive,
Wembley
Middlesex HA9 8HQ
020 8900 5800
everyone@ftv.co.uk
www.ftv.co.uk
Studio manager: Tony Edwards

Greenford Studios
5–11 Taunton Road
Metropolitan Centre, Greenford
Middlesex UB6 8UQ
020 8575 7300
studios@panavision.co.uk
www.panavision.co.uk
Studio manager: Kate Tufano

Handstand studios
13 Hope Street, Liverpool
L1 9BH
0151 708 7441
info@handstand-uk.com
www.handstand-uk.com
Studio manager: Han Duijvendak

Hillside
Merry Hill Road, Bushey
Herts WD23 1DR
020 8950 7919
mailbox@hillside-studios.co.uk
www.hillside-studios.co.uk
Operations manager: Peter Ball

Holborn Studios
49/50 Eagle Wharf Road
London N1 7ED
020 7490 4099
studiomanager@
  holborn-studios.co.uk
www.holborn-studios.co.uk
Studio manager: Marie McCartney

IAC
Moorside Road, Winchester
Hampshire S23 7US
01962 873000
info@iacl.co.uk
www.iacl.co.uk
Studio manager: Ian Rich

ICA Theatre
The Mall, London SW1 5AH
020 7930 0493
info@ica.org.uk
www.ica.org.uk
Technical manager: Lee Curran

Lichfield Studios
133 Oxford Gardens
London W10 6NE
020 8969 6161
kate@lichfieldstudios.co.uk
www.lichfieldstudios.com
Studio assistant: Kate Short

London Studios
London Television Centre
Upper Ground Floor
London SE1 9LT
020 7737 8888
sales@londonstudios.co.uk
www.londonstudios.co.uk
Managing director: Debbie Hills

Metro Imaging
76 Clerkenwell Road
London EC1M 5TN
020 7865 0000
katarina@metroimaging.co.uk
www.metroimaging.co.uk
Studio manager: Steve Jackson

Millbank Studios
4 Millbank, London SW1P 3JA
020 7233 2020
facilities@millbank-studios.co.uk
www.millbank-studios.co.uk
Studio manager: Nicola Golding

Millennium Studios
5 Elstree Way, Borehamwood
Herts WD6 1SF
020 8236 1400
info@millenniumstudios.co.uk
www.millenniumstudios.co.uk
Managing director: Ronan Willson

Park Royal Studios
1 Barretts Green Road
London NW10 7AE
020 8965 9778
info@parkroyalstudios.com
www.parkroyalstudios.com
Studio manager:
Francois van de Langkruis

Picture It Studios
50 Church Road
London NW10 9PY
020 8961 6644
chris@picit.net
www.picit.net
Studio manager: Chris Fellers

Pinewood Studios
Pinewood Road, Iver Heath
Bucks SL0 0NH
01753 651700
firstname.lastname@
  pinewood-studios.co.uk
www.pinewoodshepperton.com
Studio manager: David Wight

Production House NI/Stage
Services North
Unit 5, Prince Regent Retail Park
Prince Regent Road
Belfast BT5 6QP
028 9079 8999
info@productionhouse.net
Studio manager: Neil Lewis

Pylon Studios
Coal Hill Lane, Leeds LS13 1DJ
0113 204 7000
enquiries@pylonstudios.co.uk
www.pylonstudios.co.uk
Studio manager: Jo Scott

Q Broadcast
1487 Melton Road,
Queniborough
Leicester LE7 3FP
0116 260 8813
paul@folosite.net
Studio manager: Martin Branson

RC Film & TV Set Construction
Unit C11
Dundonald Enterprise Park
Carrowreagh Road, Dundonald
Northern Ireland BT16 1QT
028 9055 7557
Managing director: Russell Fulton

Riverside Studios
Crisp Road, Hammersmith
London W6 9RL
020 8237 1000
online@riversidestudios.co.uk
www.riversidestudios.co.uk
Centre manager: Alex Cotterill

Sands Film Studios
Grices Wharf,
119 Rotherhithe Street
London SE16 4NF
020 7231 2209
OStockman@sandsfilms.co.uk
www.sandsfilms.co.uk
Managing director:
Oliver Stockman

Savoy Hill Studios
Savoy Hill House, Savoy Hill
London WC2R 0BU
020 7497 0830
johnherbert@tabard.co.uk
Studio manager: John Herbert

Shepperton Studios
Studios Road, Shepperton
Middlesex TW17 0QD
01932 562611
firstname.lastname@
  pinewood-studios.co.uk
www.pinewoodshepperton.com
Studio manager: David Godfrey

Space Studios
Boden House
114–120 Victoria Road
London NW10 6NY
020 8961 2412
dja@basegrp.com
Managing director: David Johnson

stu-dio
Cabul Road, London SW11 2PR
020 7228 5228
info@the-studio.co.uk
www.the-studio.co.uk
Studio manager: Gemma Masters

Teddington Studios
Broom Road, Teddington
Middlesex TW11 9NT
020 8977 3252
sales@teddington.tv
www.teddington.co.uk
Studio manager: Ray Gearing

The Worx
10 Heathmans Road, Fulham
London SW6 4TJ
020 7371 9777
enquiries@theworx.co.uk
www.the-worx.co.uk
Managing directors: Jackie
Mallory, Jonathan Mallory

Twickenham Studios
The Barons
St Margarets
Twickenham, Middlesex
TW1 2AW
020 8607 8888
caroline@
  twickenhamfilmstudios.com
www.twickenhamstudios.com
Administrations manager:
Caroline Tipple

VFX Company
Dukes Island Studios
Dukes Road
London W3 0SL
020 8956 5674
info@thevfxco.co.uk
www.thevfxco.co.uk
Operations manager:
Digna Nigoumi

Waterfall Studios
2 Silver Road
Wood Lane
London W12 7SG
020 8746 2000
enquiries@waterfall-studios.com
www.waterfall-studios.com
Studio manager: Samantha Leese

TV and radio contacts : **Section 4**

117

Post-production

3sixty Media
Quay Street
Manchester M60 9EA
0161 839 0360
enquiry@3sixtymedia.com
www.3sixtymedia.com
Independent. Effects and virtual reality
Post-production manager: John Mariner
- *Island at War; Tonight with Trevor MacDonald; Blue Murder*

422 Manchester
4th Floor, South Central
11 Peter Street
Manchester M2 5QR
0161 839 6080
cooey@422.com
www.422manchester.com
Sister company 422 South. Animation, graphics, commercials, special effects and audio
Production director: Richard Wallwork
- *Chessington World of Adventures commercial; Most Haunted; Mastermind; A Question of Sport*

422 South
St John's Court
Whiteladies Road
Bristol BS8 2QY
0117 946 7222
debbiet@422.com
www.422south.com
Sister company 422 Manchester. Factual television and animation
Production director: Andy Davies-Coward
- *The Painter (Hewlett Packard); Extreme Machines; The Basil Brush Show*

Ascent Media Camden
13 Hawley Crescent
London NW1 8NP
020 7284 7900
www.ascent-media.co.uk
9 other sites. Film processing laboratory; video; tape; DVD
Managing director: Sam Webb
- *Poirot; Auf Weidersehen Pet; Hustle*

Anvil
Denham Media Park
North Orbital Road, Denham
Uxbridge, Middlesex UB9 5HL
01895 833522
firstname.secondname@thomson.net
www.anvil-post.com
Part of Technicolor (Thomson Group). Audio Studio manager: Mike Anscombe
- *The Brief; Ultimate Force; Murder in Suburbia; Inspector Morse; Midsomer Murders; Waking the Dead; Poirot*

Arena Digital
74 Newman Street, London
W1T 3EL
020 7436 4360
booking@arenadigital.co.uk
www.arenadigital.co.uk
Part of 2D video facilities. Effects; audio; documentaries; comedy
Managing directors: Terry Bettles, Dave Thompson
- *Bo' Selecta; Trouble at the Top; Scambusters; Brassed off Britain*

Arion Communications
Global House
Denham Media Park
North Orbital Road, Denham
Uxbridge Middlesex UB9 5HL
01895 834484
sales@arion.co.uk
www.arion.co.uk
Independent. Telecine; DVD duplication; editing
Managing director: Neil Mockler
- *Hitchhiker's Guide to the Galaxy; Alien vs Predator; Tomb Raider; The Cradle of Life*

Barcud Derwen
Cibyn, Caernarfon
Gwynedd LL55 2BD
01286 684300
Cardiff 02920 611515
enq@barcud-derwen.co.uk
www.barcudderwen.com
Drama, graphics
Managing director: Tudor Roberts
- *Celebrity Poker; Tracy Beaker series; Mountains and Man*

Blue
58 Old Compton Street
London W1D 4UF
020 7437 2626
info@bluepp.co.uk
www.bluepp.co.uk
VTR plc Group. Special effects; graphics; commercial; audio
Managing director: David Cadel
- *BBC Imagine; Pompeii: The Last Day; Property People*

Capital FX
2nd Floor, 20 Dering Street
London W1S 1AJ
020 7493 9998
ian@capital-fx.co.uk
www.capital-fx.co.uk
Independent. Special effects; graphics; taped film transfer
Managing director: Ian Buckton
- *Harry Potter; Troy; Lord of the Rings*

Cine Wessex
Westway House
19 St Thomas Street
Winchester, Hampshire
SO23 9HJ
01962 865454
info@cinewessex.co.uk
www.cinewessex.co.uk
Independent. Editing; camera kit and crew hire; 2D and 3D graphics; VHS, CD and DVD
Facilities director: Joe Conman
- *City Gardener; Mappin Murder; Room for Improvement*

Clear
Fenton House
55–57 Great Marlborough Street
London W1F 7JX
020 7734 5557
clear@clear.ltd.uk
www.clear.ltd.uk
Sister company Finally Cut. Visual effects, commercials and films
Senior producer/head of film: Steve Garrad
- *28 Days Later; BBC Talking Heads preview; Millions*

Clear Cut Hirers
1 Springvale Terrace
London W14 0AE
020 7605 1700
fazal@clearcutpictures.com
www.clearcutpictures.com
Sister company Clear Cut Pictures. Dry hire post-production equipment
Managing director: Fazal Shah
- *Celeb Deck; Glastonbury Festival; Liquid News*

Clear Cut Pictures
1 Springvale Terrace
London W14 0AE
020 7605 1700
reception@clearcut pictures
www.clearcutpictures.com
Sister company Clear Cut Hirers.
Graphics and digital rostrum;
video and sound
Managing director: Jo Beighton
• *Crimewatch; Horizon; Money*
  Programme

Clickstream
37 Dean Street
London W1D 4PT
020 7437 0077
info@clickstream.co.uk
www.clickstream.co.uk
Part of VTR Group. Encoding;
telestream; digital asset
management
Managing director: Neil Lane
• *E-title project for European Union;*
  Paramount; Movie Tone

Code Design
Ingestre Court, Ingestre Place
London W1F 0JL
020 7343 6449
info@codedesign.co.uk
www.codedesign.co.uk
Part of M2 Group. Storyboarding;
direction; studio shooting; graphics
Production manager: Bryony Evans
• *Troy; Q Channel Broadcasting;*
  Waking the Dead

Component
28 Newman Street
London W1T 1PR
020 7631 4477
mike@component.co.uk
www.component.co.uk
Independent. Pure graphics
Director: Mike Kenny
• *Hell's Kitchen; Destination*
  D-Day; Without Prejudice;
  SAS Jungle; Clive Anderson Now

Computamatch
117 Wardour Street
London W1F 0NU
020 7287 1316
edl@computamatch.co.uk
www.ascent-media.co.uk
Part of Ascent Group. Film negative
cutting service
Managing director: Marilyn
Sommer
• *5 Children and It; Guinness; Levi's*

Computer Film Services
66b Unit, York Road
Weybridge, Surrey KT13 9DY
01932 850034
enquiries@computerfilm.com
www.computerfilm.com
Independent. Digital disc recorders
and post-production systems
Director: Peter Holland
• *Harry Potter; Lord of the Rings*

Crow TV
12 Wendell Road
London W12 9RT
020 8749 6071
info@crowtv.com
www.crowtv.com
Independent. Graphics; editing for
television; pogle colour grade;
online/offline editing; audio
Managing director: Paul Kingsley
• *Vincent, The Full Story; South*
  Bank Show; The Challenge

Cut and Run
Cinema House
93 Wardour Street
London W1F 0UD
020 7432 9696
editors@cutandrun.co.uk
www.cutandrun.co.uk
Independent. Offline editing
Managing director:
Steve Gandalphy
• *Commercials: Castrol; Rimmel;*
  Diet Coke; UPS; Lynx

DB Dubbing
4 St Pauls Road
Clifton, Bristol, Avon BS8 1LT
0117 904 8210
miles@dbdubbing.tv
Independent. Audio
Managing director: Miles Harris
• *Secret Nature; Built for the Kill;*
  Eden Project

De Lane Lea
75 Dean Street
London W1D 3PU
020 7432 3800
info@delanelea.com
www.delanelea.com
Part of Ascent group. Sound for
post-production TV and film
Chief operating officer:
Hugh Penalt-Jones
• *Cold Mountain; Harry Potter, the*
  Prisoner of Azkaban; Two Brothers

DGP
Portland House,
12–13 Greek Street
London W1D 4DL
020 7734 4501
info@dgpsoho.co.uk
www.dgpsoho.co.uk
Independent. Editing; graphics;
DVD; authoring
Managing director: Julian Day
• *Murder City; Yahoo; Friends*

DVA Associates
7/8 Campbell Court, Bramley
Tadley, Hampshire RG26 5EG
01256 882032
info@dva.co.uk
www.dva.co.uk
Independent. Graphics; audio;
DVD; commercials
Managing director: Barrie Gibson
• *SAS Survival Secrets; Life of David*
  Kelly; Goalrush for Meridian

Editworks
Austin House, 95–97 Ber Street
Norwich, Norfolk NR1 3EY
01603 624402
info@theeditworks.co.uk
Independent. Video
Managing director: Rob Manson
• *Commercials: Norwich Union;*
  Virgin Money; Essex County
  Council for European Union

Evolutions Television
5 Berners Street, London
W1T 3LF
020 7580 3333
bookings@evolutionstelevision.com
www.evolutionstelevision.com
Independent. Graphics;
documentaries; commercials; audio
Managing director: Simon Kanjee
• *Top of the Pops titles; Jump*
  London; Other People's Houses

The Farm
13 Soho Square
London W1D 3QF
020 7437 6677
info@farmgroup.tv
www.farmgroup.tv
Partner with Home and The Shed.
Online/offline editing; audio
dubbing; high definition edit and
grading
Managing directors: Nicky Sargent,
Vikki Dunn
• *Dunkirk; Friday night with*
  Jonathan Ross; One Life

Films at 59
59 Cotham Hill, Bristol
Avon BS6 6JR
0117 906 4300
info@filmsat59.com
www.filmsat59.com
*Independent. Audio; high
definition; equipment hire;
online/offline dubbing
Managing director: Gina Lee Fucci*
• *Teachers; Big Cat Diary; Building
the Dream*

Finally Cut
1 Springvale Terrace
London W14 0AE
020 7556 6300
fclon@finalcut-edit.com
www.finalcut-edit.com
*Sister company Clear. Offline editing
Producer: Zoe Henderson*
• *Commercials: Sony PlayStation;
Mountain; Mercedes "movement"*

Finishing Post
10, Gilt Way, Giltbrook
Nottingham
Notts NG16 2GN
0115 945 8800
info@finishing-post.co.uk
www.finishing-post.co.uk
*Independent. Graphics; editing;
DVD authoring
Managing director: Mark Harwood*
• *Commercials: Jaguar; Peugeot;
Heart of the Country*

Flare DVD
Ingestre Court
Ingestre Place
London W1F 0JL
020 7343 6565
sales@flare-DVD.com
www.flare-DVD.com
*Part of M2 group. Short run
duplication; DVD design;
authoring; encoding facility
Managing director: Tom Jones*
• *Kate Rusby; Hallmark;
Fame Academy*

4x4
First Floor
21 Ormeau Avenue
Belfast BT2 8HD
028 9027 1950
4@4x4post.com
www.4x4post.com
*Independent. Effects; graphics;
commercials; audio
Directors: Katy Jackson;
Paula Campbell; Alan Perry;
Jonathan Featherstone*
• *Disability commercials; BTNI
commercial; Just for a Laugh*

Framestore CFC
9 Noel Street
London W1F 8GH
020 7208 2600
info@framestore-cfc.com
www.framestore-cfc.com
*Independent. Effects; computer
generated commercials; films
Chief executive: William Sergeant*
• *Thunderbirds; Walking with
Sea Monsters*

Frontier Post
66–67 Wells Street
London W1T 3PY
020 7291 9191
info@frontierpost.co.uk
www.frontierpost.co.uk
*Independent. Graphics; audio;
online/offline grading
Managing director: Neil Hatton*
• *Property Dreams; Howard
Goodall's 20th Century Greats;
Pagans of the Roman Empire*

Fusion Broadcast
56 Ballynahinch Road
Dromara
Dromore, County Down
BT25 2AL
028 9753 1004
www.fusionbroadcast.co.uk
*Independent. Crew supplying
Managing director: John Morriffey*
• *BBC Northern Ireland; BBC
Network*

Frontline Television
35 Bedfordbury
Covent Garden
London WC2 4DU
020 7836 0411
public@frontline-tv.co.uk
www.frontline-tv.co.uk
*Independent. Editing; graphic
design; audio; Avid online/offline
duplication
Managing director: Bill Cullen*
• *Bum Fights; VTV programme for
the Deaf; Curse of Reality TV*

Fusion Post Production
16 D'Arbly Street
London W1F 8EA
020 7758 0500
edit@fusionpost.co.uk
www.fusionpost.co.uk
*Independent. Audio; online/offline
grading; symphony online
Managing director: Adam de Wolff*
• *BBC Holiday; How Clean is your
House?; The Carrot or the Stick*

Future Post Production
25 Noel Street
London W1F 8GX
020 7434 6655
info@futurefilmgroup.com
www.futurefilmgroup.com
*Part of Future Films Group. Sound;
two dolby mix studios
Managing directors: Tim Levy,
Stephen Margolis*
• *King Arthur; Exorcist, The
Beginning; Harry Potter 3*

Glassworks
33–34 Great Pulteney Street
London W1F 9NP
020 7434 1182
nina@glassworks.co.uk
www.glassworks.co.uk
*Independent. Special effects;
animation; all online
Managing director: Hector Macleod*
• *Dream Keeper; Bjorkall is full of
love; Sprite commercials*

Goldcrest Post-Production
1 Lexington Street
36–44 Brewer Street
London W1F 9LX
020 7437 7972
reception@goldcrest-post.co.uk
www.goldcrest-post.co.uk
*Independent. Sound and telecine
Managing director: Peter Joly*
• *Cold Mountain; Lord of Rings,
Two Towers; Girl with a Pearl
Earring*

Golden Square
11 Golden Square
London W1F 9JB
020 7300 3555
info@golden-square.co.uk
www.golden-square.co.uk
*Independent. Commercials;
special effects
Managing director: Phil Gillies*
• *Campari; Tomb Raiders;
Volkswagen*

**Hackenbacker Audio Post
Production**
10 Bateman Street
London W1D 4AQ
020 7734 1324
reception@hackenbacker.com
www.hackenbacker.com
*Independent. Audio; sound effects;
films; trailers
Managing directors: Julian Slater,
Nigel Heath*
• *Shaun of the Dead; Girl with a
Pearl Earring; Spooks*

The Hive
37 Dean Street
London W12 4PT
020 7565 1000
contact@hiveuk.com
www.hiveuk.com
Part of VTR Group. Telecine; online
editing; special effects; 3 DVD and
2D graphics
Managing director:
David Southwood
• Direct Line sponsorship; BBC
Bitesize; Hell's Kitchen promotion

Home Post Productions
12–13 Richmond Buildings
Soho, London W1D 3HG
020 7292 0200
info@homepost.co.uk
www.farmgroup.tv
Independent. Graphics; audio;
effects; commercials
Managing director: Janine Martin
• Dunkirk; Friday night with
Jonathan Ross; One Life

Lip Sync Post
123 Wardour Street
London W1F 0UU
020 7534 9123
admin@lipsyncpost.co.uk
www.lipsync.co.uk
Independent. Sound; graphics;
editing
Managing director: Norman Merry
• Silent Witness; Touch the Void;
Trolleywood

Liquid TV
1–2 Portland Mews
London W1F 8JE
020 7437 2623
info@liquid.co.uk
www.liquid.co.uk
Independent. Title branding;
special effects
Managing director: Asra Alikhan
• Restoration; Film 2004; Horizon;
Troy

Lola
14–16 Great Portland Street
London W1W 8BL
020 7907 7878
info@lola-post.com
www.lola-post.com
Independent. Visual effects;
commercials; films and TV
Managing directors:
Grahame Andrew, Rob Harvey
• Troy; 5 children and It; Ancient
Egyptians

London Post
34–35 Dean Street
London W1D 4PR
020 7439 9080
dave@londonpost.co.uk
www.londonpost.co.uk
Part of Arena Digital. Audio;
graphics; sound; editing; telecine
Managing director:
Dave Thompson
• Brassed off Britain; Blag;
Celebrity Penthouse

M2 Television
Ingestre Court, Ingestre Place
London W1F 0JL
020 7343 6543
Soho 020 73436543
Camden 020 73436789
info@m2tv.com
www.m2tv.com
Edit; visual; audio
Managing director: Tom Jones
• Revenge; Human Mind;
Bodysnatchers

The Machine Room
54–58 Wardour Street
London W1D 4JQ
020 7734 3433
info@themachineroom.co.uk
www.themachineroom.co.uk
Part of VTR Group. Online editing;
telecine suites; DVD; teramix
machine; archive restoration
department
Managing director:
Danny Whybrow
• Love Actually; Bad Girls;
Footballers Wives

Mediahouse
Hogarth Business Park
3 Burlington Lane, London
W4 2TH
020 8233 5400
info@mediahouse.tv
www.mediahouse.tv/
post_production
IMG Mark McCormack Group.
Video; graphics; DVD;
transmission studio
Head of post-production:
Karen Mullins
• Bremner, Bird and Fortune;
Planet's Funniest Animals

Men-from-Mars
Unit 6, Walpole Court
Ealing Green, London W5 5ED
020 8280 9000
info@men-from-mars.com
www.men-from-mars.com
Part of Barcud Derwen. Visual
effects for film and TV
Creative director: Philip Attfield;
production director: Simon Frame
• Gladiatress; Chasing Liberty;
Jekyll and Hyde; Hamburg Cell;
Sons of the Wind; De-Lovely; Trial
and Retribution: Blue Eiderdown

Metro Broadcast
5–7 Great Chapel Street
London W1F 8FF
020 7434 7700
Metro Suffolk Street
020 7202 2000
Metro Ecosse Edinburgh
0131 554 9421
Metro Ecosse Glasgow
0141 419 1660
info@metrobroadcast.com
www.metrobroadcast.com
Editing inc HD; crewing and
equipment rental; audio and video
restoration; DVD production;
webcasting; duplications and
standards conversion
Directors: Mark Cox, Paul Beale
• EPKs for Mr Bean; Rugby World
Cup promo; NHK various
programmes, shot and edited in HD

The Mill
40–41 Great Marlborough Street
London W1F 7JQ
020 7287 4041
info@mill.co.uk
www.mill.co.uk
Independent. Commercials;
3d animation; edition
Managing director: Pat Joseph
• Commercials: Mercedes; Honda; O2

MGB Facilities
Capital House
Sheepscar Court
Meanwood Road
Leeds
West Yorkshire LS7 2BB
0113 243 6868
contact@mgbtv.co.uk
www.mgbtv.co.uk
Independent. Graphics;
commercials; DVD; animation
Managing director: Mike Gaunt
• Hasbro commercial; Brazilian
Football; DFS Furniture

TV and radio contacts : **Section 4**

Molinare
34 Fouberts Place
London W1F 7PX
020 7478 7000
bookings@molinare.co.uk
www.molinare.co.uk
Independent. Graphics; DVD; audio
Managing director: Mark Foligno
• *Faking It; Make Me Honest; Poirot*

Moving Picture Company
127 Wardour Street
London W1F 0NL
020 7434 3100
mpc@moving-picture.com
www.moving-picture.com
Independent. Commercials; effects;
animation; editing
Managing director: David Jeffers
• *Troy; Dunkirk; Guinness moth*
commercial

Nats
10 Soho Square
London W1D 3NT
020 7287 9900
bookings@nats.ltb.uk
www.nats.ltd.uk
Independent. Editing; audio;
telecine; effects; graphics
Managing director:
Charlie Leonard
• *Seven Wonders of the Industrial*
World; Grand Design; The National
Trust

Oasis Television
6–7 Great Pulteney Street
London W1F 9NA
020 7434 4133
sales@oasistv.co.uk
www.oasistv.co.uk
Independent. Audio; editing;
graphics; duplication
Managing director:
Gareth Mullaney
• *State of Play; The Young Visitors;*
May 33rd

One
71 Dean Street
London W1D 3SF
020 7439 2730
info@onepost.tv
www.onepost.tv
Part of Ascent Group. Commercials;
telecine; animation
Managing director: Paul Jones
• *Jaguar; American Express;*
Aerosmith

Optical Image
The Studio
Broome
Stourbridge
West Midlands DY9 0HA
01562 700404
info@optical-image.com
www.optical-image.com
Independent. Animation; DVD;
duplication; effects; graphics
Managing director: David Clement
• *Sindy; Jellies; Butt Ugly Martians*

Outpost Facilities
Pinewood Studios
Pinewood Road
Iver, Buckinghamshire SL0 0NH
01753 630770
helen@outpostfacilities.co.uk
www.outpostfacilities.co.uk
Independent. Commercials; films;
broadcast; TV
Managing director: Nigel Gourley
• *My Family; Everything I Know*
About Men; Teletubbies
Everywhere

P3 Post
40–42 Lexington Street
London W1F 0LN
020 7287 3006
reception@p3.tv
www.p3.tv
Independent. Effects; graphics;
DVD; commercials
Managing director: Martin Price
• *Derren Brown; Celebs Exposed;*
Audi

Pepper
3 Slingsby Place
London WC2E 9AB
020 7836 1188
mailuf@pepperpost.tv
www.pepperpost.tv
Independent. Effects; graphics;
dramas
Managing director: Patrick Holzen
• *Dirty War; Midsomer Murders;*
White Noise

Phaebus Communications Group
The Brewery Tower
The Deva centre
Trinity Way
Manchester M3 7BF
0161 605 9999
info@phaebus.co.uk
www.phaebus.co.uk
Two branches. DVD; authoring
Managing director: Steve Bettridge
• *BBC channel idents; Andy Pandy;*
Thomas Cook conference events

Pink House
33 West Park Clifton
Bristol, Avon BS8 2LX
0117 923 7087
anita.nandwami@
pinkhousepp.com
www.filmsat59.com
Part of Films at 59. Broadcast;
audio; pictures; effects;
commercials
Managing director:
Anita Nandwami
• *Building the Dream; Big Cook*
Little Cook; Animal Camera

Red Vision
Cambos House
3 Canal Street
Manchester M1 3HE
0161 907 3764
London 020 7419 2010
Bristol 0117 946 6633
info@redvision.co.uk
www.redvision.co.uk
Computer graphics for film and TV
Managing director: David Mousley
• *Touching the Void; D-Day: Men*
and Machines

Resolution
341 Old Street
London EC1V 9LL
020 7749 9300
London 020 7437 1336
info@resolution.tv
www.resolution.tv
Broadcast; commercials;
offline/online; audio; graphics
Managing director: Mike Saunders
• *Big Brother; Top Gear; Fame*
Academy

Rushes
66 Old Compton Street
London W1D 4UH
020 7437 8676
info@rushes.co.uk
www.rushes.co.uk
Part of Ascent media. Effects;
telecine for commercial video
Managing director: Joce Capper
• *Commercials: Hewlett Packard;*
Offspring; Ford Mondeo
(Tom and Jerry)

Savalas
333 Woodlands Road
Glasgow G3 6NG
0141 339 0455
all@savalas.co.uk
www.savalas.co.uk
Independent. Music production;
audio; sound design
Managing directors: Giles Lamb,
Michael MacKinnon,
Karl Henderson
• *Magdalene Sisters; Relocation,*
  Relocation, Relocation; Sea of
  Souls

2nd Sense Broadcast
Millennium Studios, Elstree Way
Borehamwood, Herts WD6 1SF
020 8236 1133
info@2ndsense.co.uk
www.2ndsense.co.uk
Independent. Audio
Managing director: Wendy Hewitt
• *Top of the Pops 2; Chuckle Vision;*
  East Enders Revealed

Skaramoosh
9–15 Neal Street
London WC2H 9PW
020 7379 9966
reception@skaramoosh.co.uk
www.skaramoosh.com
Independent. Effects; graphics;
audio
Managing director: Daniel Slight
• *Strictly Come Dancing; Football*
  Factory; Naked Science

Soho Images
8–14 Meard Street
London W1F 0EQ
020 7437 0831
www.sohoimages.com
Part of Ascent Group. Commercials;
telecine transfers; archive
restoration; DVD
Managing director: Paul Collard
• *Murder in Mind; Bloody Sunday;*
  Mrs Brown

Sound Monsters
4 Grafton Mews
London W1T 5JE
020 7387 3230
info@soundmonsters.com
www.soundmonsters.com
Independent. Audio; sound;
transfer; animation
Managing director: Cliff Jones
• *Death in Gaza; State of Texas; Real*
  Great Escapes

St Anne's Post
20 St Anne's Court
London W1F 0BH
020 7155 1500
info@saintannespost.co.uk
www.saintannespost.co.uk
Part of Ascent Group. Audio;
editing; telecine
Managing director: Keith Williams
• *Brothers Grimm; Alfie;*
  Night Detective

Stream
61 Charlotte Street
London W1T 4PF
020 7208 1567
info@streamdm.co.uk
www.streamdm.co.uk
Part of Ascent Group. DVD; design
compression; authoring facility
Managing director: Paul Kind
• *The Office; Where We're Calling*
  From; My Big Fat Greek Wedding

Suite
28 Newman Street
London W1T 1PR
020 7636 4488
shelley@suitetv.co.uk
www.suitetv.co.uk
Independent. Editing for TV
Managing director: Shelley Fox
• *The Office; Swiss Toni*

Sumners
Suite 401, Berkeley House
35 Whitworth Street West
Manchester M1 5NG
0161 228 0330
janet@sumners.co.uk
www.sumners.co.uk
Independent. Online/offline;
graphics; very reality studio
Managing directors: Janet Sumner;
Andrew Sumner
• *Best Sitcoms; Songs of Praise;*
  Bank of Mum and Dad

Television Set
22 Newman Street
London W1T 1PH
020 7637 3322
terry.bettles@tvsetgroup.co.uk
www.thetelevisionset.co.uk
2 branches. Restoration of old
archives for reuse; audio; grading;
telecine
Managing director: Terry Bettles
• *D-Day plus 60; Poirot*
  remastering; Let it Be

Television Services
International
10 Grape Street
London WC2H 8TG
020 7379 3435
enquiries@tsi.co.uk
www.tsi.co.uk
Independent. Longform and
shortform in light entertainment
and documentaries
Managing director: Simon Peach
• *Ali G; My New Best Friend; Who*
  Rules the Roost?

3 Wise Men
Ingestre Court, Ingestre Place
London W1F 0JL
020 7343 6623
daz@3wisemen.tv
martin@3wisemen.tv
www.3wisemen.tv
Independent. Offline editing
Managing directors: Martin Sage,
Darren Jonusas
• *Seven Industrial Wonders;*
  Battlefield Britain; Horizon

Todd-ao creative services
13 Hawley Crescent
London NW1 8NP
020 7284 7900
schedule@todd-ao.co.uk
www.todd-ao.co.uk
Part of Ascent Group. Telecine
grading; negative film processing;
video dailies; offline/online editing
Managing director:
Samantha Webb
• *Monarch of the Glen; Canterbury*
  Tales; Taggart

Videosonics
13 Hawley Crescent
London NW1 8NP
020 7209 0209
info@videosonics.com
www.videosonics.com
Independent. Audio
Managing director:
Denis Weinreich
• *Young Adam; Bright Young*
  Things; Sexy Beast

Vivid
68 Wells Street
London W1T 3QA
020 7290 0700
bookings@vividpost.com
www.vividpost.com
Independent. Documentaries;
audio; picture
Managing director: Robin Bextor
• *Dinner Party Inspectors; Inside*
  the Mind of a Suicide Bomber;
  Horizon Stronger

VTR
64 Dean Street
London W1D 4QQ
020 7437 0026
reception@vtr.co.uk
www.vtr.co.uk
Independent. Effects; commercials;
telecine. Managing director:
Ant Frend
• Christine Aguillera; McDonalds;
Persil

Wild Tracks Audio Studio
2nd Floor
55 Greek Street
London W1D 3DT
020 7734 6331
bookings@wildtracks.co.uk
www.wildtracks.co.uk
Independent. Audio
Managing director:
Graham Pickford
• Canon; Bob the Builder; Pingu

Yellow Moon
30 Shaw Road, Holywood
County Down BT18 9HX
028 9042 1826
general@yellowmoon.net
www.yellowmoon.net
Independent. Editing
Managing director: Greg Darby
• Citizen Alec; Christine's Children;
Sven-Goran Eriksson

Film & music libraries

BBC Pebble Mill, Information
& Archives
BBC Pebble Mill
Pebble Mill Road
Birmingham B5 7QQ
0121 432 8922
garry.campbell@bbc.co.uk
www.bbc.co.uk
Music, news requests, productions
at Pebble Mill Studio

BFI National Film and TV
Archives
Kingshill Way, Berkhamsted
Herts HP4 3TP
01442 876301
david.pierce@bfi.org.uk
www.bfi.org.uk
Large collection from 1895 to the
present

East Anglian Film Archive
University of East Anglia
Norwich NR4 7TJ
01603 592 664
eafa@uea.ac.uk
www.uea.ac.uk/eafa
East Anglia

Film and Video Archive, Imperial
War Museum
Department of Art
Lambeth Road
London SE1 6HZ
020 7416 5211
film@iwm.org.uk
www.iwm.org.uk/collections/
film.htm
Large collection

Film Institute of Ireland/ Irish
Film Archive
6 Eustace Street
Temple Bar
Dublin 2
00 353 1 679 5744
info@irishfilm.ie
www.irishfilm.ie
Films worldwide. Every Irish film
ever made

GMTV Library Sales
London TV Centre, Upper Ground
London SE1 9TT
020 7827 7363 /6
librarysales@gmtv.co.uk
www.gmtv.co.uk

Huntley Film Archive
191 Wardour Street
London W1F 8ZE
020 7287 8000
films@huntleyarchives.com
www.huntleyarchives.com
Rare and vintage documentary film
from 1895

Images Of War
31a Regents Park Road
London NW1 7TL
020 7267 9198
derek@dircon.co.uk
www.warfootage.com
Images of war archive. 1900 to
first Gulf war

ITN Archive
200 Grays Inn Road
London WC1X 8XZ
020 7833 3000
sales@itnarchive.com
www.itnarchive.com
More than 500,000 hours of news
and feature material

ITV Central
Gas Street, Birmingham B1 2JT
0121 643 9898
www.itv.com

JW Media Music
4 Whitfield Street, London
W1T 2RD
020 7681 8900
info@jwmediamusic.com
www.jwmediamusic.com
Music

Media Archive for Central
England
The Institute of Film Studies
University of Nottingham
University Park
Nottingham NG7 2RD
0115 846 6448
james.patterson@nottingham.ac.uk
www.nottingham.ac.uk/film/mace
East Midlands

National Screen and Sound
Archive of Wales
Aberystwyth, Ceredigion
SY23 3BU
01970 628 2828
agssc@llgc.org.uk
http://screenandsound.llgc.org.uk
Wales

North West Film Archive
Minshull House,
47–49 Chorlton Street
Manchester M1 3EU
0161 247 3097
n.w.filmarchive@mmu.ac.uk
www.nwfa.mmu.ac.uk
The North-west, 1897 to present day

Northern Region Film and
Television Archive
University of Teesside,
Borough Road
Middlesbrough TS1 3BA
01642 384022
leo@nrfta.org.uk
www.nrfta.org.uk
The North

Pathé Pictures
14–17 Market Place
London W1W 8AR
020 7323 5151
www.pathe.co.uk
Worldwide images

Royal Television Society, Library & Archive
Holborn Hall, 100 Grays Inn Road
London WC1X 8AL
020 7430 1000
info@rts.org.uk
www.rts.org.uk
Archive TV pictures, award ceremonies and monthly dinners

Scottish Screen Archive
1 Bowmont Gardens
Glasgow G12 9LR
0141 337 7400
archive@scottishscreen.com
www.scottishscreen.com/archivelive
Scotland since the 1890s

South East Film & Video Archive
University of Brighton
Grand Parade, Brighton BN2 0JY
01273 643 213
sefva@brighton.ac.uk
www.bton.ac.uk/sefva/
sefilmarchivenews
The South-east: Kent, Surrey, East and West Sussex

South West Film and Television Archive
Melville Building, Royal William Yard
Stonehouse, Plymouth PL1 3RP
01752 202 650
info@tswfta.co.uk
www.tswfta.co.uk
Bristol to Dorset

Wessex Film and Sound Archive
Hampshire Record Office
Sussex Street, Winchester
SO23 8TH
01962 847742
sadedm@hants.gov.uk
www.hants.gov.uk/
record-office/film
Hants film and sound archive

Wiener Library
4 Devonshire Street
London W1W 5BH
020 7636 7247
info@wienerlibrary.co.uk
www.wienerlibrary.co.uk
Modern Jewish history

Yorkshire Film Archive
Yorkshire St John College
Mayors Walk, York
YO31 7EX
01904 716 550
yfa@yorksj.ac.uk
Yorkshire only

TV associations

Association of Motion Picture Sound
28 Knox Street
London W1H 1FS
020 7723 6727
admin@amps.net
www.amps.net
Film and TV sound technicians

Bafta (British Academy of Film and Television Arts)
195 Piccadilly
London W1J 9LN
020 7734 0022
www.bafta.org
Awards, training and education

Barb (Broadcasters' Audience Research Board)
18 Dering Street
London W1S 1AQ
020 7529 5531
enquiries@barb.co.uk
www.barb.co.uk
Industry-owned audience data

Bectu (Broadcasting, Entertainment, Cinematograph and Theatre Union)
373–377 Clapham Road
London SW9 9BT
020 7346 0900
www.bectu.org.uk
Union for broadcasting, entertainment and theatre

British Film Council International
10 Little Portland Street
London W1W 7JG
020 7861 7860
info@ukfilmcouncil.org.uk
wwwukfilmcouncil.org.uk
Promotes UK as production centre

British Film Institute
21 Stephen Street
London W1T 1LN
020 7255 1444
publishing@bfi.org.uk
www.bfi.org.uk
Education, exhibitions and resources

British Universities Film and Video Council
77 Wells Street
London W1T 3QJ
020 7393 1500
ask@bufvc.ac.uk
www.bufvc.ac.uk

Broadcasting Press Guild
Tiverton, The Ridge
Woking, Surrey GU22 7EQ
01483 764895
torin.douglas@bbc.co.uk

Cinema and Television Benevolent Fund
22 Golden Square
London W1F 9AD
020 7437 6567
charity@ctbf.co.uk
www.ctbf.co.uk
Trade charity

Drama Association of Wales
The Old Library Building
Singleton Road, Splott
Cardiff CF24 2ET
029 2045 2200
aled.daw@virgin.net

DigiTAG (Digital Terrestrial Television Action Group)
17a Ancienne Route
CH-1218 Grand Saconnex
Geneva
Switzerland
+41 22 717 2716
projectoffice@digitag.org
www.digitag.org
Not-for-profit international association

Digital Television Group
7 Old Lodge Place
St Margarets
Twickenham TW1 1RQ
020 8891 1830
office@dtg.org.uk
www.dtg.org.uk
Director-general: Marcus Coleman International industry-led consortium

Digital Video Broadcasting Project (DVB)
Project Office,
17a Ancienne Route
CH-1218 Grand Saconnex,
Geneva
Switzerland
+41 22 717 2719
dvb@dvb.org
www.dvb.org
Not-for-profit international association

Directors' Guild of Great Britain
Acorn House
314–320 Gray's Inn Road
London WC1X 8DP
020 7278 4343
guild@dggb.org
www.dggb.org

Documentary Film-makers Group
225a Brecknock Road
London N19 5AA
020 7428 0882
info@dfglondon.com
www.dfglondon.com

Cable & Satellite International
Perspective Publishing
402 The Fruit and Wool Exchange
Brushfield Street,
London E1 6EP
020 7426 0101
justin@cable-satellite.com
www.cable-satellite.com
6pa. Editor: John Moulding

Channel 21 International magazine
C21 Medial, Top Floor
25 Phipp Street
London EC2A 4NP
020 7729 7460
press@c21media.net
www.c21media.net
10pa. Editor: David Jenkins

Commonwealth Broadcaster
Commonwealth Broadcasting
Association
17 Fleet Street
London EC4Y 1AA
020 7583 5550
cba@cba.org.uk
www.cba.org.uk
Quarterly. Editor: Elizabeth Smith

Contacts
The Spotlight
7 Leicester Place
London WC2H 7RJ
020 7437 7631
info@spotlightcd.com
www.spotlightcd.com
Annual. Contacts for stage, film, TV and radio. Editor: Kate Poynton

Crewfinder
Adleader Publications
15 Chartwell Park, Belfast
BT8 6NG
028 9079 7902
mail@adleader.co.uk
www.crewfinderwales.co.uk
Annual. Wales' film, TV and video directory. Proprietor: Stan Mairs

Digilook
7 Burgess Green, Deal
Kent CT14 0AU
07709 118854
andi@digilook.net
www.digilook.net
*Web. Digital TV & radio
Editors: Andi Gasking, Alex Oughton*

Digital Spy
6 Queen's Elm Square
London SW3 6ED
07814 776894
nwilkes@digitalspy.co.uk
www.digitalspy.co.uk
Web. Digital TV. Editor: Neil Wilkes

FilmBang
Marianne Mellin
43 Hyndland Road
Glasgow G12 9UX
0141 334 2456
info@filmbang.com
www.filmbang.com
Annual. Scotland's film and video directory. Editor: Marianne Mellin

IBE
DMG Business Media
Queensway House,
2 Queens Way
Redhill, Surrey RH1 1QS
01737 855224
info@ibeweb.com
www.ibeweb.com
12pa. International broadcast engineering. Editor: Neil Nixon

Kemps Film, TV, Video Handbook (UK edition)
Reed Business Information
Windsor Court
East Grinstead House
East Grinstead
West Sussex RH19 1XA
01342 332073
kemps@reedinfo.co.uk
www.kftb.com
Annual. Guide to international production. Editor: Pat Huwson

The Knowledge
CMP Information
Riverbank House
Angel Lane
Tonbridge
Kent TN9 1SE
01732 377591
knowledge@cmpinformation.com
www.theknowledgeonline.com
Annual. Production directory

Line Up
Line Up Publications
The Hawthornes
4 Conference Grove
Crowle WR7 4SF
01905 381725
editor@lineup.biz
www.ibs.org.uk
6pa. Journal of the Institute of Broadcast Sound. Editor: Hugh Robjohns

Multichannel News
Chilton Company
37 The Towers
Lower Mortlake Road
Richmond TW9 2JR
020 8948 8561
chrisforrester@compuserve.com
www.multichannel.com
Weekly. Editor: Chris Forester

Pact directory of Independent producers
Producers Alliance for Cinema
and Television (PACT)
45 Mortimer Street
London W1W 8HJ
020 7331 6000
enquiries@pact.co.uk
www.pact.co.uk
Annual. Directory of independent producers. Editor: Louise Bateman

Pro Sound News
CMP Information
Ludgate House
245 Blackfriars Road
London SE1 9UR
020 7921 8319
info@cmpinformation.com
www.cmpinformation.com
*12pa. Audio industry
Editor: David Robinson*

The Production Guide
Emap Information
33–39 Bowling Green Lane
London EC1R 0DA
020 7505 8000
theproductionguide@Emap.com
www.productionguideonline.com
*Annual. Information on production
Editor: Mei Mei Rogers*

Satellite Finance
Thompson Stanley Publishers
1–3 Leonard Street
London EC2A 4AQ
020 7251 2967
oliver.cann@satellitefinance.com
www.telecomfinance.com
*11pa. Finance journal for executives
Editor: Oliver Cann*

Screen Digest
Screen Digest
Lymehouse Studios
38 Georgiana Street
London NW1 0EB
020 7424 2820
editorial@screendigest.com
www.screendigest.com
Monthly. Editor: David Fisher

Screen International
Emap Media
33–39 Bowling Green Lane
London EC1R 0DA
020 7505 8080
screeninternational@hotmail.com
www.screendaily.com
Weekly. News service for global film industry. Editor: Colin Brown

Sports TV Yearbook
Perspective Media
PO Box 22499
London W6 9YS
020 7937 3636
pnicholson@sportsvisionnews.com
www.sportscentric.com
Annual. Editor: Jay Stuart

Stage Screen and Radio
Bectu
373–377 Clapham Road
London SW9 9BT
020 7346 0900
janice@
 stagescreenandradio.org.uk
www.bectu.org.uk
10pa. Broadcasting union
Editor: Janice Turner

Televisual
Centaur Communications
50 Poland Street
London W1F 7AX
020 7970 4000
mundy.ellis@centaur.co.uk
www.mad.co.uk
Monthly. Trade magazine for TV
Editor: Mundy Ellis

TV International
Informa Media and Telecoms
Mortimer House
37–41 Mortimer Street
London W1T 3JH
020 7017 4269
toby.scott@informa.com
www.informamedia.com
Daily. International TV listings
Editor: Stewart Clarke

TBI (Television Business International)
Informa Media and Telecoms
Mortimer House
37–41 Mortimer Street
London W1T 3JH
020 7453 2300
kevin.scott@informa.com
www.informamedia.com
Annual. Directory to businesses
Editor: Kevin Scott

TV Technology and Production
IMAS Publishing UK
Atlantica House
11 Station Road
St Ives, Cambs PE27 5BH
01480 461555
tvteurope@aol.com
www.imaspub.com
6pa. Broadcasting and production
technology. Editor: Mark Hallinger

TVB Europe
CMP Information,
Prospect House
1 Prospect Road
Dublin 9
00 353 1 882 4444
sgrice@cmpinformation.com
www.tvbeurope.com
Monthly. Broadcasting innovation
and technology.
Editor: Fergal Ringrose

VLV Bulletin
Voice of the Listener and Viewer
101 Kings Drive
Gravesend DA12 5BQ
01474 352835
vlv@btinternet.com
www.vlv.org.uk
Quarterly. Consumer campaigning
body. Editor: Jocelyn Hay

Zerb
The Deeson Group
Ewell House, Gravney Road
Faversham, Kent ME13 8UP
01795 535468
alichap@mac.com
www.gtc.org.uk
2pa. For camera operators
Editor: Alison Chapman

Radio Contacts

BBC radio

Broadcasting House
Portland Place
London W1A 1AA
020 7580 4468

Director of radio and music:
Jenny Abramsky,
020 7765 4561
Head of radio news:
Stephen Mitchell
Head of radio current affairs:
Gwyneth Williams
Controller, radio production:
Graham Ellis, 020 7765 4809
Controller, radio & music new media: Simon Nelson,
020 7765 2545
Publicity: Sue Lynas,
020 7765 4990
Digital radio publicist:
Jamie Austin, 020 7765 0426

BBC Radio 1/1xtra
Yalding House
152–156 Great Portland Street
London W1N 6AJ
www.bbc.co.uk/radio1
www.bbc.co.uk/1xtra
Controller: Andy Parfitt; head of mainstream programmes: Ben Cooper, 020 7765 2236; head of specialist live music: Ian Parkinson, 020 7765 0365; breakfast show: Chris Moyles (Radio 1), Rampage (1xtra); press: Julian Payne, 020 7765 1030

BBC Radio 2
Western House
99 Great Portland Street
London W1A 1AA
www.bbc.co.uk/radio2
Controller: Lesley Douglas, 020 7765 3493; managing editor: Antony Bellekom, 020 7765 4612; editor, mainstream programmes: Phil Hughes, 020 7765 4159; editor, specialist programmes: Dave Barber, 0121 432 9854; breakfast show: Terry Wogan; press: Hester Nevill, 020 7765 5712

BBC Radio 3
Broadcasting House
Portland Place
London W1A 1AA
www.bbc.co.uk/radio3
Controller: Roger Wright, 020 7765 2523; head of speech programmes: Abigail Appleton, 020 7765 3277; head of music programming: John Evans, 020 7765 0481; controller, Proms, events & TV classical music: Nicholas Kenyon, 020 7765 4928; press: Sian Davis, 020 7765 5887

BBC Radio 4
Broadcasting House
Portland Place
London W1A 1AA
www.bbc.co.uk/radio4
Controller: Helen Boaden, 020 7765 3836; network manager: Denis Nowlan, 020 7765 4615; head of radio drama: Gordon House, 020 755 71006; editor, drama and entertainment: Caroline Raphael, 020 7765 1870; editor, radio light entertainment: John Pidgeon, 020 7765 4220; editors, general factual: Jane Ellison (features) 020 7765 0631, Prue Keely (strands) 020 7765 2585; editor, specialist factual: Andrew Caspari, 020 7765 2660; press: Marion Greenwood, 020 7765 2629
Today programme
Room G630, Stage 6
Television Centre, Wood Lane
London W12 7RJ
www.bbc.co.uk/radio4/today
Editor: Kevin Marsh; presenters: John Humphrys, James Naughtie, Ed Stourton, Sarah Montague

BBC Radio Five Live & Five Live Sports Extra
Television Centre, Wood Lane
London W12 7RJ
www.bbc.co.uk/fivelive
Controller: Bob Shennan, 020 8624 8956; head of radio sport: Gordon Turnbull, 020 8225 6206; head of news, Radio Five Live: Ceri Thomas, 020 8624 8946; commissioning editor: Moz Dee, 020 8624 8948; press: Andy Bate, 020 8576 1694

BBC 6 Music
Western House
99 Great Portland Street
London W1A 1AA
www.bbc.co.uk/6music
Controller: Lesley Douglas, 020 7765 3493; head of programmes: Ric Blaxill; breakfast show: Phill Jupitus; see also Radio 2 contacts

BBC Asian Network
Epic House, Charles Street
Leicester LE1 3SH
0116 251 6688
www.bbc.co.uk/asiannetwork
Controller: Bijay Sharma; breakfast: Gagan Grewal; publicity: Dimple Poojara, 020 8225 6373

BBC 7
Broadcasting House
Portland Place
London W1A 1AA
www2.thny.bbc.co.uk/bbc7
Controller: Helen Boaden, 020 7765 3836; see also Radio 4 contacts

BBC World Service
Bush House, Strand
London WC2B 4PH
020 7557 2941
www.bbc.co.uk/worldservice
Director: Mark Byford

Nations & regions

BBC Radio Scotland
Queen Margaret Drive
Glasgow G12 8DG
0141 339 8844
scottishplanning@bbc.co.uk
www.bbc.co.uk/scotland
Controller: Ken MacQuarrie; news editor: Blair Jenkins. 92–95 FM; 810 AM

BBC Radio Nan Gaidheal
52 Church Street, Stornoway
Isle of Lewis HS1 2LS
01851 705000
feedback@bbc.co.uk
www.bbc.co.uk/scotlandalba/radio
Editor: Marion MacKinnon; news editor: Norrie Maclennan. 103–105 FM

BBC Radio Wales/Cymru
Broadcasting House
Llandaff,
Cardiff
CF5 2YQ
0870 010 0110
radiowales@bbc.co.uk
www.bbc.co.uk/radiowales
Managing editor: Julie Barton;
head of news: Geoff Williams;
breakfast show: Richard Ellis/
Felicity Evans. 93-104 FM

BBC Radio Ulster
Broadcasting House
Belfast
BT2 8HQ
028 9033 8000
radioulster@bbc.co.uk
www.bbc.co.uk/radioulster
Head of radio: Ana Leddy;
head of music: Declan McGovern;
head of news: Andrew Colman.
92-95.4 FM

BBC Radio Foyle
Northland Road, Derry
Londonderry
BT48 7GD
028 7137 8600
radiofoyle@bbc.co.uk
www.bbc.co.uk/radiofoyle
Head of radio: Ana Leddy; head of
news: Eimear O'Callaghan.
792 AM; 93.1 FM

BBC local radio

BBC Radio Berkshire
PO Box 1044,
Reading RG4 8FH
0118 946 4200
berkshireonline@bbc.co.uk
www.bbc.co.uk/berkshire
Editor: Marianne Bell; breakfast
show: Jim Cathcart/Maggie
Filburn. 104.1 FM; 95.4 FM; 104.4
FM; 94.6 FM

BBC Radio Bristol and Somerset Sound
PO Box 194,
Bristol BS99 7QT
01179 741111
radio.bristol@bbc.co.uk
www.bbc.co.uk/radiobristol and
www.bbc.co.uk/bristol
Managing editor, Bristol: Jenny
Lacey; assistant editors: Dawn
Trevett (Bristol), Simon Clifford
(Somerset Sound); breakfast show:
Nigel Dando/ Rachael Burden.
95.5, 94.9 FM; 1548, 1566 AM

BBC Radio Cambridgeshire
PO Box 96, 104 Hills Road
Cambridge CB2 1LD
01223 259696
cambs@bbc.co.uk
www.bbc.co.uk/cambridgeshire
News editor: Alison Daws;
managing editor: David Martin;
breakfast show: Trevor Dann &
Emma McLean.
96 FM; 95.7 FM

BBC Radio Cleveland
PO Box 95FM, Newport Road
Middlesbrough TS1 5DG
01642 225211
bbcradiocleveland@bbc.co.uk
www.bbc.co.uk/tees
Managing editor: Andrew Glover;
news editor: Peter Harris; breakfast
show: Ken Snowdon. 95 FM

BBC Radio Cornwall
Phoenix Wharf
Truro, Cornwall TR1 1UA
01872 275421
radio.cornwall@bbc.co.uk
www.bbc.co.uk/cornwall
Managing editor: Pauline Causey;
news editor: Ed Goodrich; breakfast
show: Pam Spriggs & James
Churchfield. 103.9 FM; 95.2 FM

BBC Radio Cumbria
Annetwell Street, Carlisle
CA3 8BB
01228 592444
radio.cumbria@bbc.co.uk
www.bbc.co.uk/radiocumbria
Managing editor: Nigel Dyson;
news editor: Tom Stight; breakfast
show: Richard Corrie & Richard
Nankivell.
95.6 FM; 96.1 FM; 104.1 FM

BBC Radio Derby
PO Box 104.5, Derby
DE1 3HL
01332 361111
radio.derby@bbc.co.uk
www.bbc.co.uk/radioderby
Managing editor: Simon Cornes;
news editor: John Atkin; breakfast
show: Andy Whitaker. 1116 AM;
104.5 AM; 95.3 FM; 96FM

BBC Radio Devon
PO Box 1034, Plymouth
PL3 5BD
01752 260323
radio.devon@bbc.co.uk
www.bbc.co.uk/devon
Managing editor: Sarah Softley;
news editor: David Farwig;
breakfast show: Monica Ellis.
103.4 FM

BBC Essex
198 New London Road
Chelmsford, Essex
CM2 9XB
01245 616000
essex@bbc.co.uk
www.bbc.co.uk/essex
Managing editor: Margaret Hyde;
news editor: Alison Hodgkins-
Brown; breakfast show: Etholle
George & John Hayes. 103.5 FM;
95.3 FM; 765 AM; 1530 AM;
729 AM

BBC Radio Gloucestershire
London Road
Gloucester
GL1 1SW
01452 308585
radio.gloucestershire@bbc.co.uk
www.bbc.co.uk/gloucestershire
Managing editor: Mark Hurrell;
news editor: Ivor Ward-Davis;
breakfast show: Vernon Harwood.
104.7 FM; 1413 AM

BBC GMR
PO Box 951
Oxford Road
Manchester M60 1SD
0161 200 2000
gmr.newsdesk@bbc.co.uk
www.bbc.co.uk/england/gmr
Managing editor: Mike Briscoe;
news editor: Matt Elliott;
breakfast show: Heather Stott &
Mark Edwardson.
95.1 FM; 104.6 FM

BBC Radio Guernsey
Bulwer Avenue
St Sampsons
Guernsey GY2 4LA
01481 200600
radio.guernsey@bbc.co.uk
www.bbc.co.uk/guernsey
Managing editor: Rod Holmes; news
editors: Simon Alexander & Kay
Longlay; breakfast show: Adrian
Gidney.
93.2 FM; 1116 AM

BBC Hereford and Worcester
Hylton Road
Worcester
WR2 5WW
01905 748485
bbchw@bbc.co.uk
www.bbc.co.uk/worcester
or /hereford
Managing editor: James Coghill;
news editor: Jo Baldwin; breakfast
show: Mike George. 104 FM; 104.6
FM; 94.7 FM

BBC Radio Humberside and BBCi Hull
Queens Court, Queens Gardens
Hull HU1 3RP
01482 323232
radio.humberside@bbc.co.uk
www.bbc.co.uk/humber
Managing editor: Simon Pattern; news editor: Mike Morris; breakfast show: Andy Comfort. 95.9 FM; 1485 AM

BBC Radio Jersey
18 Parade Road, St Helier
Jersey JE2 3PL
01534 870000
radio.jersey@bbc.co.uk
www.bbc.co.uk/jersey
Managing editor: Denzil Dudley; news editor: Sarah Scriven; breakfast show: Colin Bray. 88.8 FM

BBC Radio Kent
The Great Hall, Mount Pleasant Road
Tunbridge Wells, Kent TN1 1QQ
01892 670000
radio.kent@bbc.co.uk
www.bbc.co.uk/kent
Managing editor: Robert Wallace; news editors: Sally Dunk & Simon Longprice; breakfast show: Steve Ladner. 96.7 FM; 97.6 FM; 104.2 FM

BBC Radio Lancashire and BBC Open Centre
26 Darwen Street, Blackburn
Lancs BB2 2EA
01254 262411
radio.lancashire@bbc.co.uk
www.bbc.co.uk/lancashire
Managing editor: John Clayton; news editor: Chris Rider; breakfast show: Mike West. 95.5 FM

BBC Radio Leeds
Broadcasting Centre
2 St Peters Square, Leeds
LS9 8AH
0113 244 2131
radio.leeds@bbc.co.uk
www.bbc.co.uk/leeds
Managing editor: John Ryan; news editor: Andy Evans; breakfast show: Andrew Edwards & Liz Rhodes. 92.4 FM

BBC Radio Leicester
Epic House, Charles Street
Leicester LE1 3SH
0116 251 6688
radio.leicester@bbc.co.uk
www.bbc.co.uk/leicester
Managing editor: Kate Squire; breakfast show: Ben Jackson. 104.9 FM

BBC Radio Lincolnshire
PO Box 219, Newport
Lincoln LN1 3XY
01522 511411
radio.lincolnshire@bbc.co.uk
www.bbc.co.uk/lincolnshire
Managing editor: Charlie Partridge; news editor: Andy Farrant; breakfast show: William Wright. 94.9 FM; 1368 FM; 104 FM

BBC London 94.9
35 Marylebone High Street
London W1U 4QA
020 7224 2424
yourlondon@bbc.co.uk
www.bbc.co.uk/london
Managing editor: David Robey; breakfast show: Danny Baker. 94.9 FM

BBC Radio Merseyside and BBC Open Centre
55 Paradise Street
Liverpool L1 3BP
0151 708 5500
radio.merseyside@bbc.co.uk
www.bbc.co.uk/liverpool
Managing editor: Mick Ord; news editor: Lee Bennion; breakfast show: Linda McDermot & Andy Ball. 95.8 FM

BBC Radio Newcastle
Broadcasting Centre
Barrack Road
Newcastle upon Tyne NE99 1RN
0191 232 4141
radio.newcastle@bbc.co.uk
www.bbc.co.uk/england/radionewcastle
Managing editor: Sarah Drummond; news editor: Doug Morris; breakfast show: Mike Parr. 95.4 FM

BBC Radio Norfolk
The Forum, Millennium Plain
Norwich NR2 1BH
01603 617411
radionorfolk@bbc.co.uk
www.bbc.co.uk/norfolk
Managing editor: David Clayton; news editor: Sarah Kings; breakfast show: Graham Barnard. 104.1 FM; 95.1 FM; 855 AM; 873 AM

BBC Radio Northampton
Broadcasting House,
Abington Street
Northampton NN1 2BH
01604 239100
northampton@bbc.co.uk
www.bbc.co.uk/northamptonshire
Managing editor: Laura Moss; news editor: Mark Whall; breakfast show: Liz Caroll-Wheat. 104.2 FM; 103.6 FM

BBC Radio Nottingham
London Road
Nottingham
NG2 4UU
0115 955 0500
radio.nottingham@bbc.co.uk
www.bbc.co.uk/nottingham
Managing editor: Mike Bettison; news editor: Steve Beech; breakfast show: Karl Cooper. 103.8 FM

BBC Radio Oxford
PO Box 95.2
Oxford OX2 7YL
01865 311444
radio.oxford@bbc.co.uk
www.bbc.co.uk/radiooxford
Managing editor: Steve Taschini; news editor: Neil Bennett. 95.2 FM

BBC Radio Sheffield and BBC Open Centre
54 Shoreham Street
Sheffield S1 4RS
0114 273 1177
radio.sheffield@bbc.co.uk
www.bbc.co.uk/england/radiosheffield
Managing editor: Angus Moorat; news editor: Mike Woodcock; breakfast show: Everard Davy. 88.6 FM

BBC Radio Shropshire
2–4 Boscobel Drive
Shrewsbury
SY1 3TT
01743 248484
radio.shropshire@bbc.co.uk
www.bbc.co.uk/shropshire
Managing editor: Tim Pemberton; news editor: John Shone; breakfast show: Eric Smith. 96 FM; 95.7 FM

BBC Radio Solent
Broadcasting House,
Havelock Road
Southampton
SO14 7PW
02380 631311
solent@bbc.co.uk
www.bbc.co.uk/radiosolent
Managing editor: Mia Costello; breakfast show: Julian Clegg. 96.1 FM

BBC Southern Counties Radio
Broadcasting Centre
Guildford GU2 7AP
01483 306306
southern.counties.radio@bbc.co.uk
www.bbc.co.uk/southerncounties
Managing editor: Mike Hapgood; news editor: Mark Carter; breakfast show: Sarah Gorrell, Ed Douglas, John Radford. 104–104.8 FM; 95–95.3 FM

BBC Radio Stoke and BBC Open Centre
Cheapside, Hanley
Stoke on Trent ST1 1JJ
01782 208080
radio.stoke@bbc.co.uk
www.bbc.co.uk/stoke
Managing editor: Sue Owen;
news editor: Roy Hill; breakfast
show: Kevin Fernihough, Janine
Machin. 94.6 FM

BBC Radio Suffolk
Broadcasting House
St Matthew's Street,
Ipswich
Suffolk IP1 3EP
01473 250000
radiosuffolk@bbc.co.uk
www.bbc.co.uk/suffolk
Managing editor: Gerald Main;
news editor: Lis Henderson;
breakfast show: Mark Murphy.
105.5 FM; 104.5 FM; 103 FM

BBC Radio Swindon
PO Box 1234
Swindon SN1 3RW
01793 513626
radio.swindon@bbc.co.uk
www.bbc.co.uk/wiltshire
Managing editor: Tony Worgan;
news editor: Kirsty Ward; breakfast
show: Peter Heaton-Jones. 103.6 FM

BBC Three Counties Radio
PO Box 3CR, Luton
Bedfordshire LU1 5XL
01582 637400
3cr@bbc.co.uk
www.bbc.co.uk/threecounties
Managing editor: Mark Norman;
breakfast show: Roberto Perrone.
95.5 FM; 104.5 FM; 103 FM

BBC Radio Wiltshire
PO Box 1234
01793 513626
radio.wiltshire@bbc.co.uk
www.bbc.co.uk/wiltshire
Managing editor: Tony Worgan;
news editor: Kirsty Ward; breakfast
show: Sue Davies. 103.5 FM; 104.3
FM; 104.9 FM

BBC WM (Birmingham)
Pebble Mill Road
Birmingham B5 7QQ
0121 432 9000
radio.wm@bbc.co.uk
www.bbc.co.uk/birmingham
or
www.bbc.co.uk/blackcountry
Managing editor: Keith Beech;
breakfast show: Adrian Goldberg

BBC WM (Coventry)
1 Holt Court
Greyfriars Road
Coventry CV1 2WR
02476 860086
coventry.warwickshire@bbc.co.uk
www.bbc.co.uk/coventry
Managing editor: David Clargo;
breakfast show: Ann Othen, Colin
Hazelden, Sandie Dunleavy. 103.7
FM; 94.8 FM; 104 FM

BBC North Yorkshire – Radio York
20 Bootham Row
York YO30 7BR
01904 641351
northyorkshire.news@bbc.co.uk
www.bbc.co.uk/northyorkshire
Managing editor: Matt Youdale;
news editor: Elly Fiorentini;
breakfast show: Allan Watkiss,
Anna Wallace
1260 AM; 666 AM; 104.5 FM;
103.7 FM; 95.5 FM

Resources

BBC Radio Resources
Brock House
19 Langham Street
London W1A 1AA
020 7765 5394
radio.facilities@bbc.co.uk
www.bbcradioresources.com
Senior operations manager:
Martin Hollister; head of research:
Miles Hosking; marketing
manager: Amanda Bates

Event Services
Brock House
19 Langham Street
London W1A 1AA
020 7765 5100
rr-events-team@bbc.co.uk
Events manager: Mark Diamond;
events assistant: Joanne Surtees

Outside Broadcasts
Brock House
19 Langham Street
London W1A 1AA
020 7765 4889
duncan.smith@bbc.co.uk
Operations manager: Will Garrett;
radio outside broadcasts manager:
Duncan Smith

Studios

Birmingham Studios
Pebble Mill,
Pebble Mill Road
Edgbaston,
Birmingham
West Midlands B5 7QQ
0121 432 8888
bryn.george@bbc.co.uk
www.bbc.co.uk/birmingham
Operations co-ordinator: Liz
Treacher; deputy controller:
David Holdsworth

Bristol Broadcasting House
Whiteladies Road,
Bristol BS8 2LR
0117 973 2211
www.bbc.co.uk/bristol
Operations co-ordinator: Maria
Clutterbuck; open team leader:
Iain Hunter

Broadcasting House Studios
Brock House,
19 Langham Street
London W1A 1AA
020 8743 8000
Communications and marketing
manager: Amanda Bates; senior
operations manager:
Martin Hollister

Maida Vale Studios
1–129 Delaware Road
London W9 2LG
020 7765 2091
Facilities manager: John Hakrow

Manchester Studios
New Broadcasting House
PO Box 27
Oxford Road
Manchester M60 1SJ
0161 244 4607
Operations co-ordinator:
Lilian O'Callaghan; operations
manager: Richard Savage

Commercial radio

Commercial Radio Companies Association
77 Shaftesbury Avenue
London W1D 5DU
020 7306 2603
info@crca.co.uk
www.crca.co.uk
*Chief executive: Paul Brown;
research & commercial manager:
Alison Winter*

Main commercial radio groups

CN Group
Dalston Road, Carlisle
Cumbria CA2 5UA
01228 612600
news@cumbrian-
newspapers.co.uk
www.cumbria-online.co.uk
*Chief executive: Robin Burgess;
director of technical services: Peter
Simpson; general manager:
Christopher Bisco*

Capital Radio
30 Leicester Square
London WC2H 7LA
020 7766 6000
info@capitalradio.com
www.capitalradio.plc.uk
*Chairman: Ian Irvins; chief
executive: David Mansfield;
operations director: Paul Davies;
programme controller:
Keith Pringle*

Chrysalis Radio Group
The Chrysalis Building
13 Bramley Road
London W10 6SP
020 7221 2213
info@chrysalis.com
www.chrysalis.com
*PLC chairman: Chris Wright;
chief executives: Richard
Huntingford (whole group),
Phil Riley (radio); programming
director: Jim Hicks; head of network
news: Jonathan Richards; senior
press officer: Huw Davies*

Classic Gold Digital
Network Centre, Chiltern Road
Dunstable LU6 1HQ
01582 676200
www.classicgolddigital.com
*Chairman: Tim Blackmore;
managing director: John Baish;
programme controller: Paul Baker*

Emap Performance Network
Mappin House
4 Winsley Street
London W1W 8HF
020 7436 1515
www.emap.com
*Group managing director:
Marcus Rich; advertising director:
Dave King; programme director:
Phil Roberts*

GWR Group
Chiseldon House, Stonehill Green
Westlea, Swindon SN5 7HB
0118 928 4313
www.gwrgroup.musicradio.com
*Executive chairman:
Ralph Bernard; group operations
director UK: Steve Orchard*

Lincs FM
Witham Park
Waterside South
Lincoln LN5 7JN
01522 549900
enquiries@lincsfm.co.uk
www.lincsfm.co.uk
*Chief executive: Michael Betton;
director of programming: Jane Hill*

SMG
200 Renfield Street
Glasgow G2 3PR
0141 300 3300
www.smg.plc.uk
*Chief executive: Andrew Flanagan;
chief executive, SMG Radio:
John Pearson*

Scottish Radio Holdings
Clydebank Business Park
Clydebank
Glasgow G81 2RX
0141 565 2200
www.srhplc.com
*Chairman: Lord Gordon of
Strathblane; chief executive:
Richard Findlay; MD, radio:
David Goode; MD, Score Digital:
Grae Allan*

The Wireless Group
18 Hatfields
London SE1 8DJ
020 7959 7800
www.talksport.net
*Chairman and chief executive:
Kelvin MacKenzie; MD, ILRS:
Ashley MacKenzie; group
programme director: Paul Chantler*

Tindle Radio Holdings
Weaver's Yard, 6 West Street
Farnham, Surrey GU9 7DN
01252 735667
www.tindleradio.com
*Chairman: Sir Ray Tindle; deputy
chairman: Robert Stiby; directors:
Colin Christmas, Kevin Stewart*

UKRD Group
Cam Brea Studios
Wilson Way
Redruth
Cornwall TR15 3XX
01209 310435
enquiries@ukrd.co.uk
www.ukrd.com
*Chairman: James St Aubyn;
general managing director:
William Rogers; commercial
director: Rob van Pooss;
programme director: Phil Angell;
marketing director: Mark Beever*

National commercial radio: AM, Digital One and Freeview

Digital One
7 Swallow Place
London W1B 2AG
020 7288 4600
Press 07813 783181
info@digitalone.co.uk
www.ukdigitalradio.com
*Chief executive: Quentin Howard
Joint venture backed by GWR
and NTL*

Freeview
Broadcast Centre,
201 Wood Lane
London W12 7TP
0870 880 9980
www.freeview.co.uk
*General manager:
Matthew Seaman*

Capital Disney
30 Leicester Square
London WC2H 7LA
020 7766 6000
kevin.palmer@
capitalradiogroup.com
www.capitaldisney.co.uk
*Head of Communications Group
Radio: Elly Smith; programme
controller: Will Chambers.
Digital One*

Classic FM
7 Swallow Place
Oxford Circus
London W1B 2AG
020 7343 9000
www.classicfm.com
*Editorial contact: Rob Weinberg;
managing editor: Darren Henley.
Digital One; 99.9–101.9 FM*

Core
PO Box 2269
London W1A 5UQ
GWR Group
020 7911 7300
fresh@corefreshhits.com
www.corefreshhits.com
Digital content manager:
Nick Piggott.
Digital One, Sky, cable & internet

The Hits
Castle Quay
Castlefields
Manchester M15 4PR
0161 288 5000
studio@thehitsradio.com
www.thehitsradio.com
Station manager: Phil Mackenzie;
programme controller:
Anthony Gay.
Freeview; DAB Digital Radio:
Greater London

Jazz FM
26–27 Castlereagh Street
London W1H 5DL
020 7706 4100
jazzinfo@jazzfm.com
www.jazzfm.com
Managing director: Carter Tanner;
programme director: Mark Walker.
Freeview; DAB Digital Radio:
central Scotland; Greater London;
south Wales and Severn estuary;
West Midlands; 102.2FM

Kerrang!
Kerrang House
20 Lionel Street
Birmingham
B3 1AQ
Emap Performance Network
0845 053 1052
brendan.moffett@emap.com
www.Emapdigitalradio.com
Programme controller:
Andrew Jefferies; managing
director: Lyn Wood.
Freeview, satellite & Cable
Kerrang! Digital is broadcast
from Mappin House, London.
Tel: 020 7436 1515

Kiss
Mappin House
4 Winsley Street
London W1W 8HF
Emap Performance Network
020 7975 8100
brendan.moffett@emap.com
www.kiss100.com
Managing director: Mark Story;
programme director: Andy Roberts.
100 FM; Greater London; Freeview,
Sky, satellite, digital

Life
30 Leicester Square
London WC2H 7LA
020 7766 6000
studio@listentolife.com
Programme manager:
Kevin Palmer.
Digital One

Magic
900 Herries Road
Sheffield S6 1RH
0114 209 1034
natalie.johnson@emap.com
www.Emapdigitalradio.com
Managing director: Ian Clasper;
programme director: Gary Stein
Freeview, Sky and cable

Oneword Radio
Landseer House
19 Charing Cross Road
London WC2H OES
020 7976 3030
info@oneword.co.uk
www.oneword.co.uk
Managing director:
Simon Blackmore.
Digital One, Freeview, Sky and
internet

Planet Rock
PO Box 2269
London W1A 5UQ
GWR Group
020 7911 7300
joinus@planetrock.com
www.planetrock.com
Digital content manager:
Nick Piggott.
Digital One

Prime Time Radio
PO Box 5050
London SW1E 6ZR
0870 050 5050
david.atkey@primetimeradio.org
www.primetimeradio.org
Managing director: Ron Coles;
operations director: David Atkey.
Digital One, Sky, cable & internet

Q Radio
Mappin House
4 Winsley Street
London W1W 8HF
Emap Performance Network
020 7436 1515
brendan.moffett@emap.com
www.q4music.com
Managing director: Mark Story;
programme director: Simon Long.
Freeview, Sky and cable

Smash! Hits
Mappin House
4 Winsley Street
London W1W 8HF
Emap Performance Network
020 7436 1515
brendan.moffett@emap.com
www.Emapdigitalradio.com
Managing director: Ian Clasper;
programme director: Andy Roberts.
Freeview, Sky and cable

TalkSport
18 Hatfields
London SE1 8DJ
The Wireless Group
020 7959 7800
www.talksport.net
Managing director: Michael
Franklyn; programme director:
Mike Parry.
Digital One; 1107 AM; 1053 AM;
1071 AM; 1089 AM

Virgin Radio
No 1 Golden Square
London W1F 9DJ
020 7434 1215
reception@virginradio.co.uk
www.virginradio.co.uk
Station manager: Steve Taylor;
programme director: Paul Jackson.
Digital One; 1197 AM; 1215 AM;
1233 AM; 1242 AM; 1260 AM, Sky

News services

ITN Radio
200 Grays Inn Road
London WC1X 8XZ
020 7430 4090
newsdesk: 020 7430 4814
radio@itn.co.uk
www.itn.co.uk
Provides news service for
Independent Radio News (IRN),
plus other feeds
Managing director: John Perkins;
editor: Jon Godel

Independent Radio News (IRN)
6th Floor
200 Grays Inn Road
London WC1X 8XZ
020 7430 4090
newsdesk: 020 7430 4814
irn@itn.co.uk
news@irn.co.uk
www.irn.co.uk
Managing director: John Perkins;
editor: Jon Godel

Commercial local radio: England

107.3 Time FM
Abbey Road
London SE2 OEW
020 8311 3112
www.timefm.com
South-east London. Station director: Neil Remain; head of news: Alex Hornall; breakfast show: Richard Price.
107.3 FM. Owner: London Media Group. All time favourites

95.8 Capital FM
30 Leicester Square
London WC2H 7LA
020 7766 6000
info@capitalradio.com
www.capitalfm.com
Greater London. Managing director: Keith Pringle; head of news: Justin Kings; breakfast show: Johnny Vaughan.
95.8 FM. Owner: Capital Radio. Pop

Capital Gold (1548)
30 Leicester Square
London WC2H 7LA
020 7766 6000
info@capitalradio.com
www.capitalgold.com
Greater London. Programme director: Andy Turner; head of news: Justin King; breakfast show: Mick Brown & Emma Hignett.
1548 AM. Owner: Capital Radio. Hits of the 60s, 70s and 80s

Choice 107.1 FM
291–299 Borough High Street
London SE1 1JG
020 7378 3969
info@choicefm.com
www.choicefm.com
North London. Programme controller: Ivor Etienne; news editor: Pam Joseph; breakfast show: Martin Jay & Asher.
107.1 FM. Owner: Capital Group. R&B

Club Asia
Asia House
227–247 Gascoigne Road
Barking, Essex IG11 7LN
020 8594 6662
info@clubasiaonline.com
www.clubasiaonline.com
Greater London. Managing director: Humerah Khan; creative director: Sumerah Ahmad; breakfast show: Missy D. 972 AM. Independent. London's young Asian hit music station

Easy Radio London
43–51 Wembley Hill Road
London HA9 8AU
020 8795 1035
info@easy1035.com
www.easy1035.com
Greater London. Programme controller & head of music: Natalie King; breakfast show: Chris Townsend.
1035 AM. Owner: Easy Radio Limited.
Easy listening

Heart 106.2
The Chrysalis Building,
Bramley Road
London W10 6SP
020 7468 1062
www.heart1062.co.uk
Greater London. MD: Steve Parkinson; programme director: Francis Currie; head of news: Jonathan Richards; breakfast show: Jono Coleman & Harriet Scott. 106.2 FM. Owner: Chrysalis Radio. Adult contemporary

Jazz FM 102.2
26–27 Castlereagh Street
London W1H 5DL
020 7706 4100
jazzinfo@jazzfm.com
www.jazzfm.com
Greater London. Managing director: Carter Tanner; programme director: Mark Walker; head of news: Nick Hatfield; breakfast show: Jon Scragg. 102.2FM. Owner: Guardian Media Group Radio. Smooth jazz & classic soul

Kiss 100
Mappin House
4 Winsley Street
London W1W 8HF
020 7975 8100
firstname.lastname@kiss100.com
www.kiss100.com
Greater London. Managing director: Mark Story; programme director: Simon Long; breakfast show: Bam Bam
100 FM. Owner: Emap Performance Network. Garage, R&B

LBC 97.3 FM
The Chrysalis Building
Bramley Road
London W10 6SP
020 7314 7300
firstname.lastname@lbc.co.uk
www.lbc.co.uk
Greater London. Managing director: Mark Flanagan; programme director: Steve Kyte; head of news: Tom Bateman; breakfast show: Howard Hughes & Nick Ferrari. 97.3 FM. Owner: Chrysalis Group PLC. Talk radio

LBC News 1152 AM
The Chrysalis Building,
Bramley Road
London W10 6SP
020 7314 7309
newsroom@lbc.co.uk
www.lbc.co.uk
Greater London. Head of network news: Jonathan Richards. 1152 AM. Owner: Chrysalis Group. News

London Greek Radio
437 High Road
London N12 OAP
0871 288 1000
sales@lgr.co.uk
www.lgr.co.uk
North London. Programme controller and head of news: G Gregoriou; breakfast show: Soula Viola Ri.
103.3 FM. Independent. Greek music

London Turkish Radio LTR
185B High Road, Wood Green
London N22 6BA
020 8881 0606
info@londontv.org
www.londonturkishradio.org
North London. Programme controller: Umit Dandul; head of news: Erkan Pastirmacioglu; breakfast show: Fatos Sarman. 1584 AM. Independent. Turkish & English music

Magic 105.4 FM
Mappin House
4 Winsley Street
London W1W 8HF
020 7955 1054
firstname.lastname@emap.com
www.magic1054.co.uk
*Greater London. Programming
director: Trevor White; station
director: Mark Storey; breakfast
show: Graham Dean. 105.4 FM.
Owner: Emap Performance
Network. Adult contemporary*

Premier Christian Radio
22 Chapter Street
London SW1P 4NP
020 7316 1300
premier@premier.org.uk
www.premier.org.uk
*Greater London. Programme
controller: Charmaine Noble-
Mclean; head of news: Victoria
Lawrence; breakfast show: John
Pantry. 1413 AM; 1305 AM; 1413
AM; 1332 AM. Owner: Premier
Media Group. Christian music*

Spectrum Radio
4 Ingate Place
Battersea
London SW8 3NS
020 7627 4433
name@spectrumradio.net
www.spectrumradio.net
*Greater London. General manager:
Paul Hogan; sales: Millie Bentham.
558 AM. Independent. Multi-ethnic*

Sunrise Radio
Sunrise House,
Merrick Road
Southall, Middlesex UB2 4AU
020 8574 6666
Reception@sunriseradio.com
www.sunriseradio.com
*Greater London. Chief executive:
Tony Lit; MDs: Dr Avtar Lit
(London), Andrew Housley
(Midlands); head of news: David
Landau; breakfast show:
Tony Patti. 1458 AM. Independent.
Asian music*

Time FM
2–6 Basildon Road
Abbey Wood
London SE2 OEW
020 8311 3112
mark@time1068.com
www.1068.com
*Thamesmead, Greater London.
Station director: Mark Rasen; head
of news: Alex Hornall; breakfast
show: Gary Mulligan. 106.8 FM.
Owner: London Media Group. Pop*

Virgin 105.8
1 Golden Square
London W1F 9DJ
020 7434 1215
reception@virginradio.co.uk
www.virginradio.co.uk
*Greater London. Programme
director: Paul Jackson; head of
news: Andrew Bailey; breakfast
show: Pete & Geoff.
105.8 FM. Owner: SMG. Rock*

Xfm
30 Leicester Square
London WC2H 7LA
020 7766 6600
info@xfm.co.uk
www.xfm.co.uk
*Greater London. Managing
director: Graham Bryce;
programme controller:
Andrew Phillips; head of news:
Justin King. 104.9 FM. Owner:
Capital Radio. Adult contemporary*

SOUTH-EAST

103.2 Power FM
Radio House, Whittle Avenue
Segensworth
West Fareham PO15 5SH
01489 589911
info@powerfm.co.uk
www.powerfm.com
*South Hampshire. Managing
director: Peter Harris; programme
controller: Craig Morris; head of
news: Alison Law; breakfast show:
Rick Jackson & Rachel Brooks.
103.2 FM. Owner: Capital Radio.
20 years to up-to-date pop*

107.4 The Quay
Flagship Studios
PO Box 1074
Portsmouth PO2 8YG
023 9236 4141
mail@quayradio.com
www.quayradio.com
*Portsmouth. Programme controller:
Paul Owen; head of news: Sam
Mattersace; breakfast show:
Simon Rose. 107.4 FM. Owner:
Radio Investments. Pop*

107.5 Sovereign Radio
14 St Mary's Walk, Hailsham
East Sussex BN27 1AF
01323 442700
info@1075sovereignradio.co.uk
www.1075sovereignradio.co.uk
*Eastbourne. Brand manager: Nigel
Ansell; commercial manager:
Karen Dyball; breakfast show:
Nigel Ansell. 107.5 FM. Owner:
Radio Investments. Music*

107.6 Kestrel FM
Paddington House,
Festival Place
Basingstoke RG21 7LJ
01256 694000
studio@kestrelfm.com
www.kestrelfm.com
*Basingstoke. Managing director:
Paul Allen; programme manager:
Andy Green; head of news: Mel
Barham; breakfast show: Mandy
O'Neil. 107.6 FM. Milestone Group.
70s, 80s, 90s and today*

107.8 Arrow FM
Priory Meadow Centre,
Hastings
East Sussex TN34 1PJ
01424 461177
info@arrowfm.co.uk
www.arrowfm.co.uk
*Hastings. Managing director:
Stuart Woodford; programme
controller: Mike Buxton;
head of news: Vicky Jones;
breakfast show: Andy Knight
107.8 FM. Owner: Radio
Investments. Adult contemporary*

107.8 Radio Jackie
The Old Post Office
110–112 Tolworth Broadway
Surbiton, Surrey KT6 7JD
020 8288 1300
info@radiojackie.com
www.radiojackie.com
*Kingston Upon Thames. Managing
director: Peter Stremes; programme
controller: Dave Owen; head of
news: Rod Bradbury; breakfast
show: Neil Long. 107.8 FM.
Independent. Adult contemporary*

107.8 SouthCity FM
City Studios,
Marsh Lane
Southampton
SO14 3ST
023 8022 0020
info@southcityfm.co.uk
www.southcityfm.co.uk
*Southampton. Managing director:
Gary Haberfield; programme
director: Stuart McGinley; head of
news: Stuart McGinley; breakfast
show: Pat Sissons. 107.8 FM.
Independent. Adult contemporary*

2-Ten FM
PO Box 2020
Calcot, Reading
Berkshire RG31 7FG
0118 945 4400
tim.parker@creation.com
www.musicradio.com
*Reading, Basingstoke, Newbury
and Andover. Managing director:
Jonathan Bradley; programme
controller: Tim Parker; head of
news: Susie Southgate; breakfast
show: The Morning Crew. 103.4
FM; 97 FM; 102.9 FM. Owner:
GWR Group. All types of music*

96.4 The Eagle
Dolphin House, North Street
Guildford GU1 4AA
01483 300964
onair@964eagle.co.uk
www.964eagle.co.uk
*Guildford. Managing director:
Valeria Handley; programme
director: Peter Gordon; head of
news: Lucy Skitmore; breakfast
show: Dave Johns. 96.4 FM. Owner:
UKRD Group. Adult contemporary*

Bright 106.4
The Market Place Shopping
Centre, Burgess Hill
West Sussex RH15 9NP
01444 248127
reception@bright1064.com
www.bright1064.com
*Burgess Hill and Haywards Heath.
Managing director: Allan Moules;
programme director: Mark Chapple;
head of news: Alan Lewis; breakfast
show: Mark Chappel. 106.4 FM.
Independent. 70s, 80s, 90s & latest*

Capital Gold (1170 and 1557)
30 Leicester Square
London WC2H 7LA
020 7766 6000
info@capitalgold.com
www.capitalgold.com
*South Hampshire. Programme
director: Andy Turner; head of
news: Justin King; breakfast show:
Kevin King. 1557 AM; 1170 AM.
Owner: Capital Radio. Hits of the
60s, 70s and 80s*

Capital Gold (1242 and 603)
30 Leicester Square
London WC2H 7LA
020 7766 6000
info@invictaradio.co.uk
www.capitalgold.com
*Maidstone, Medway and East Kent.
Programme director: Andy Turner;
head of news: Justin King. 603 AM;
1242 AM. Owner: Capital Radio.
Hits of the 60s, 70s and 80s*

Capital Gold (1323 and 945)
30 Leicester Square
London WC2H 7LA
020 7766 6000
info@capitalgold.co.uk
www.capitalgold.com
*Brighton, Eastbourne and Hastings.
Programme director: Andy Turner;
head of news: Justin King;
breakfast show: Kevin King. 945
AM; 1323 AM. Owner: Capital
Radio. Hits of the 60s, 70s and 80s*

Classic Gold 1431/1485
The Chase, Calcot
Reading RG31 7RB
0118 945 4400
enquiries@classicgolddigital.com
www.classicgolddigital.com
*Reading, Basingstoke and Andover.
Managing director: Jonathan
Bradley; programme controller:
Don Douglas; head of news:
Susie Southgate.
1431 AM; 1485 AM. Owner: Classic
Gold Digital. 80s, 90s and modern*

Classic Gold 1521
The Stanley Centre, Kelvin Way
Crawley, West Sussex RH10 2SE
01293 519161
studio@musicradio.com
www.musicradio.co.uk
*Reigate and Crawley. Station
manager: Amanda Masters;
programme controller: Don Douglas;
head of news: Gareth Davies;
breakfast show: Dan Jennings &
Emma Richards. 1521 AM. Owner:
Classic Gold Digital. 60s & 70s*

County Sound Radio 1566 AM
Dolphin House North Street
Guildford GU1 4AA
01483 300964
onair@countysound.co.uk
www.ukrd.com
*Guildford. Managing director:
Valerie Handley; programme
director: Peter Gordon; head of
news: Lucy Skitmore; breakfast
show: Dave Johns. 1566 AM.
Owner: UKRD Group. Adult
contemporary*

CTR 105.6 FM
6 Mill Street, Maidstone
ME15 6XH
01622 662500
enq@ctrfm.com
www.ctrfm.com
*Maidstone. Managing director:
John Maxfield; head of news:
Helen Fisher & Moira Mitchell;
breakfast show: Mike Russell.
105.6 FM. Independent. Adult
contemporary*

Delta FM
65 Weyhill, Haslemere
Surrey GU27 1HN
01428 651971
studio@deltaradio.co.uk
www.deltaradio.co.uk
*Alton, Hampshire. Managing
director: David Way; sales
manager: Andy Wise; head of news:
Stuart Ireland; breakfast show:
Bill Sheldrake. 101.6 FM; 102 FM;
97.1 FM; 101.6 FM
Owner: UKRD Group and Tindell
Newspapers. Yesterday and today*

FM 103 Horizon
14 Vincent Avenue Crownhill
Milton Keynes MK8 0ZP
01908 269111
reception@horizon.musicradio.com
www.musicradio.com
*Milton Keynes. Station manager:
Ian Stuart; programme controller:
Trevor Marshall; breakfast show:
Trevor Cueball & Roz. 103.3 FM.
Owner: GWR Group. 80s, 90s
and today*

Invicta FM
Radio House
John Wilson Business Park
Whitstable, Kent CT5 3QX
01227 772004
info@invictaradio.co.uk
www.invictafm.com
*Maidstone, Medway and East Kent.
Sales director: Jake Worrall;
programme controller:
Rebecca Trbojevich; head of news:
Clare Martin; breakfast show:
The Morning Zoo.
95.9 FM; 102.8 FM; 96.1 FM;
97 FM; 103.1 FM. Owner: Capital
Radio. Pop music*

Isle of Wight Radio
Dodnor Park Newport
Isle of Wight PO30 5XE
01983 822557
admin@iwradio.co.uk
www.iwradio.co.uk
*Isle of Wight. Programme
controller: Tom Stroud; head of
news: Andrew Carter; breakfast
show: Andy Shier. 102 FM; 107 FM.
Owner: Radio Investments. Adult
contemporary & Pop*

Juice 107.2
170 North Street
Brighton BN1 1EA
01273 386107
info@juicebrighton.com
www.juicebrighton.com
Brighton. Managing director:
Stephen Stark; programme
controller: Matt Bashford;
head of news: Graham Levitt;
breakfast show: Marc Brooks.
107.2 FM. Owner: Brighton & Hove
Ltd. Commercial Dance

Kick FM
The Studios 42 Bone Lane
Newbury
Berkshire RG14 5SD
01635 841600
mail@kickfm.com
www.kickfm.com
Newbury. Managing director:
Jeff Lee; head of news: John
Statford; programme controller:
Mark Watson; breakfast show:
Mark Watson. 105.6 FM; 107.4 FM.
Owner: Milestone Group. Adult
contemporary

KMfm Canterbury
9 St George's Place, Canterbury
Kent CT1 1UU
01227 475950
reception@kmfm.co.uk
www.kentonline.co.uk/kmfm
Canterbury. Group programme
controller: Mike Osborne; head of
news: Julia Walsh; breakfast show:
Chris Finn. 106 FM. Owner:
KM Radio. Adult Contemporary

KM-FM for Folkestone and Dover
93–95 Sandgate Road
Folkestone
Kent CT20 2BQ
01303 220303
Scork@kmfm.co.uk
www.kentonline/kmfm
Dover and Folkestone. Group
programme controller:
Mike Osborne; Head of Sales:
Christine Saffrey; breakfast show:
Johnny Lewis. 106.8 FM; 96.4 FM.
Owner: KM Radio. 60s, 70s, 80s
& 90s

Medway's KM-FM
Medway House, Ginsbury Close
Sir Thomas Longley Road
Stroud ME2 4DU
01634 227808
pcarter@kmfm.co.uk
www.kentonline.co.uk/kmfm
Medway Towns. Group programme
controller: Mike Osborne; breakfast
show: Russ Lowe. 100.4 FM; 107.9
FM. Owner: KM Radio. Adult
contemporary

Mercury FM
The Stanley Centre
Kelvin Way
Crawley
West Sussex RH10 9SE
01293 519161
studio@musicradio.com
www.musicradio.com
Reigate and Crawley. Station
manager: Amanda Masters;
programme controller: Tim Parker;
head of news: Gareth Davies;
breakfast show: Dan Jennings &
Emma Richards. 97.5 FM; 102.7
FM. Owner: GWR Group. 60s & 70s

Mix 96
Friars Square Studios
11 Bourbon Street
Aylesbury HP20 2PZ
01296 399396
info@mix96.co.uk
www.mix96.co.uk
Aylesbury. Managing director:
Rachael Faulknet; programme
controller: Nathan Cooper; head of
news: Penny Marsh; breakfast
show: James O'Neil. 96.2 FM.
Owner: Radio Investments. 70 to
present day

Ocean FM
Radio House
Whittle Avenue
Segensworth
West Fareham
PO15 5SH
01489 589911
info@oceanfm.co.uk
www.oceanfm.com
South Hampshire. Programme
controller: Stuart Ellis; head of
news: Alison Law; breakfast show:
Pippa Head & David Perry. 96.7
FM; 97.5 FM. Owner: Capital Radio.
70s, 80s & 90s

Reading 107 FM
Radio House
Madejski Stadium
Reading,
Berkshire RG2 0FN
0118 986 2555
firstname@reading107fm.com
www.reading107fm.com
Reading. Managing director:
Tony Grundy; programme
controller: Tim Grundy;
marketing director:
Joannah Bishop; breakfast show:
Tim Grundy.
107 FM. Independent. Beatles to
Bangles

Soul City 107.5
Lambourne House
7 Western Road
Romford, Essex RM1 3LD
0870 607 1075
info@soulcity1075.com
www.soulcity1075.com
Havering. Managing director:
Chris Slack; sales director:
Flip Pearce; programme director:
Chris Slack; breakfast show:
Tracy Young.
107.5 FM. Independent. Soul

Southern FM
Radio House
PO Box 2000
Brighton BN41 2SS
01273 430111
news@southernfm.co.uk
www.southernfm.com
Brighton/Eastbourne and Hastings.
Sales director: Jack Manzoor;
programme controller:
Tony Aldridge; head of news:
Lawrence King; breakfast show:
Chris Baughen.
103.5 FM; 96.9 FM; 102.4 FM;
102 FM. Owner: Capital Radio. Pop

Spirit FM
9–10 Dukes Court
Bognor Road
Chichester PO19 8FX
01243 773600
info@spiritfm.net
www.spiritfm.net
Chichester, Bognor Regis,
Littlehampton.
Managing director: Stephen Oates;
programme controller:
Duncan Barkes; head of news:
Caroline Kingsmill. 102.3 FM;
96.6 FM. Independent. Easy
listening

Splash FM
Guildbourne Centre
Worthing
West Sussex BN11 1LZ
01903 233005
mail@splashfm.com
www.splashfm.com
Worthing. Managing director:
Roy Stannard; programme
controller: Simon Osborne;
news editor: Justin Stacey;
breakfast show: Simon Osborne.
107.7 FM. Independent. 60s, 70s,
80s, 90s & today

Star 106.6
The Observatory Shopping Centre
Slough SL1 1LH
01753 551066
onair@star1066.co.uk
www.star1066.co.uk
Slough, Maidenhead, Windsor.
Programme controller:
Anthony Ballard; head of news:
Rob Harris; breakfast show:
Anthony Ballard. 106.6 FM.
Owner: UKRD Group. Adult
contemporary

Swan FM
PO Box 1107, High Wycombe
Buckinghamshire HP13 6WQ
01494 446611
sales@swanfm.co.uk
www.swanfm.co.uk
High Wycombe. Commercial
director: Rachael Faulkner;
programme director and Head of
News: Andy Muir; breakfast show:
Andy Muir.107.7 FM. Owner: Radio
Investments. Adult contemporary

Thanet's KM-FM
Imperial House, 2–14 High Street
Margate, Kent CT9 1DH
01843 220222
initialsurname@kmgroup.co.uk
www.kentonline.co.uk/kmfm
Thanet. Group programme
controller: Mike Osborne; head of
news: Julia Walsh; breakfast show:
Adam John. 107.2 FM. Owner: KM
Radio. Classic hits from 70s and
current

Wave 105 FM
5 Manor Court, Barnes Wallis
Road, Segensworth East
Fareham, Hampshire PO15 5TH
01489 481057
martin.ball@wave105.com
www.wave105.com
Solent. Managing director:
Martin Ball; programme controller:
John Dash; head of news:
Jason Beck; breakfast show:
Steve Power. 105.2 FM; 105.8 FM.
Owner: ScottishRadio Holdings.
70s, 80s & 90s hits

West Kent's KM-FM
1 East Street, Tonbridge
Kent TN9 1AR
01732 369200
tonbridgestudio@kmfm.co.uk
www.kentonline.co.uk/radio
Tunbridge Wells and Sevenoaks.
Group programme controller:
Mike Osborne; head of news:
Julia Walsh; breakfast show:
Steve Watts. 96.2 FM; 101.6 FM.
Owner: KM Radio. Adult
contemporary

Win 107.2
PO Box 107
The Brooks Shopping Centre
Winchester, Hants SO23 8FT
01962 841071
jo@winfm.co.uk
www.winfm.co.uk
Winchester. Station manager:
Jo Talbot; head of news:
Julie Massitter; breakfast show:
David Adams. 107.2 FM. Owner:
Radio Investments. Adult
contemporary

104.7 Island FM
12 Westerbrook
St Sampsons
Guernsey GY2 4QQ
01481 242000
firstname@islandfm.guernsey.net
www.islandfm.guernsey.net
Guernsey. Managing director:
Nick Cread; programme controller:
Gary Burgess; head of news:
Katie Collins; breakfast show:
Gary Burgess.
104.7 FM; 93.7 FM. Owner: Tindle
Radio. Chart music. Rock show in
evenings

107.5 3TR FM
Riverside Studios
Boreham Mill
Bishopstow
Warminster BA12 9HQ
01985 211111
admin@3trfm.com
www.3trfm.com
Warminster. Brand manager:
Jonathan Fido; sales manager:
Ann Holmes; head of news:
Louisa Jackson; breakfast show:
Kev Scott. 107.5 FM. Owner:
Radio Investments. Classics

2CR FM
5–7 Southcote Road
Bournemouth
Dorset BH1 3LR
01202 259259
newsbournemouth@creation.com
www.musicradio.com
Bournemouth & Hampshire.
Programme controller: Graham
Mack; sales director: Jane Suttie;
breakfast show: Graham Mack.
102.3 FM. Owner: GWR Group. 80s
and 90s and chart music

97 FM Plymouth Sound
Earl's Acre
Plymouth PL3 4HX
01752 275600
mail@
plymouthsound.musicradio.com
www.musicradio.com
Plymouth. Programme controller:
Dave England; head of news: Lisa
Hay; breakfast show: Leigh-Ann
Venning & Martin Mills. 97 FM;
96.6 FM. Owner: GWR Group. 80s,
90s and today

97.4 Vale FM
Longmead Studios, Shaftesbury
Dorset SP7 8PL
01747 855711
studio@valefm.co.uk
www.valefm.co.uk
Shaftesbury. Programme controller:
Stewart Smith; head of news:
Kevin Gover; breakfast show:
Karen Smith.
97.4 FM; 96.6 FM. Owner: Radio
Investments. Adult contemporary

Bath FM
Station House, Ashley Avenue
Lower Weston, Bath BA1 3DS
01225 471571
news@bath.fm
www.bath.fm
Bath. Managing director: Jo Woods;
programme controller and head of
news: Steve Collins. 107.9 FM.
Independent. Adult contemporary

BCRfm
Royal Clarence House,
York Buildings
High Street
Bridgwater TA6 3AT
01278 727701
studio@bcrfm.co.uk
www.bcrfm.co.uk
Bridgwater. Managing director:
Mark Painter; programme
controller: David Englefield;
breakfast show: David Englefield.
107.4 FM. Independent. Music from
last four decades

Channel 103 FM
6 Tunnell Street, St Helier
Jersey JE2 4LU
01534 888103
firstname@channel103.com
www.channel103.com
Jersey. Managing director:
Linda Burnham; programme
director: Matt Howells; head of
news: Phil Bouchard; breakfast
show: Peter Mac. 103.7 FM.
Owner: Tindle Radio. Broad
mix of pop and rock

Classic Gold 1152 AM
Earl's Acre
Plymouth PL3 4HX
01752 275600
Peter.Greig@musicradio.com
www.classicgolddigital.com
Plymouth. Programme controller:
Don Douglas; head of news:
Lisa Hay; breakfast show:
Tony Blackburn. 1152 AM. Owner:
GWR Group. 70s, 80s & 90s

Classic Gold 1260
One Passage Street
Bristol BS99 7SN
0117 984 3200
admin@classicgolddigital.com
www.classicgolddigital.com
Bristol and Bath. Managing
director: Dirk Anthony;
programme controller:
Don Douglas; head of news:
Vickie Brakewell; breakfast show:
Tony Blackburn. 1260 AM. Owner:
GWR Group. Chart music

Classic Gold 666/954
Hawthorn House
Exeter Business Park
Exeter EX1 3QS
01392 444444
colin.slade@musicradio.com
www.musicradio.com
Exeter/Torbay. Programme
controller: Colin Slade; breakfast
show: Tony Blackburn &
Laura Pittson. 954 AM; 666 AM.
Owner: GWR Group. Classic hits

Classic Gold 774
Bridge Studios, Eastgate Centre
Gloucester GL1 1SS
01452 313200
reception@musicradio.com
www.classicgolddigital.com
Gloucester/Cheltenham.
Programme controller:
Russel Wilcox; head of news:
Mark Smith. 774 AM. Owner:
Classic Gold Digital. Various
sounds

Classic Gold 828
5 Southcote Road, Bournemouth
Dorset BH1 3LR
01202 259259
newsbournemouth@creation.com
www.classicgolddigital.co.uk
Bournemouth. Programme
controller: Don Douglas; breakfast
show: Tony Blackburn. 828 AM.
Owner: Classic Gold Digital.
Popular music

Classic Gold 936/1161 AM
Lime Kiln Studio, Lime Kiln
Wooton Bassett, Swindon
SN4 7EX
01793 842600
reception@musicradio.com
www.musicradio.com
Swindon. Managing director:
Dirk Anthony; programme
controller: Sue Carter; breakfast
show: Matt & H. 936 AM; 1161 AM.
Owner: Classic Gold Digital.
Popular music

Fire 107.6FM
Quadrant Studios
Old Christchurch Road
Bournemouth BH1 2AD
01202 318100
firstname@fire1076.com
www.fire1076.com
Bournemouth and Poole.
Programme controller: Max Hailey;
head of news: Justin Gladdis;
breakfast show: Max & Northern.
107.6 FM. Owner: Radio
Investments. Rhythmic &
contemporary

FOX FM
Brush House, Pony Road
Oxford OX4 2XR
01865 871000
reception@foxfm.co.uk
www.foxfm.co.uk
Oxford and Banbury. Programme
controller: Sam Walker; head of
news: Hugh James; breakfast show:
Carl & Jo. 102.6 FM; 97.4 FM.
Owner: Capital Radio. Adult
contemporary

Gemini FM
Hawthorn House
Exeter Business Park
Exeter EX1 3QS
01392 444444
gemini@geminifm.musicradio.com
www.musicradio.com
Exeter/Torbay. Programme
controller: Gavin Marshall; head of
news: Michelle Horsley; breakfast
show: Ben Clarke & Rachael Hicks.
97 FM; 103 FM; 96.4 FM. Owner:
GWR Group. Top 40

GWR FM and Classic Gold Digital
PO Box 2000
Woottonbassett SN4 7EX
01793 842600
reception@musicradio.com
www.musicradio.com
Swindon and West Wiltshire.
Programme controller: Sue Carter;
head of news: Deb Evans;
breakfast show: Matt & H and
Tony Blackburn.
102.2 FM; 96.5 FM; 97.2 FM.
Owner: GWR Group. 70s, 80s &
90s & today

GWR FM (Bristol and Bath)
PO Box 2000
One Passage Street
Bristol BS99 7SN
0117 984 3200
reception@gwrfm.musicradio.com
www.musicradio.com
Bristol and Bath. Managing
director: Dirk Anthony;
programme controller:
Paul Andrew; head of news:
Vickie Brakewell; breakfast show:
Tony & Michaela. 103 FM; 96.3
FM. Owner: GWR Group. Chart
music

Ivel FM
The Studios, Middle Street
Yeovil, Somerset BA20 1DJ
01747 848488
all@ivelfm.co.uk
www.ivelfm.co.uk
Yeovil (Somerset). Programme
controller: Steve Carpenter; head of
news: Catherine DeCosta; breakfast
show: Steve Carpenter. 105.6 FM.
Owner: Radio Investments. 60s,
70s, 80s to present day

Lantern FM
2b Lauder Lane
Roundswell Business Park
Barnstable EX31 3TA
01271 340340
jim.trevelyan@creation.com
www.musicradio.com
Barnstable. Sales director:
Jim Trevelyan; programme
controller: Paul Hopper; head of
news: Dave Lewis; breakfast show:
PJ and Spanky. 97.3 FM; 96.2 FM.
Owner: GWR Group. Late 90s to
present day

Orchard FM
Haygrove House, Taunton
Somerset TA3 7BT
01823 338448
orchardfm@musicradio.com
www.musicradio.com
Yeovil & Taunton. Programme
controller: Steve Bulley; journalists:
Nicola Maxey & Darren Bevan.
102.6 FM; 97.1 FM; 96.5 FM.
Owner: GWR Group. Top 40

Passion 107.9
270 Woodstock Road
Oxford OX2 7NW
01235 547825
info@passion1079.com
www.passion1079.com
Oxford. Programme controller and
station manager: Andy Green;
breakfast show: Bodge at Breakfast.
107.9 FM. Owner: Milestone Group.
Dance & pop

Pirate FM102
Carn Brea Studios
Wilson Way
Redruth, Cornwall TR15 3XX
01209 314400
enquiries@piratefm102.co.uk
www.piratefm102.co.uk
Cornwall & West Devon.
Managing director: Beverley
Warne; programme director:
Bob McCreadie; head of news:
Alistair Jell; breakfast show:
Bob McCreadie. 102.2 FM; 102.8
FM. Owner: UKRD Group.
Various pop

Quay West Radio
The Harbour Studios
The Esplanade, Watchet
Somerset TA23 0AJ
01984 634900
studio@quaywest.fm
www.quaywest.fm
West Somerset. Programme
director: David Mortimer; head of
news: Spencer Bishop; breakfast
show: David Mortimer. 102.4 FM.
Independent. Adult contemporary

Severn Sound
Bridge Studios,
Eastgate Centre
Gloucester GL1 1SS
01452 313200
reception@musicradio.com
www.musicradio.com
Gloucester/Cheltenham.
Programme controller:
Russ Wilcox; sales manager:
Mark Right; head of news:
Mark Smith; breakfast show: Russ,
Nicola & Darcy. 103 FM; 102.4
FM. Owner: GWR Group.
Various sounds

South Hams Radio
Unit 1G, South Hams
Business Park
Churchstow,
Kingsbridge
Devon TQ7 3QH
01548 854595
southams@musicradio.com
South Hams. Station manager:
David Fitzgerald; head of news:
Stephanie Wright; breakfast show:
Ian Calvert. 101.9 FM; 100.8 FM;
100.5 FM; 101.2 FM. Owner:
GWR Group/ Independent.
Adult contemporary

Spire FM
City Hall Studios
Malthouse Lane
Salisbury, Wiltshire
SP2 7QQ
01722 416644
admin@spirefm.co.uk
www.spirefm.co.uk
Salisbury. Managing director:
Ceri Hurford-Jones; programme
controller: Roger Clark;
breakfast show: Daren Cee. 102 FM.
Owner: Radio Investments. Chart hits

Star 107
Unit 3 Brunel Mall
London Road
Stroud, Gloucester GL5 2BP
01453 767369
studio@star1079.co.uk
www.star1079.co.uk
Stroud. Head of sales:
Rebecca Tansley; programme
controller: Marie Greenwood;
head of news: Alan Wood; breakfast
show: Roger Noble. 107.2 FM; 107.9
FM. Owner: UKRD Group. 70s, 80s
& 90s and greatest hits

Star 107.5
Cheltenham Film Studios
1st Floor
West Suite Arle Court
Hatherley Lane
Cheltenham GL51 6PN
01242 699555
studio@star1075.co.uk
www.star1075.co.uk
Cheltenham. Managing director:
Alan Knight; programme manager:
Ian Timms; head of news:
Dannielle Crawshaw. 107.5 FM.
Owner: UKRD Group. 80s to today

Star 107.7 FM
11 Beaconsfield Road
Weston Super Mare
BS23 1YE
01934 624455
name@star1077.co.uk
www.star1077.co.uk
Weston Super Mare. Programme
controller: Scott Temple; head of
news: Hayley Mellers; breakfast
show: Derek Thompson. 107.7 FM;
107.1 FM; 106.5 FM. Owner: UKRD
Group. 70s, 80s & 90s popular
music

Vibe 101
26 Baldwin Street
Bristol BS1 1SE
0117 901 0101
info@vibe101.co.uk
www.vibe101.co.uk
South Wales & Severn Estuary.
Managing director:
Beverley Cleall-Harding;
programme controller:
Jason Staveley; head of news:
Ben Moss; breakfast show:
Ben & Alison.
97.2 FM; 101 FM. Scottish Radio
Holdings. Dance and R&B

Wessex FM
Radio House
Trinity Street
Dorchester DT1 1DJ
01305 250333
admin@wessexfm.co.uk
www.wessexfm.com
Weymouth and Dorchester.
Programme controller: Martin Lee;
head of news: Kevin Gover;
breakfast show: Phil Stocks. 97.2
FM; 96 FM. Owner: Radio
Investments. Hits of 60s, 70s, 80s

EASTERN ENGLAND

102.7 Hereward FM
PO Box 225
Queensgate Centre
Peterborough PE1 1XJ
01733 460460
paul.green@musicradio.com
www.musicradio.com
Greater Peterborough. Programme
controller: Paul Green; head of
news: Sarah Spence; breakfast
show: Matt & Sarah. 102.7 FM.
Owner: GWR Group. Adult
contemporary

103.4 The Beach
PO Box 103.4
Lowestoft, Suffolk NR32 2TL
0845 345 1035
sue.taylor@thebeach.co.uk
www.thebeach.co.uk
Great Yarmouth and Lowestoft.
Managing director: David Blake;
news editor: Kirsty Taylor;
breakfast show: Tom Kay. 103.4
FM. Owner: Tindle Radio. Chart
past and present

96.9 Chiltern FM
55 Goldington Road
Bedford, Beds MK40 3LT
01234 272400
simon.marshall@musicradio.com
www.musicradio.com
Bedford. Sales manager:
Sharon Rush; programme
controller: Stuart Davies; head of
news: Mark Grinnell; breakfast
show: Andy Gelder. 96.9 FM. Owner:
GWR Group. 80s, 90s to today

97.6 Chiltern FM
Chiltern Road, Dunstable
Beds LU6 1HQ
01582 676200
stuart.davies@musicradio.co.uk
www.musicradio.com
Herts/Beds/Bucks. Programme
controller: Stuart Davies; sales
manager: Francis Flannigan;
head of news: Mark Grinnell;
breakfast show: Gareth Wesley &
Karen Carpenter. 97.6 FM. Owner:
GWR Group. Easy listening

Broadland 102
St George's Plain
47–49 Colgate
Norwich NR3 1DB
01603 630621
chris.marston@musicradio.com
www.musicradio.com
Norfolk and North Suffolk. Sales
centre manager: Sophie Crocker;
programme controller: Steve
Martin; head of news: Harry
Mitchell; breakfast show: Rob &
Chrissy. 102.4 FM. Owner: GWR
Group. 80s, 90s and today

Classic Gold 1332 AM
PO Box 225, Queensgate Centre
Peterborough PEI IXJ
01733 460460
don.douglas@
  classicgolddigital.com
www.classicgolddigital.com
Peterborough. Programme
controller: Don Douglas; head of
news: Sarah Spence; breakfast show:
Tony Blackburn. 1332 AM. Owner:
Opus Group. Classic Gold Digital.
Classic hits

Classic Gold 792/828
Chiltern Road
Dunstable, Beds LU6 1HQ
01582 676200
john.baish@classicgolddigital.com
www.classicgolddigital.com
Luton/Bedford. Programme
controller: John Baish; sales centre
manager: Francis Flannighan;
head of news: Mark Grinnell;
breakfast show: Tony Blackburn &
Laura Pitson. 792 AM; 828 AM.
Owner: Opus Group. Classic Gold
Digital. 60s to modern

Classic Gold Amber
St George's Plain
47–49 Colgate
Norwich NR3 1DB
01603 630621
paul.baker@classicgolddigital.com
www.classicgolddigital.com
Norwich. Programme controller:
Paul Baker; sales centre manager:
Sophie Crocker; breakfast show:
Rob & Chrissy. 1152 AM. Owner:
GWR Group. Classic Gold Digital.
80s, 90s and today

Classic Gold Amber
Alpha Business Park
6–12 White House Road
Ipswich IP1 5LT
01473 461000
paul.baker@classicgolddigital.com
www.classicgolddigital.com
Ipswich and Bury St Edmunds.
Programme controller: Paul Baker;
breakfast show: Tony Blackburn.
1251 AM; 1170 AM. Owner: Classic
Gold Digital. 70s and 80s

Classic Gold Breeze
Radio House, Clifftown Road
Southend on Sea
Essex SS1 1SX
01702 333711
david.baker@
  classicgolddigital.com
www.classicgolddigital.com
Southend and Chelmsford.
Programme controller: David
Baker; head of news: Lee Murphy;
breakfast show: David Baker. 1359
AM; 1431 AM. Owner: Opus Group.
Classic Gold Digital. Classic 60s,
70s, 80s

Dream 100 FM
Northgate House
St Peter's Street
Colchester, Essex CO1 1HT
01206 764466
info@dream100.com
www.dream100.com
North Essex/South Suffolk.
Managing director: Jamie Brodie;
programme controller:
Jonathan Hemmings; head of news:
Andre Kimche; breakfast show:
Chris Sturgess. 100.2 FM. Owner:
Tindle Radio. 70s to today

Dream 107.7
Cater House, High Street
Chelmsford CM1 1AL
01245 259400
firstname.surname@
  dream107.com
www.dream107.com
Chelmsford. Managing director:
Martyn Davies; programme
controller and head of news:
Nick Hull. 107.7 FM. Owner: Tindle
Radio. Adult Contemporary

Essex FM
Radio House, Clifftown Road
Southend on Sea
Essex SS1 1SX
01702 333711
Lee.murphy@creation.com
www.musicradio.com
Southend and Chelmsford.
Programme controller:
Chris Cotton; head of news:
Lee Murphy; breakfast show:
David Baker. 102.6 FM; 96.3 FM;
97.5 FM. Owner: GWR Group.
Classic 60s, 70s, 80s

Fen Radio 107.5 FM
5 Church Mews, Wisbech
Cambridgeshire PE13 1HL
01945 467107
studio@fenradio.co.uk
www.sound-wave.co.uk
Fenland. Station manager and
programme director: Mark Pryke;
programme manager:
Richard Grant; sales director:
Jason Smith; breakfast show:
Richard Grant. 107.1 FM; 107.5
FM. Owner: UKRD Group. 70s to
today

Hertbeat FM
The Pump House
Knebworth Park
Hertford
Hertfordshire SG3 6HQ
01438 810900
info@hertbeat.com
www.hertbeat.com
Hertfordshire. Station manager:
Darrell Thomas; programme
controller: Robert Owen; news
editor: Rita Gibbon; breakfast
show: Steve Folland. 106.9 FM;
106.7 FM. Independent. 80s/90s,
specialist programmes weekend

KL.FM 96.7
18 Blackfriars Street
Kings Lynn
Norfolk
PE30 1NN
01553 772777
admin@klfm967.co.uk
www.klfm967.co.uk
Kings Lynn and West Norfolk.
Managing director: William Rogers;
Station manager: Mark Pryke;
programme controller: Steve Bradley;
head of news: Euan Monahan;
breakfast show: Steve Bradley. 96.7
FM. Owner: UKRD Group. Best of
last 30 years

Lite FM
5 Church Street
Peterborough
PE1 1XB
01733 898106
kev@lite1068.co.uk
www.lite1068.co.uk
Peterborough. Managing director:
David Myatt; programme
manager: Kevin Lawrence; head of
news: Simon Potter; breakfast show:
Kevin Lawrence. 106.8 FM. Owner:
Forward Media Group. Adult
contemporary

North Norfolk Radio
PO Box 962
The Studio
Breck Farm
Stody
Norfolk NR24 2ER
01263 860808
info@northnorfolkradio.com
www.northnorfolk.com
North Norfolk. Programme
controller: Steve Wells;
head of news: John Bultitude;
breakfast show: Mike Ahern.
103.2 FM; 96.2 FM. Independent.
Adult contemporary

Q103 FM
Enterprise House, The Vision Park
Chivers Way, Histon
Cambridgeshire CB4 9WW
01223 235255
firstname.surname@
q103.musicradio.com
www.musicradio.com
Cambridge and Newmarket. Area
programme controller: Paul Green;
sales director: Phil Caborn; head of
news: Sarah Spence; breakfast show
"Q103". 97.4 FM; 103 FM. Owner:
GWR Group. Mix of today

SGR Colchester
Abbey Gate Two,
9 Whitewell Road
Colchester CO2 7DE
01206 575859
sgrcolchester@musicradio.com
www.musicradio.com
Colchester. Programme controller:
Paul Morris; sales director:
Brent Coulson; head of news:
Peter Cook; senior Presenter:
Paul Morris. 96.1 FM. Owner:
GWR Group. 80s, 90s and today

SGR FM
Alpha Business Park
6–12 White House Road
Ipswich, Suffolk IP1 5LT
01473 461000
tracy.cooper@musicradio.com
www.musicradio.com
Suffolk. Programme controller:
Tracy Cooper; head of news:
Mike Jackson; breakfast show:
Chris Skinner. 96.4 FM; 97.1 FM.
Owner: GWR Group. 80s, 90s and
current hits

Star 107.9
Radio House, Sturton Street
Cambridge CB1 2QF
01223 722300
admin@star107.co.uk
www.star1079.co.uk
Cambridge, Ely, New Market.
Managing director: James Keen;
programme controller: James Keen;
head of news: Mathew Barratt;
breakfast show: Andy Gall.
107.1 FM. Owner: UKRD Group.
Mainstream adult contemporary

Ten 17
Latton Bush Centre
Southern Way
Harlow, Essex CM18 7BB
01279 431017
jill.adams@musicradio.com
www.musicradio.com
East Herts/west Essex. Programme
director: Jeff O'Brien; news editor:
Lee Murphy; breakfast show:
Ian Burrage. 101.7 FM. Owner:
GWR Group. Pop

Vibe FM
Reflection House
The Anderson Centre
Olding Road
Bury St Edmunds IP33 3TA
01284 715300
general@vibefm.co.uk
www.vibefm.co.uk
East of England. Managing director
& programme controller:
Gary Robinson; news editors:
Dawn Ferguson & Neil Didsbury;
breakfast show: Stuart Grant.
105–108 FM. Owner: ScottishRadio.
Dance station

Watford's Mercury 96.6
Unit 5, The Metro Centre
Dwight Road, Watford
WD18 9UP
01923 205470
firstname.surname@
musicradio.com
www.musicradio.com
St Albans and Watford. Programme
controller: Rebecca Dundon;
head of news: Tricia Bullen;
breakfast show: Danny Lacey.
96.6 FM. Owner: GWR Group.
Popular music

EAST MIDLANDS

102.8 RAM FM
35–36 Irongate
Derby DE1 3GA
01332 205599
ramfm@musicradio.com
www.musicradiocom
Derby. Programme controller:
James Dening; Regional director:
Chris Hughes; head of news:
Lewis Scrimshaw; breakfast show:
Rachael & Deano. 102.8 FM.
Owner: GWR Group. All current
pop music

107 Oak FM
7 Waldron Court
Prince William Road
Loughborough
Leicestershire LE11 5GD
01509 211711
studio@oak107.co.uk
www.oak107.co.uk
Charnwood/NW Leicestershire.
Managing director: Bill Johnston;
programme manager: Mike Vitti;
head of news: Yvonne Radley;
breakfast show: Dave James. 107
FM. Owner: CN Group. 60s to today

96 Trent FM
29–31 Castle Gate
Nottingham
NG1 7AP
0115 952 7000
dick.stone@musicradio.com
www.musicradio.com
Nottinghamshire. Area Regional
director: Chris Hughes; programme
controller: Dick Stone; head of
news: Lewis Scrimshaw; breakfast
show: Jo & Twiggy. 96.2 FM.
Owner: GWR Group. All types of
music

Centre FM
5-6 Aldergate
Tamworth
Staffordshire B79 7DJ
01827 318000
studio@centrefm.com
www.centre.fm
South-east Staffordshire. Managing
director: Phil Richardson;
programme manager: Mike Vitti;
head of news: Chris Mills; breakfast
show: Neil Jackson. 101.6 FM; 102.4
FM. Owner: CN Group. 80s, 90s
and today

106 Century FM
City Link, Nottingham
NG2 4NG
0115 910 6100
info106@centuryfm.co.uk
www.106centuryfm.com
East Midlands. Brand Managing
director: Nick Davidson; Brand
programme director: Giles Squire;
breakfast show: Jim & Paula.
106 FM. Owner: Capital Radio.
Contemporary 80s, 90s

Classic Gold 1557
Northamptonshire
19–21 St Edmunds Road
Northampton NN1 5DY
01604 795600
firstname.surname@
  classicgolddigital.com
www.classicgolddigital.com
Northampton. Managing director:
Colin Wilsher; programme
controller: Don Douglas; head of
news: Fiona Pryor; breakfast show:
Lucinda Holman. 1557 AM. Owner:
Classic Gold Digital. Classic music

Classic Hits
PO Box 262
Worcester WR6 5ZE
01905 740600/ 01432 360246
info@classicgolddigital.fm
www.classichits.co.uk
Hereford and Worcester.
Managing director: Chris Jefferies;
programme controller:
Tim Boswell; head of news:
Andrew Currie; breakfast show:
Tim Boswell. 954 AM; 1530 AM.
Owner: Murfin Media
International. Last four or five
decades of hits

Classic Gold GEM
29–31 Castle Gate
Nottingham NG1 7AP
0115 952 7000
don.douglas@
  classicgolddigital.com
www.classicgolddigital.com
Nottingham/Derby. Managing
director: John Daish; programme
controller: Don Douglas; head of
news: Lewis Scrimshaw; breakfast
show: Tony Blackburn. 999 AM;
945 AM. Owner: Classic Gold
Digital. Classic chart hits

Connect FM
Unit 1, Centre 2000
Kettering
Northants NN16 8PU
01536 412413
info@connectfm.com
www.connectfm.com
Kettering, Corby, Wellingborough.
Group Managing director:
David Myatt; Station manager:
Martin Barr; programme manager:
Danny Gibson; head of news:
John Reading; breakfast show:
Gregg Nunney. 107.4 FM; 97.2 FM.
Owner: Forward Media Group. 70s,
80s & 90s and today

Dearne FM
PO Box 458,
Barnsley S71 1YP
01226 321733
enquiries@dearnefm.co.uk
www.dearnefm.co.uk
Barnsley. Managing director:
Keith Briggs; programme manager:
Paul Bromley; head of news:
Leanne Goacher; breakfast show:
Kev Wilson. 97.1 FM; 102 FM.
Owner: Lincs FM Group. 60s, 70s,
80s & 90s and current hits

Fosseway Radio
PO Box 107, Hinckley
Leicestershire LE10 1WR
01455 614151
enquiries@fossewayradio.co.uk
www.fossewayradio.co.uk
Hinckley/Nuneaton. Chief
executive: Michael Betton;
programme manager: Ian Ison;
head of news: James Wall; breakfast
show: Nick Guerney. 107.9 FM.
Owner: Lincs FM. 70s, 80s & 90s
and hits of today

Leicester Sound
6 Dominus Way
Meridian Business Park
Leicester LE19 1RP
0116 256 1300
reception@
  leicesterfm.musicradio.com
www.musicradio.com
Leicester. Programme controller:
Craig Boddy; head of sales:
Bina Chauhan; head of news:
Liz Gameson; breakfast show:
Rae & Kev. 105.4 FM. Owner:
GWR Group. 90s and today

Lincs FM
Witham Park
Waterside South
Lincoln LN5 7JN
01522 549900
enquiries@lincsfm.co.uk
www.lincsfm.co.uk
Lincoln. Chief executive: Michael
Betton; programme manager: John
Marshall; news editor: Shaun
Dunderdale; breakfast show: John
Marshall. 102.2 FM; 97.6 FM; 96.7
FM. Owner: Lincs FM. Pop

Mansfield 103.2
The Media Suite
Brunts Business Centre
Samuel Brunts Way
Mansfield
Notts NG18 2AH
01623 646666
info@mansfield103.co.uk
www.mansfield103.co.uk
Mansfield and District. Managing
director: Tony Delahunty;
programme controller & head
of news: Katie Trinder;
breakfast show: Katie Trinder.
103.2 FM. Independent. 70s, 80s
& 90s and present day

Northants 96
19–21 St Edmunds Road
Northampton NN1 5DY
01604 795600
firstname.surname@
musicradio.com
www.musicradio.com
Northampton. Managing director:
Colin Wilsher; programme
controller: Richard Neale; head of
news: Fiona Pryor; breakfast show:
Lucinda Holman. 96.6 FM. Owner:
GWR Group. Pop

Peak 107 FM
Radio House, Foxwood Road
Chesterfield S41 9RF
01246 269107
info@peak107.com
www.peak107.com
Chesterfield/north Derbyshire/
south Sheffield/Peak District.
Group programme controller:
John Evington; head of news:
Naz Premiji; breakfast show:
Sean Goldsmith. 102 FM; 107.4 FM.
Owner: TWG Wireless Group.
50/50 music mix

Rutland Radio
40 Melton Road
Oakham, Rutland LE15 6AY
01572 757868
enquiries@rutlandradio.co.uk
www.rutlandradio.co.uk
Rutland and Stamford. Station
manager: Julie Baker; head of
news: Richard Harding; breakfast
show: Rob Persani. 97.4 FM;
107.2 FM. Owner: Lincs FM.
Last 40 years' hits

Sabras Radio
Sabras Sound Ltd, Radio House
63 Melton Road
Leicester LE4 6PN
0116 261 0666
enq@sabrasradio.com
www.sabrasradio.com
Leicester. Managing director and
programme controller: Don Kotak.
1260 AM. Independent. Asian music

Saga 106.6 FM
Saga Radio House, Alder Court
Riverside Business Park
Nottingham NG2 1RX
0115 986 1066
reception@saga1066fm.co.uk
www.saga1066fm.co.uk
East Midlands. Managing director:
Phil Dixon; programme director:
Paul Robey; head of news:
Lisa Teanby; breakfast show:
John Peters. 106.6 FM. Owner: Saga
Group. Easy listening from past six
decades

Signal 1
Stoke Road
Stoke on Trent ST4 2SR
01782 441300
info@signalradio.com
www.signal1.co.uk
Stoke on Trent. Group programme
director: John Evington; managing
director: Chris Hurst; head of news:
Paul Sheldon; breakfast show:
Andy Golding & Louise Stone.
96.4 FM; 102.6 FM; 96.9 FM.
Owner: The Wireless Group.
Pop music

Signal Two
Stoke Road
Stoke on Trent ST4 2SR
01782 441300
info@signalradio.com
www.signal1.co.uk
Stoke on Trent. ILR group
programme director:
Kevin Howard; managing director:
Chris Hurst; head of news:
Paul Sheldon; breakfast show:
Johnny Owen. 1170 FM. Owner:
The Wireless Group. Pop music

Trax FM
PO Box 444, Worksop
Notts S80 1HR
01909 500611
enquiries@traxfm.co.uk
www.traxfm.co.uk
Bassetlaw. Station manager:
Paula Spence; programme
controller: Rob Wagstaff; head of
news: Tina Masters; breakfast
show: Warren Miller. 107.9 FM.
Owner: Lincs FM. Adult
contemporary

WEST MIDLANDS

100.7 Heart FM
1 The Square
111 Broad Street
Birmingham B15 1AS
0121 695 0000
news@heartfm.co.uk
www.heartfm.co.uk
West Midlands. Managing director:
Paul Fairburn; programme
director: Alan Carruthers; head of
news: Chris Kowalik; breakfast
show: Ed James. 100.7 FM. Owner:
Chrysalis Radio. Easy listening

107.1 Rugby FM
Dunsmore Business Centre
Spring Street
Rugby CV21 3HH
01788 541100
mail@rugbyfm.co.uk
www.rugbyfm.co.uk
Rugby. Managing director &
head of news: Martin Mumford.
107.1 FM. Owner: Milestone Radio
Group. 60s, 70s, 80s & 90s and
contemporary

107.4 Telford FM
PO Box 1074
Telford TF1 5HU
01952 280011
staff@telfordfm.co.uk
www.telfordfm.co.uk
Telford. Programme director:
Pete Wagstaff; head of news:
Ian Perry; breakfast show:
Paul Shuttleworth. 107.4 FM.
Independent. Easy listening

107.7 The Wolf
10th Floor
Mander House
Wolverhampton WV1 3NB
01902 571070
firstname@thewolf.co.uk
www.thewolf.co.uk
Wolverhampton. Group
programme director:
John Evington; head of news:
Julia Rae; breakfast show:
Dickie Dodd. 107.7 FM. Owner:
Wireless Group. 50/50 mix of
yesterday and today

96.4 FM BRMB
Nine Brindley Place
4 Ozells Square
Birmingham B1 2DJ
0121 245 5000
info@brmb.co.uk
www.brmb.co.uk
Birmingham. Commercial
controller: Jane Davis; programme
controller: Adam Bridge; breakfast
show: "The Big Brum Breakfast".
96.4 FM. Owner: Capital Radio.
Chart music

Beacon FM
267 Tettenhall Road
Wolverhampton WV6 ODE
01902 461300
firstname.surname@creation.com
www.musicradio.com
Wolverhampton. Programme
director: Chris Pegg; head of news:
Adam Edward; breakfast show:
Mark Jeeves & Jo Jesmond.
97.2 FM; 103.1 FM. Owner:
GWR Group. Popular mix

Capital Gold (1152)
30 Leicester Square
London WC2H 7LA
020 7766 6000
info@capitalgold.co.uk
www.capitalgold.com
Birmingham. Programme director:
Andy Turner; head of news:
Justin King; breakfast show:
Tom Ross. 1152 AM. Owner: Capital
Radio. Hits of the 60s, 70s and 80s

Classic Gold 1359
Hertford Place
Coventry CV1 3TT
02476 868200
firstname.surname@
  classicgolddigital.com
www.classicgolddigital.com
Coventry. Programme controller:
Luis Clark; breakfast show:
Tony Blackburn. 1359 AM. Owner:
Classic Gold Digital. 70s, 80s & 90s

Classic Gold WABC
267 Tettenhall Road
Wolverhampton WV6 0DE
01902 461300
firstname.surname@
  classicgolddigital.com
www.classicalgolddigital.com
Wolverhampton, Shrewsbury and
Telford. Head of news:
Adam Edward; breakfast show:
Tony Blackburn. 990 AM; 1017 AM.
Owner: Classic Gold Digital. Classic
80s, 90s onward

FM 102 – The Bear
The Guard House Studios
Banbury Road
Stratford Upon Avon CV37 7HX
01789 262636
info@thebear.co.uk
www.thebear.co.uk
Stratford Upon Avon. Station
director: Chris Arnold; programme
manager: Mike Vitti; head of news:
Daniel Bruce; breakfast show:
Howard Bentham. 102 FM. Owner:
CN Group. Classic & current hits

Galaxy 102.2
1 The Square
111 Broad Street
Birmingham B15 1AS
0121 695 0000
galaxy1022@galaxy1022.co.uk
www.galaxy1022.co.uk
Birmingham. Managing director:
Paul Fairburn; programme
director: Neil Greenslade;
head of news: Chris Kowalik;
breakfast show: Ed James.
102.2 FM. Owner: Chrysalis Radio.
Easy listening

Kix 96
Watch Close Spon Street
Coventry CV1 3LN
024 7652 5656
firstname@kix.fm
www.kix.fm
Coventry. Sales director: Greg
Parker; programme manager: Mike
Vitti; head of news: Magdalene
Kent; breakfast show: Stefan
Latouche. 96.2 FM. Owner: CN
Group. Pop and Dance

Mercia FM
Hertford Place
Coventry CV1 3TT
024 7686 8200
merciafm@musicradio.com
www.musicradio.com
Coventry. Programme controller:
Luis Clark; head of news: Tony
Attwater; breakfast show: Ru,
Simon and James.
102.9 FM; 97 FM. Owner: GWR
Group.
80s, 90s & modern

Radio XL 1296 AM
KMS House Bradford Street
Birmingham B12 0JD
0121 753 5353
arun@radioxl.net
www.radioxl.net
Birmingham. Managing director:
Arun Bajaj; programme director:
Sukjoinder Ghataore. 1296 AM.
Independent. Indian and Asian
mixes

Saga 105.7 FM
3rd Floor, Crown House
Beaufort Court, 123 Hagley Road
Edgbaston B16 8LD
0121 452 1057
onair@saga1057fm.co.uk
www.saga1057fm.co.uk
West Midlands. Managing director:
Peter Tomlinson; programme
director: Brian Savin; news editor:
Colin Palmer; breakfast show: Les
Ross.
105.7 FM. Owner: Saga Group. 40s
upwards

Wyvern FM
5–6 Barbourne Terrace
Worcester WR1 3JZ
01905 612212
simon.monk@creation.com
www.musicradio.com
Hereford and Worcester.
Programme controller: Simon
Monk; head of news: Jonathan
Dunbar; breakfast show: Lee Stone.
102.8 FM; 97.6 FM; 96.7 FM.
Owner: GWR Group. Pop music

NORTH-EAST

Alpha 103.2
Radio House,
11 Woodland Road
Darlington Co., Durham
DL3 7BJ
01325 255552
sales@alpha1032.com
www.alpha1032.com
Darlington. Managing director:
Angela Bridgen; programme
manager: Ricky Durkin; head of
news: Steve Mackay; breakfast
show: Ricky Durkin. 103.2 FM.
Owner: Radio Investments. Classic
hits from last 30 years

Century FM
Church Street
Gateshead NE8 2YY
0191 477 6666
info@centuryfm.co.uk
www.100centuryfm.com
North-east England. Programme
controller: Paul Drogan; head of
news: Rick Martin; breakfast show:
Liz and Gary. 96.2 FM; 96.4 FM;
100.7 FM; 101.8 FM. Owner:
Capital Radio. 80s, 90s and today

Galaxy 105–106
Kingfisher Way
Silverlink Business Park
Tyne & Wear NE28 9NX
0191 206 8000
matt.mcclure@galaxy1056.co.uk
www.galaxy1056.co.uk
North-east England. Programme
director: Matt McClure; Journalist:
Mandy Simpson; breakfast show:
Kate Fox. 105.3 FM; 105.6 FM;
105.8 FM; 106.4 FM. Owner:
Chrysalis Radio. Dance and R&B

Magic 1152
Longrigg, Swalwell
Newcastle upon Tyne
NE99 1BB
0191 420 0971
tony.mckenzie@
  metroandmagic.com
www.magic1152.co.uk
Tyne and Wear. Managing director:
Sally Aitchaison; programme
director: Tony McKenzie; breakfast
show: Brian Moore. 1152 AM.
Owner: Emap Performance
Network. Classic 60s and 70s

Magic 1170
Radio House, Yales Crescent
Thornaby
Stockton-on-Tees TS17 6AA
01642 888222
colin.paterson@tfmradio.com
www.tfmradio.co.uk
Teesside. Managing director:
Catherine Ellington; programme
director: Colin Paterson; head of
news: Myles Ashley; breakfast
show: Peter Grant. 1170 AM.
Owner: Emap Performance
Network. Adult contemporary

Metro Radio
Longrigg, Swalwell
Newcastle upon Tyne NE99 1BB
0191 420 0971
tony.mckenzie@
  metroandmagic.com
www.magic1152.co.uk
Tyne and Wear. Managing director:
Sally Aitchison; programme
director: Tony McKenzie; breakfast
show: Brian Moore. 97.1 FM; 102.6
FM; 103 FM; 103.2 FM. Owner:
Emap Performance Network. Adult
contemporary & chart

Sun FM
PO Box 1034,
Sunderland
SR5 2YL
0191 548 1034
progs@sun-fm.com
www.sun-fm.com
Sunderland. Brand controller:
Simon Grundy; head of news:
Mark Selling; breakfast show:
Simon Grundy & Jill Hope.
103.4 FM. Owner: Radio
Investments. Adult contemporary

TFM
Radio House
Yales Crescent
Thornaby
Stockton-on-Tees
TS17 6AA
01642 888222
colin.paterson@tfmradio.com
www.tfmradio.co.uk
Teesside. Managing director:
Catherine Ellington; programme
director: Colin Paterson; head of
news: Myles Ashley; breakfast
show: Mojo & Cara. 96.6 FM.
Owner: Emap Performance
Network. Adult contemporary

YORKSHIRE AND HUMBERSIDE

96.3 Radio Aire
51 Burley Road
Leeds LS3 1LR
0113 283 5500
firstname.lastname@
  radioaire.com
www.radioaire.co.uk
Leeds. Managing director:
Alexis Thompson; programme
director: Stuart Baldwin; head of
news: Richard Pervis; breakfast
show: Cameron & Jamie. 96.3 FM.
Owner: Emap Performance
Network. Adult contemporary

96.9 Viking FM
The Boat House
Commercial Road
Hull HU1 2SG
01482 325141
reception@vikingfm.co.uk
www.vikingfm.co.uk
Hull. Programme director:
Darrell Woodman; head of news:
Kirsty Moore; breakfast show:
Foxy & Tom. 97.2 FM. Owner:
Radio Investments. Variety

97.2 Stray FM
The Hamlet
Hornbeam Park Avenue
Harrogate HG2 8RE
01423 522972
mail@972strayfm.co.uk
www.strayfm.com
Harrogate. Managing director:
Sarah Barry; programme director:
Ray Stroud; head of news:
Patrick Dunlop; breakfast show:
Ed George. 97.2 FM. Owner:
Radio Investments. 60s & 70s

Classic Gold 1278/1530 AM
Pennine House, Forster Square
Bradford, West Yorkshire
BD1 5NE
01274 203040
general@pulse.co.uk
www.pulse.co.uk
Bradford, Halifax and
Huddersfield. ILR group
programme director:
John Evington; managing director:
Esther Morton; head of news:
Richard Murie; breakfast show:
Matt and Elisa. 1278 AM;
1530 AM. Owner: The Wireless
Group. Oldies

Compass FM
26a Wellowgate
Grimsby DN32 0RA
01472 346666
enquiries@compassfm.co.uk
www.compassfm.co.uk
Grimsby. Programme director:
Jane Hill; programme manager:
Andy Marsh; head of news:
Shaun Dunderdale; breakfast show:
Richard Lyon. 96.4 FM. Owner:
Lincs FM. Easy listening

Fresh Radio
Fresh Radio Ltd, Firth Mill,
Firth Street
Skipton, North Yorkshire
BD23 2PT
01756 799991
info@freshradio.co.uk
www.freshradio.co.uk
Yorkshire Dales with Skipton.
Managing director: Dave Parker;
head of news: James Wilson;
breakfast show:
1431 AM; 1413 AM; 936 AM.
Independent. Adult contemporary

Galaxy 105
Joseph's Well
Hannover Walk, off Park Lane
Leeds LS3 1AB
0113 213 0105
mail@galaxy105.co.uk
www.galaxy105.co.uk
Yorkshire. Managing director:
David Lloyd; head of news &
programme director: Mike Cass;
breakfast show: Hirsty, Danny &
JoJo. 105.8 FM; 105.6 FM;
105.1 FM; 105.6 FM; DAB; Sky;
cable. Owner: Chrysalis Radio.
Dance and R&B. Biggest station
outside London

Hallam FM
Radio House 900 Herries Road
Sheffield S6 1RH
0114 209 1000
Programmes@hallamfm.co.uk
www.hallamfm.co.uk
South Yorkshire. Managing
director: Iain Clasper; head of news
& Programming: Chris Straw;
breakfast show: Big John Breakfast
Show. 102.9 FM; 103.4 FM;
97.4 FM. Owner: Emap
Performance Network. All types
of music

Home 107.9
The Old Stableblock
Lockwood Park
Huddersfield HD1 3UR
01484 321107
info@home1079.com
www.home1079.com
Huddersfield. Programme
controller: Nick Hancock;
sales director: Phil Chadderton;
head of news: Steven Naylor;
breakfast show: Nick Hancock.
107.9 FM. Owner: Radio
Investments. Pop from last three
decades

Magic 1161 AM
Commercial Road
Hull HU1 2SG
01482 325141
reception@magic1161.co.uk
www.magic1161.co.uk
Humberside (east Yorkshire
and north Lincolnshire).
Managing director: Mike Baldwin;
programme director:
Darrell Woodman; head of news:
Kirsty Moore; breakfast show:
Steve Jordan. 1161 AM. Owner:
Emap Performance Network.
60s to present day

Magic 828
51 Burley Road
Leeds LS3 1LR
0113 283 5500
firstname.lastname@radioaire.com
www.radioaire.co.uk
Leeds. Managing director: Alexis
Thompson; programme director:
Stuart Baldwin; head of news:
Richard Pervis; breakfast show:
Paul Carrington. 828 AM. Owner:
Emap Performance Network. Adult
contemporary

Magic AM
Radio House, 900 Herries Road
Sheffield S6 1RH
0114 209 1000
Programmes@magicam.co.uk
www.magicam.co.uk
South Yorkshire. Managing
director: Iain Clasper; head of news
& Programming: Chris Straw;
breakfast show: Howie & Emma
at breakfast. 990 AM; 1.305 AM;
1545 AM. Owner: Emap
Performance Network. Popular
music

Minster FM
PO Box 123, Dunnington
York YO19 5ZX
01904 488888
general@minsterfm.com
www.minsterfm.com
York. Commercial station
manager: Sarah Barry;
programme controller: Ed Bretton;
head of news: Tristan Hunkin;
breakfast show: Ed Bretton.
104.7 FM; 102.3 FM. Owner: Radio
Investments. Last few decades

Real Radio (Yorkshire)
Sterling Court, Capitol Park
Leeds WF3 1EL
0113 238 1114
info@realradiofm.com
www.realradiofm.com
South and West Yorkshire.
Managing director:
Mike Pennington; programme
director: Terry Underhill; Head of
News: James Rea; breakfast show:
Terry Underhill. 107.6 FM;
106.2 FM; 107.7 FM. Owner:
Guardian Media Group Radio.
90s and popular contemporary

Ridings FM
PO Box 333
Wakefield WF2 7YQ
01924 367177
enquiries@ridingsfm.co.uk
www.ridingsfm.co.uk
Wakefield. Programme manager:
Phil Butler; head of news:
Andy Smith; breakfast show:
Danny Lacey. 106.8 FM. Owner:
Lincs FM. Popular music

Sunrise FM
Sunrise House, 30 Chapel Street
Little Germany
Bradford BD1 5DN
01274 735043
usha@sunriseradio.fm
www.sunriseradio.fm
Bradford. Managing director &
programme controller:
Usha Parmar; head of news:
Gail Papworth. 103.2 FM.
Independent. Asian music

The Pulse
Pennine House, Forster Square
Bradford, West Yorkshire
BD1 5NE
01274 203040
general@pulse.co.uk
www.pulse.co.uk
Bradford, Huddersfield and
Halifax. ILR group programme
director: John Evington;
managing director: Esther Morton;
head of news: Richard Murie.
102.5 FM; 97.5 FM. Owner:
The Wireless Group. Oldies

Trax FM
PO Box 44, Doncaster
DN4 5GW
01302 341166
events@traxfm.co.uk
www.traxfm.co.uk
Doncaster. Programme controller:
Rob Wagstaff; sales manager:
Peggy Watson; head of news:
Tine Master. 107.1 FM. Owner:
Lincs FM. All sorts

Yorkshire Coast Radio
PO Box 962 Scarborough
North Yorkshire YO11 3ZP
01723 581700
studio@yorkshirecoastradio.com
www.yorkshirecoastradio.com
Bridlington, Scarborough, Whitby.
Station manager & programme
controller: Chris Sigsworth; head of
news: Wesley Mallin; breakfast
show: Chris Belly Bell. 96.2 FM;
103.1 FM. Owner: Radio
Investments. Chart hits

Yorkshire Coast Radio
Bridlington's Best
PO Box 1024 Bridlington
East Yorkshire YO15 2YW
01262 404400
info@yorkshirecoastradio.com
www.yorkshirecoastradio.com
Bridlington. Programme controller:
Chris Sigsworth; sales director:
Gaynor Preston-Routledge; head of
news: Wesley Mallin; breakfast
show: Belly at Breakfast. 102.4 FM.
Owner: Radio Investments. Adult
contemporary

102.4 Wish FM
Orrell Lodge, Orrell Road
Orrell, Wigan WN5 8HJ
01942 761024
studio@wish_fm.com
*Wigan. Programme director:
John Evington; head of news:
Alistair Clark; breakfast show:
Danny & Jo. 102.4 FM. Owner: The
Wireless Group. 80s, 90s, up to date*

106.9 Silk FM
Radio House, Bridge Street
Macclesfield, Cheshire
SK11 6DJ
01625 268000
mail@silkfm.com
www.silkfm.com
*Macclesfield. Commercial manager:
Rachael Barker; programme
manager: Andy Bailey; head of
news: Helen Croydon; breakfast
show: Andy Clewes 106.9 FM.
Owner: Radio Investments.
Adult contemporary*

107.2 Wire FM
Warrington Business Park,
Long Lane
Warrington WA2 8TX
01925 445545
info@wirefm.com
www.wirefm.com
*Warrington. ILR group programme
director: John Evington; station
director: Mathew Allitt; head of
news: Mark Bell; breakfast show:
Dominic Walker. 107.2 FM. Owner:
The Wireless Group. Adult
contemporary*

2BR
Imex Lomeshaye Business Village
Nelson, Lancs BB9 7DR
01282 690000
info@2br.co.uk
www.2br.co.uk
*Burnley. Managing director:
Mark Matthews. 99.8 FM*

96.2 The Revolution
PO Box 962
Oldham OL1 3JF
0161 621 6500
info@therevolution.uk.com
www.revolutiononline.co.uk
*Oldham. Managing director:
Dave Stankler; programme
controller & head of news:
Chris Gregg; breakfast show:
Lee Clasby & Big Al. 96.2 FM.
Owner UKRD & Hurst Kidd &
Renny. Hits from yesteryear to
current day*

97.4 Rock FM
PO Box 974
Preston PR1 1YE
01772 477700
firstname.lastname@rockfm.co.uk
www.rockfm.co.uk
*Preston and Blackpool. Programme
director: Brian Paige; head of news:
Clare Hannah; breakfast show:
Dixie. 97.4 FM. Owner: Emap
Performance Network. Adult
contemporary*

Asian Sound Radio
Globe House, Southall Street
Manchester M3 1LG
0161 288 1000
info@asiansoundradio.co.uk
www.asiansoundradio.com
*East Lancashire. Managing
director & programme director:
Shujat Ali; head of news:
Fiaz Mohammed; breakfast show:
Sophie. 963 AM; 1377 AM.
Independent. Asian hip-hop*

The Bay
PO Box 969, St Georges Quay
Lancaster LA1 3LD
01524 848747
information@thebay.fm
www.thebay.fm
*Morecambe Bay. 102.3 FM;
96.9 FM. Owner: CN Group*

Century 105
Laser House, Waterfront Quay
Salford Quays
Manchester M5O 3XW
0161 400 0105
info1054@centuryfm.co.uk
www.1054centuryfm.com
*North West England. Managing
director: Nick Davidson; Brand
programme director: Giles Squire;
head of news: Matt Bowen; breakfast
show: Tony Horne. 105.4 FM.
Owner: Capital Radio. Pop*

Classic Gold Marcher 1260 AM
The Studios, Mold Road
Wrexham LL11 4AF
01978 752202
firstname.surname@
classicgolddigital.com
www.classicgolddigital.com
*Wrexham and Chester. Programme
controller: Don Douglas; head of
news: Elina Cavanagh; breakfast
show: Tony Blackburn. 1260 AM.
Owner: Classic Gold Digital.
Classical music*

Dee 106.3
2 Chantry Court, Chester
CH1 4QN
01244 391000
info@dee1063.com
www.dee1063.com
*Chester. Sales director: Sarah Vel;
Head of news: Lucy Liddard;
breakfast show: Mike James.
106.3 FM. Independent. Adult
contemporary*

Dune FM
The Power Station, Victoria Way
Southport PR8 1RR
01704 502500
studio@dunefm.co.uk
www.dunefm.co.uk
*Southport. Managing director:
David Myatt; programme
manager: Jonathan Dean; head of
news: Charlotte Maher; breakfast
show: Derek Marks. 107.9 FM.
Media Forward Group. Adult
contemporary*

Galaxy 102
5th Floor, The Triangle,
Hanging Ditch
Manchester M4 3TR
0161 279 0300
mail@galaxy102.co.uk
www.galaxy102.co.uk
*Manchester. Managing director:
David Lloyd; programme director:
Vaughan Hobbs; Editorial:
Lynsey Horn; breakfast show:
Nicksy in the morning. 102 FM.
Owner: Chrysalis Radio. Dance and
R&B*

Imagine FM
Regent House, Heaton Lane
Stockport SK4 1BX
0161 609 1400
info@imaginefm.com
www.imaginefm.co.uk
*Stockport. ILR group programme
director: John Evington; head of
news & programme controller:
Ashley Burne; breakfast show:
Mathew Rudd. 104.9 FM. Owner:
The Wireless Group. Hits 70s to
90s and today*

Jazz FM 100.4
8 Exchange Quay
Manchester M5 3EJ
0161 877 1004
jazzinfo@jazzfm.com
www.jazzfm.com
*North West England. Managing
director: Roy Bennett; programming
director: Steve Collins; programme
controller: Derek Webster; breakfast
show: Chris Best. 100.4 FM. Owner:
Guardian Media Group Radio.
Smooth and R&B*

Juice 107.6
27 Fleet Street
Liverpool L1 4AR
0151 707 3107
mail@juiceliverpool.com
www.juice.fm
Liverpool. Managing director:
Donna O'Driscoll; programme
director: Grainne Landowski; head
of news: Mike Baker; breakfast show:
Paul Curran. 107.6 FM. Owner:
Forever Broadcasting. R&B

KCR FM
The Studios, Cables Retail Park
Prescot
Knowsley L34 5NQ
0151 290 1501
kcrmusic@btconnect.com
www.kcr.fm
Knowsley. Managing director
and programme controller:
Ray Ferguson; head of news:
John Donnelly; breakfast show:
Dan & Jeff. 106.7 FM. Independent.
60s to modern

Key 103
Castle Quay, Castlefield
Manchester M15 4PR
0161 288 5000
first.name@key103.co.uk
www.key103.com
Manchester. Managing director:
Gus McKenzie; programme
director: Anthony Gay; head of
news: John Pickford; breakfast
show: "K". 103 FM. Owner: Emap
Performance Network. Mainstream

Lakeland Radio
Lakeland Food Park, Plumgarths,
Crook Road
Kendal, Cumbria LA8 8QJ
01539 737380
info@lakelandradio.co.uk
www.lakelandradio.co.uk
Kendal and Windermere. Station
manager: Peter Fletcher; head of
music: Colin Yare; breakfast show:
Darren Milby. 100.8 FM; 100.1 FM.
Independent. 60s to modern

Magic 1548
St Johns Beacon
1 Houghton Street
Liverpool L1 1RL
0151 472 6800
firstname@magic1548.com
www.radiocity.co.uk
Liverpool. Managing director:
Tom Hunter; programme director:
Richard Maddock; head of news:
Steve Hothersell; breakfast show:
Phil Easton. 1548 AM. Owner: Emap
Performance Network. Adult
contemporary

Magic 999
St Pauls Square, Preston
PR1 1YE
01772 477700
name.surname@magic999.co.uk
www.magic999.co.uk
Preston and Blackpool. Programme
director: Brian Page; head of news:
Clare Hannah; breakfast show:
Dave Asher. 999 AM. Owner: Emap
Performance Network. Adult
contemporary

Manchester's Magic 1152
Castle Quay, Castlefield
Manchester M15 4PR
0161 288 5000
first.lastname@key103.co.uk
www.key103.co.uk
Manchester. Managing director:
Gus McKenzie; programme
director: Anthony Gay; head of
news: John Pickford; breakfast
show: Justin Moorhouse. 1152 AM.
Owner: Emap Performance
Network. 80s, 90s

MFM 103.4
The Studios, Mold Road,
Gwersyllt
Nr Wrexham LL11 4AF
01978 752202
sarah.smithard@musicradio.com
www.mfmradio.co.uk
Wrexham and Chester. Area
programme director:
Graham Ledger; head of news:
Elina Cavenagh; breakfast show:
Dave & Beck. 103.4 FM. Owner:
GWR Group. Pop music

Radio City 96.7
St Johns Beacon,
1 Houghton Street
Liverpool L1 1RL
0151 472 6800
firstname.surname@
    radiocity967.com
www.radiocity.co.uk
Liverpool. Managing director:
Tom Hunter; programme director:
Richard Maddock; head of news:
Steve Hothersell; breakfast show:
Kev Seed. 96.7 FM. Owner: Emap
Performance Network. Pop

Tower FM
The Mill, Brownlow Way
Bolton BL1 2RA
01204 387000
info@towerfm.co.uk
www.towerfm.co.uk
Bolton and Bury. Sales director: Matt
Ramsbottom; programme director:
Gary Stein; head of news: Matt
Hardman; breakfast show: Bix &
Fairclough. 107.4 FM. Owner: Wire
Group. Traditional music

Wave 96.5
965 Mowbray Drive, Blackpool
Lancashire FY3 7JR
01253 304965
wave@thewavefm.co.uk
www.wave965.com
Blackpool. Regional MD:
Esther Morton; programme
director: Helen Bowden; Station
director: Mel Booth; breakfast show:
Roy Lynch and Hayley Kay.
96.5 FM. Owner: The Wireless
Group. Chart and retro

Wirral's Buzz 97.1
Media House, Claughton Road
Birkenhead CH41 6EY
0151 650 1700
sarah.smithard@musicradio.com
www.musicradio.com
Wirral. Managing director:
Sarah Smithard; area programme
controller: Graham Ledger; head
of news: Alina Cavanagh; breakfast
show: Loraine Gabriel & Jamie
Scott. 97.1 FM. Owner: GWR Group.
Chart 80s & 90s

Commercial local radio:
Wales

106.3 Bridge FM
PO Box 1063
Bridgend CF31 1WF
01656 647777
firstname.surname@bridge.fm
www.bridge.fm
Bridgend. Managing director:
Mark Franklyn; programme
controller: Lee Thomas; head of
news: Kayley Thomas; breakfast
show: Mark Franklyn. 106.3 FM.
Owner: Tindle Radio.
Adult contemporary

96.4 FM The Wave
PO Box 1170, Swansea
SA4 3AB
01792 511964
info@thewave.co.uk
www.thewave.co.uk
Swansea. ILR group programme
director: John Evington; managing
director: Esther Morton; head of
news: Emma Thomas; breakfast
show: Mark Powell. 96.4 FM.
Owner: The Wireless Group. Chart
hits

Capital Gold (1305 and 1359)
30 Leicester Square
London WC2H 7LA
020 7766 6000
first.surname@capitalgold.com
www.capitalgold.com
Cardiff and Newport. Programme
director: Andy Turner; head of
news: Justin King; breakfast show:
Tony Wright. 1305 AM; 1359 AM.
Owner: Capital Radio. 60s, 70s and
80s hits

Champion FM
Llys y Dderwen Parc Menai
Bangor LL57 4BN
01248 671888
sarah.smithard@musicradio.com
www.musicradio.com
Caenafon. Managing director:
Sarah Smithard; Area programme
controller: Graham Ledger; head of
news: David Grundy; breakfast
show: Kevin Williams. 103 FM.
Owner: GWR Group. Modern music

Coast FM
PO Box 963, Bangor LL57 4ZR
01248 673272
sion.pritchard@musicradio.com
www.coastfm.co.uk
North Wales Coast. Managing
director: Sarah Smithard; Area
programme controller:
Graham Ledger; head of news:
David Grundy; breakfast show:
Kevin Williams. 96.3 FM. Owner:
GWR Group. Modern music

Radio Ceredigion
Yr Hen Ysgol Gymraeg Ffordd
Alexandra Aberystwyth
Ceredigion SY23 1LF
01970 627999
admin@ceredigionfmf9.co.uk
www.ceredigionradio.co.uk
Ceredigion. Programme controller:
Mark Simon; head of news:
Ceriel Davis; breakfast show: Thomo.
97.4 FM; 103.3 FM; 96.6 FM.
Independent. Adult contemporary
Welsh

Radio Maldwyn
The Studios, The Park, Newtown
Powys SY16 2NZ
01686 623555
radio.maldwyn@ukonline.co.uk
www.magic756.net
Montgomeryshire. Managing
director & Operations director
& programme controller:
Austin Powell; head of news:
Andrew Curry; breakfast show:
Mark Edwards. 756 AM. Owner:
Murfin Media International. Adult
contemporary

Radio Pembrokeshire
Unit 14 The Old School Estate
Station Road, Narbarth
Pembrokeshire SA67 7DU
01834 869384
enquiries@
radiopembrokeshire.com
www.radiopembrokeshire.com
Pembrokeshire/West
Carmarthenshire.
Managing director and programme
controller: Keri Jones; head of news:
Tim John; breakfast show:
Keri Jones.102.5 FM; 107.5 FM.
Independent. Adult contemporary
rock

Real Radio (South Wales)
PO Box 6105 Ty-Nant Court
Cardiff CF15 8YF
029 2031 5100
info@realradiofm.com
www.realradiofm.com
South Wales Regional. Programme
director: Sarah Graham; head of
news: Gareth Setter; breakfast
show: Sam Graham & Steve Clark.
105.9 FM; 106 FM; 105.2 FM;
105.4 FM. Owner: Guardian Media
Group Radio. 70s to modern

Red Dragon FM & Capital Gold
Atlantic Wharf
Cardiff Bay CF10 4DJ
029 2066 2066
mail@reddragonfm.co.uk
www.reddragonfm.co.uk
Cardiff and Newport. Programme
controller: David Rees; head of
news: Angharad Thomas;
breakfast show: Jason Harrold &
Zoe Hampson. 103.2 FM; 97.4 FM.
Owner: Capital Radio. Chartmusic

Star 107.2
Bristol Evening Post Building
Temple Way,
Bristol BS99 7HD
0117 910 6600
dev@star1072.co.uk
www.star1073.co.uk
Bristol. Station manager &
Managing director:
Dev Chakraborty; head of news:
Stephanie Worman; breakfast
director: Ian Downef. 107.2 FM.
Owner: UKRD Group. Adult
contemporary & soul

Sunshine 855
Unit 11, Burway Trading Estate,
Ludlow
Shropshire SY8 1EN
01584 873795
sunshine855@ukonline.co.uk
www.sunshine855.com
Ludlow. Managing director:
Ginny Murfin; programme
controller: Ginny Murfin; head of
news: Andrew Currie; breakfast
show: Nick Jones. 855 AM. Owner:
Murfin Media International. Adult
contemporary

Swansea Sound
PO Box 1170, Swansea
SA4 3AB
01792 511170
info@swanseasound.co.uk
www.swanseasound.co.uk
Swansea. ILR group programme
director: John Evington; managing
director: Esther Morton; head of
news: Emma Thomas; head of
music: Andy Miles; breakfast show:
Kevin Johns. 1170 AM. Owner: The
Wireless Group. Chart hits

Valleys Radio
Festival Park Victoria
Ebbw Vale NP23 8XW
01495 301116
admin@valleysradio.co.uk
www.valleysradio.co.uk
Heads of South Wales valleys.
ILR group programme director:
John Evington; managing director:
Chris Hurst; head of news:
Emma Thomas; breakfast show:
Tony Peters. 1116 AM; 999 AM.
Owner: The Wireless Group.
Adult contemporary

Commercial local radio: Scotland

96.3 QFM
65 Sussex Street
Glasgow G41 1DX
0141 429 9430
sales@q-fm.com
www.q96.net
Paisley. ILR group programme
director: John Evington; managing
director: Aaron Shields; head of
news: Chris Martin; breakfast
show: Derek McIntyre. 96.3 FM.
Owner: The Wireless Group. All
types

Argyll FM
27–29 Longrow, Campbeltown
Argyll PA28 6ER
01586 551800
argyllradio@hotmail.com
Kintyre, Islay and Jura. Managing director: Colin Middleton; programme controller: Kenny Johnson; head of news: Ian Henderson; breakfast show: Bill Young. 107.7 FM; 107.1 FM; 106.5 FM. Independent. Adult contemporary

Beat 106
Four Winds Pavilion, Pacific Quay
Glasgow G51 1EB
0141 566 6106
info@beat106.com
www.beat106.com
Central Scotland. Programme controller: Claire Pattenden; news editor: Vicky Lee; breakfast show: Paul Harper & Des Clarke. 106.1 FM; 105.7 FM. Owner: Capital Radio. Dance music

Central FM
201 High Street
Falkirk FK1 1DU
01324 611164
mail@centralfm.co.uk
www.centralfm.co.uk
Stirling and Falkirk. Programme controller: Tom Bell; head of news: Tadek Pszywa; breakfast show: Malky Brown. 103.1 FM. Owner: Radio Investments. Hits & memories

CFM (Carlisle)
PO Box 964
Carlisle CA1 3NG
01228 818964
reception@cfmradio.com
www.cfmradio.com
Carlisle. Managing director: Cathy Kirk; programme controller: David Bain; head of news: Bill McDonald; breakfast show: Robbie Dee. 96.4 FM; 102.5 FM. Owner: Scottish Radio Holdings. Best mix of music

CFM (West Cumbria)
PO Box 964
Carlisle CA1 3NG
01228 818964
reception@cfmradio.com
www.cfmradio.com
West Cumbria. Managing director: Cathy Kirk; programme controller: David Bain; head of news: Bill McDonald; breakfast show: Robbie Dee. 103.4 FM; 102.2 FM. Owner: Scottish Radio Holdings. Best mix of music

Clan FM
Radio House, Rowantree Avenue
Newhouse Ind. Estate,
Newhouses
Lanarkshire ML1 5RX
01698 733107
reception@clanfm.com
www.clanfm.com
North Lanarkshire. Station manager: Janis Melville; programme controller: Darren Stenhouse; breakfast show: David Ross; Head of news: Andrew Thompson. 107.9 FM; 107.5 FM. Owner: Kingdom Group. Adult contemporary

Clyde 1 FM
Clydebank Business Park
Glasgow G81 2RX
0141 565 2200
info@clyde1.com
www.clyde1.com
Glasgow. Managing director: Paul Cooney; programme controller: Ross Macfadyen; head of news: Russell Walker; breakfast show: George Bowis. 97 FM; 103.3 FM; 102.5 FM. Owner: Scottish Radio Holdings. Pop

Clyde 2
Clydebank Business Park
Glasgow G81 2RX
0141 565 2200
info@clyde2.com
www.clyde2.com
Glasgow. Managing director: Paul Cooney; programme controller: Ross Macfadyen; head of news: Russell Walker; breakfast show: Mike Riddoch. 1152 AM. Owner: Scottish Radio Holdings. Hits from last few decades

Forth AM
Forth House, Forth Street
Edinburgh EH1 3LE
0131 556 9255
info@forth2.com
www.forth2.com
Edinburgh. Managing director: Sandy Wilkie; programme director: Nik Goodman; head of news: Paul Robertson; breakfast show: Darren Adam. 1548 AM. Owner: Scottish Radio Holdings. 60s, 70s, 80s, 90s & today

Forth FM
Forth House, Forth Street
Edinburgh EH1 3LE
0131 556 9255
info@forthone.com
www.forthone.com
Edinburgh. Managing director: Sandy Wilkie; programme director: Nik Goodman; head of news: Paul Robertson; breakfast show: Boogie & Vicky. 97.6 FM; 102.2 FM; 97.3 FM. Owner: Scottish Radio Holdings. Adult contemporary

Heartland FM
Atholl Curling Rink, Lower Oakfield Pitlochry
Perthshire PH16 5HQ
01796 474040
mailbox@heartlandfm.co.uk
Pitlochry and Aberfeldy. Programme controller: Peter Ramsden; head of news: Margaret Stevenson; breakfast show: Bruce Patterson. 97.5 FM; 102.7 FM. Independent. Classic hits

Isles FM
PO Box 333
Stornoway, Isle of Lewis
HS1 2PU
01851 703333
studio@isles.fm
www.isles.fm
Western Isles. Director of operations: David Morrison; head of news: Ian Maclver. 103 FM. Independent. Adult contemporary

Kingdom FM
Haig House, Haig Business Park
Markinch, Fife KY7 6AQ
01592 753753
info@kingdomfm.co.uk
www.kingdomfm.co.uk
Fife. Chief executive: Ian Sewell; programme director: Kevin Brady; head of news: Chris Hodge; breakfast show: Ian Gilmore. 95.2 FM; 105.4 FM; 96.6 FM; 1 06.3 FM; 96.1 FM. Independent. Across the board mix

Lochbroom FM
Radio House, Mill Street
Ullapool
Ross-shire IV26 2UN
01854 613131
radio@lochbroomfm.co.uk
www.lochbroomfm.co.uk
Ullapool. Chairman: Iain Boyd; head of music: Tiffany McCaulay. 96.8 FM; 102.2 FM. Independent. Adult contemporary

Moray Firth Radio (MFR)
Scorguie Place,
Inverness IV3 8UJ
01463 224433
mfr@mfr.co.uk
www.mfr.co.uk
*Inverness. Managing director:
Danny Gallagher; senior presenter:
Ray Atkins; breakfast show:
Tich McCooey & Nicky Marr.
96.6 FM; 96.7 FM; 97.4 FM;
102.5 FM; 102.8 FM. Owner:
Scottish Radio Holdings.
Contemporary and chart*

NECR
The Shed, School Road, Kintore
Aberdeenshire AB51 0UX
01467 632909
necrradio102.1fmsales@
supanet.com
*Inverurie. Managing director:
Colin Strong; programme
controller: John Dean; head of
news: John Dean; breakfast show:
John Dean. 102.1 FM; 102.6 FM;
97.1 FM; 103.2 FM; 101.9 FM;
106.4FM. Independent. Recent hits
& classic gold. Specialist country,
Irish and Scottish*

Nevis Radio
Ben Nevis Estate, Claggan
Fort William PH33 6PR
01397 700007
studio@nevisradio.co.uk
www.nevisradio.co.uk
*Fort William and parts of Lochaber.
Head of News, Station manager
and programme controller:
Willie Cameron; breakfast show:
Michael McCrae. 96.6 FM;
102.4 FM; 97 FM; 102.3 FM
Independent. Daily chart music.
Evening specialist*

Northsound One
Abbotswell Road, West Tullos
Aberdeen AB12 3AJ
01224 337000
northsound@srh.co.uk
www.northsound1.co.uk
*Aberdeen, north-east Scotland.
Managing director: Adam Finlay;
programme controller:
Luke McCullough; head of news:
Ross Govans; breakfast show:
Andy James.96.9 FM; 97.6 FM;
103 FM. Owner: Scottish Radio
Holdings. Modern music*

Northsound Two
Abbotswell Road, West Tullos
Aberdeen AB12 3AJ
01224 337000
northsound@srh.co.uk
www.northsound2.co.uk
*Aberdeen, north-east Scotland.
Managing director: Adam Finlay;
programme controller:
Luke McCullough; head of news:
Ross Govans. 1035 AM. Owner:
Scottish Radio Holdings. Modern
music*

Oban FM
132 George Street, Oban
Argyll PA34 5NT
01631 570057
obanfmradio@btconnect.com
www.obanfm.tk
*Oban. Managing director:
Neil Horne; programme director:
Tina Tobertson; head of news:
Coll McDougall. 103.3 FM.
Independent. Gaelic to modern pop*

Radio Borders
Tweedside Park
Galashiels TD1 3TD
01896 759444
programming@radioborders.com
www.radioborders.com
*Borders. Programme controller:
Stuart McCulloch; head of news:
Denise Glass; breakfast show:
Keith Clarkson. 96.8 FM; 103.1 FM;
103.4 FM; 97.5 FM. Owner:
Scottish Radio Holdings. Hits &
memories*

Real Radio (Scotland)
PO Box 101, Parkway Court,
Glasgow Business Park
Glasgow G69 6GA
0141 781 1011
contact.name@realradiofm.com
www.realradiofm.com
*Central Scotland. Managing
director: Shaun Bowron;
programme director: Jay Crawford;
head of news: Heather Kane;
breakfast show: Robin Galloway.
100.3 FM; 101.1 FM. Owner:
Guardian Media Group Radio.
Wide variety*

River FM
Stadium House, Alderstone Road
Livingstone, West Lothian
EH54 7DN
01506 420975
office@river-fm.com
www.river-fm.com
*West Lothian. Programme
controller: Donny Hughes; sales
director: Susan Dignon; news
editor: Campbell Hart; breakfast
show: Mike Arthur. 107.7 FM;
103.4 FM. Kingdon Radio Group.
Adult contemporary & charts*

RNA FM
Radio North Angus Ltd
Abroath Infirmary
Rosemount Road
Abroath, Angus DD11 2AT
01241 879660
info@radionorthangus.co.uk
www.radionorthangus.co.uk
*Arbroath/Carnoustie. Managing
director and head of news:
Malcolm Finlayson. 96.6 FM.
Independent. Classic/Scottish
and pop*

SIBC
Market Street, Lerwick
Shetland ZE1 0JN
01595 695299
info@sibc.co.uk
www.sibc.co.uk
*Shetland. Managing director
& programme controller:
Inga Walterson; head of news:
Ian Anderson. 96.2 FM; 102.2 FM.
Independent. Rock & pop*

South West Sound
Unit 40, The Loreburne Centre
High Street, Dumfries DG1 2BD
01387 250999
info@westsound.co.uk
www.westsound.co.uk
*Dumfries and Galloway. Managing
director: Sheena Borthwick;
programme director: Alan Toomey;
head of news: Ian Wilson; breakfast
show: Tommy Jargon. 96.5 FM;
97 FM; 103 FM. Owner: Scottish
Radio Holdings. Chart music*

Tay AM
6 North Isla Street
Dundee DD3 7JQ
01382 200800
tayam@radiotay.co.uk
www.radiotay.co.uk
*Dundee/ Perth. Managing director
& programme director:
Arthur Ballingail; head of news:
Amanda Mezullo; breakfast show:
Grant Reed. 1584 AM; 1161 AM.
Owner: Scottish Radio Holdings.
Various music*

Tay FM
6 North Isla Street
Dundee DD3 7JQ
01382 200800
tayam@radiotay.co.uk
www.radiotay.co.uk
Dundee/ Perth. Managing
director & programme director:
Arthur Ballingail; head of news:
Amanda Mezullo; breakfast show:
Graham Waggott. 102.8 FM;
96.4 FM. Owner: Scottish Radio
Holdings. Various music

Two Lochs Radio
The Harbour Centre, Pier Road
Gairloch IV21 2BQ
01445 712712
info@2lr.co.uk
www.2lr.co.uk
Gairloch and Loch Ewe.
Programme director:
Colin Pickering; Chairman &
Station manager: Alex Gray;
breakfast show: Campbell Elder.
106.6 FM. Independent. Broad mix
& Scottish Gaelic

Wave 102
8 South Tay Street
Dundee DD1 1PA
01382 901102
studio@wave102.co.uk
www.wave102.co.uk
Dundee. ILR group programme
director: Peter Mas; managing
director: Mike Robertson; head of
news: Rebecca Wallis; breakfast
show: Peter Mac. 102 FM. Owner:
The Wireless Group.
70s to modern

Waves Radio Peterhead
7 Blackhouse Circle
Peterhead AB42 1BW
01779 491012
waves@radiophd.freeserve.co.uk
www.wavesfm.com
Peterhead. Managing director
& programme controller:
Norman Spence; head of news:
Glenn Moir; breakfast show:
Kenny King. 101.2 FM.
Independent. Current & classic

West FM
Radio House, 54a Holmston Road
Ayr KA7 3BE
01292 283662
info@westfm.co.uk
www.westfmonline.com
Ayr. Managing director:
Sheena Borthwick; programme
director: Alan Toomey; head of
news: Ian Wilson; breakfast show:
Alan Toomey. 97.5FM; 96.7 FM.
Owner: Scottish Radio Holdings.
Wide variety including music

West Sound AM
Radio House, 54a Holmston Road
Ayr KA7 3BE
01292 283662
info@westsound.co.uk
www.west-sound.co.uk
Ayr. Managing director:
Sheena Borthwick; programme
director: Alan Toomey; head of
news: Ian Wilson; breakfast show:
Alan Toomey. 1035 AM. Owner:
Scottish Radio Holdings. Wide
variety of music

Your Radio
Pioneer Park Studios, Unit 1–3
80 Castlegreen Street
Dumbarton G82 1JB
01389 734422
info@yourradio.com
www.yourradiocom
Dumbarton. Chairman:
Jim Duncan; programme
controller: Steven Scott; sales
manager: Scott Gusfogg; breakfast
show: Gary Pews. 103 FM; 106.9
FM. Independent. Popular music

Commercial local radio: Northern Ireland

City Beat 96.7
PO Box 967
Belfast BT9 5DF
028 9020 5967
misic@citybeat.co.uk
www.citybeat.co.uk
Belfast. Station director:
Dorothy McDide; head of news:
Mark Malett; breakfast show:
Morris Jay. 96.7 FM. Owner:
CN Group. Commercial chart

Cool FM
PO Box 974
Belfast BT1 1RT
028 9181 7181
music@coolfm.co.uk
www.coolfm.co.uk
Northern Ireland. Programme
controller: David Sloan MBE; head
of news: Harry Castles; breakfast
show: Carl Kinsman. 97.4 FM.
Owner: Scottish Radio Holdings. Pop

Downtown Radio
Newtownards, Co Down
Northern Ireland BT23 4ES
028 9181 5555
Programmes@downtown.co.uk
www.downtown.co.uk
Northern Ireland. Programme
controller: David Sloan MBE; head
of news: Harry Castles; breakfast
show: Caroline & Roy. 97.1 FM;
103.1 FM; 103.4 FM; 102.4 FM;
1026 AM; 96.6 FM; 102.3 FM;
96.4 FM. Owner: Scottish Radio
Holdings. Adult contemporary

Mid 106
2c Park Avenue, Burn Road
Cookstown BT80 8AH
028 8675 8696
firstnamelastname@
midfm106fm.co.uk
www.mid106.co.uk
Mid-Ulster. Station director:
Neil McLeod Berriskell; news
manager: Donagh McKeown;
senior Presenter: Francie Quinn;
breakfast show: Francie Quinn.
106 FM. Owner: CN Group. 80s,
90s mix.

Q101.2 FM West
42A Market Street, Omagh
Co. Tyrone BT78 1EH
028 8224 5777
Manager@q101west.fm
www.q101west.fm
Omagh and Enniskillen.
Programme controller:
Frank McLaughlin; head of news:
Sophie Wheeler; breakfast show:
Stuart Gorclon. 101.2 FM. Owner:
Q Radio Group. Chart & pop

Q102.9 FM
The Riverview Suite
87 Rossdowney Road, Waterside
Londonderry BT47 5SU
028 7134 4449
Manager@q102.fm
www.q102.fm
Londonderry. Managing director
and programme controller:
Frank McLaughlin; head of news:
Roger Donnelly; breakfast show:
Pete Wilson. 102.9 FM.
Independent. 70s to today

Q97.2 Causeway Coast Radio
24 Cloyfin Road, Coleraine
Co Londonderry BT52 2NU
028 7035 9100
Manager@q972.fm
www.q972.fm
Coleraine. Programme controller:
Frank McLaughlin; head of
news: Bob Lee; breakfast show:
Barrie Owler. 97.2 FM. Owner: Q
Radio Group. Adult contemporary

Community radio

All FM
Manchester
0161 273 4072
info@allfm.org
www.allfm.org
Programme organiser:
Dave Lenaghan
96.9 FM. Adult contemporary

Angel Community Radio
Havant
02392 481988
angelradio@37.com
www.cssd.com
Managing director: Tony Smith
101.1 FM

BCB 96.7 FM
Bradford
01274 771677
info@bcb.yorks.com
www.bcb.yorks.com
Managing director: Mary Dowson;
programme controller:
Jonathan Pinfield
96.7 FM

Cross Rhythms City Radio
Stoke on Trent
0870 011 8008
admin@crossrhythms.co.uk
www.crossrhythms.co.uk
Chief executive officer: Chris Cole;
programmes controller: Steve Perry
101.8 FM. Digital satellite channel
876

Desi Radio
Southall, London
020 8574 9591
info@desiradio.org.uk
www.desiradio.org.uk
Chair of the trustees: Amarjit
Khera; programme controller:
Ajit Singh
1602 AM. Panjabi, satellite,digital

Forest Of Dean Radio
Gloucester
01594 820722
contactus@fodradio.org
www.fodradio.org
Programme manager: Roger Drury
1503 AM; 1521 AM. All ages

GTFM
Pontypridd
01443 406111
news@gtfm.fsnet.co.uk
www.gtfm.co.uk
Manager: Andrew Jones
106.9 FM. Adult contemporary

New Style Radio 98.7 FM
Birmingham
0121 456 3826
c_r_t@lineone.net
www.newstyleradio.co.uk
Manager: Barbara Richards;
programme controller:
Denis Edwards
98.7 FM. Reggae, all types music

Resonance 104.4 FM
London
020 7836 3664
info@resonance.com
www.resonancefm.com
Studio manager: Knut Aufermann;
programmer: Ed Baxter
104.4 FM. Adult contemporary/pop

Sound Radio
Hackney, east London
020 8533 8899
info @soundradio.info
www.svt.org.uk
Chief executive: Lol Gellor
1503 AM. Multilingual station

Takeover Radio
Leicester
0116 299 9600
office@takeoverradio.com
www.takeoverradio.com
Station manager: Graham Coley
103.2 FM. Children's

Wythenshawe FM
Manchester
0161 499 7982
info@wfmradio.org
www.wfmradio.org
Programme manager:
Christine Brennan; programme
organiser: Jason Kenyon
97.2 FM. Adult contemporary

Hospital, student and sporting event radio

1287 AM Insanity
01784 414268
studio@rhul.ac.uk
www.su.rhul.ac.uk
Station manager: Matt Jones
1287 AM. Student radio

1503 AM Radio Diamonds
01933 652000
mathew.rowe@airwair.co.uk
www.thediamonds.co.uk
General manager: Mathew Rowe
1503 AM. Matchday service for
Rushden and Diamonds FC

Auckland Hospital radio
01388 455452
secretary@aucklandradio.com
www.aucklandradio.com
Station manager: Craig Robinson
1386 AM

Acorn FM
0781 640177
www.acornfm.co.uk
Programme controller:
Niall Hayley
87.7 FM. North Devon College

Bailrigg FM
01524 593902
Manager@bailriggfm.co.uk
www.bailriggfm.co.uk
Station manager: Ali Cordrey
87.7 FM. Lancaster University

Basildon Hospital Radio
01268 282828
1287am@bhr.co.uk
www.bhr.org.uk
Chairman: Alan Newman
1287 AM

BFBS
01494 878703
bfbs@bfbs.com
www.bfbs.com
Station manager: Charles Foster
1287 AM. Forces radio

Blast 1386
0118 967 5068
blast1386@reading-college.ac.uk
www.blast1386.com
Station manager: Bob Goertz
1386 AM. Student radio

Bridge FM
01382 423000 x25151
studio@bridgefm.org.uk
www.bridgefm.org.uk
Chairman: Barry Hampton;
programme controller:
Bob McNally
87.7 FM. Hospital, Tayside

C4 Radio
01227 782424
c4radio@cant.ac.uk
www.c4radio.com
Station manager: Ian Eason
999 AM. Christchurch College radio

Canterbury Hospital Radio
01227 864161
www.chradio.org.uk
Studio manager: Martin Pauley
945 AM

Chichester Hospital Radio
01243 788122 x3000
studio@chr1431.org.uk
www.chr1431.org.uk
Presenter: Bill Barwell
1431 AM

City & Hemel Hospital Radio
01442 262222
general@hemelradio.com
www.hemelradio.com
Programme controller:
Alan Etchells
1287 AM

Crush
01707 285005
uhsu.comms@herts.ac.uk
www.uhsu.herts.ac.uk
Programme controller:
Ollie Cadman
1278 AM. College radio

CUR
committee@cur1350.co.uk
1350 AM

Dorton Radio Station
01732 592600
karen.campbell@risb.org.uk
www.rslb.org.uk
Station manager: Karen Campbell
1350 AM. Dorton College

Freak 1c
01772 894895
www.freak1c.co.uk
Station manager: Emily Bull
1350 AM
University of Central Lancashire

Frequency
01772 513200
surecreation@uclan.ac.uk
www.yourunion.co.uk
Station manager: Emily Bull
1350 AM. Student radio

Gara Sound
01623 464220
admin@garibaldi.org.uk
www.garibaldi.org.uk
Station manager: Dave Kenny
1386 AM. School radio

Garrison Radio
01748 830050
hq@garrisonradio.com
www.garrison.com
Station manager: Mark Page
1287 AM; 1350 AM. Army radio

GU2
01483 681350
studio@gu2.co.uk
www.gu2.co.uk
Station manager: Nathan
Whittaker
1350 AM. Student

Hospital Radio Basingstoke
01256 313521
mail@hrbasingstoke.co.uk
www.hrbasingstoke.co.uk
Programme controller: Neil Ogden
945 AM

Hospital Radio Gwendolen
0116 256 1686
jsmethurst@ntlworld.com
www.beehive.thisisleicestershire.
   co.uk
Station manager: Dave Wilcocks
1287 AM

Hospital Radio Plymouth
01752 763441
www.plymouthhospitals.org.uk
Communications: Corinne Glen
87.7 FM

Hospital Radio Pulse
01527 512048
studio@hospitalradiopulse.com
www.hospitalradiopulse.com
Programme controller: Ian Barstow
1350 AM

Hospital Radio Reading
0118 950 7420
requests@hospitalradioreading.
   co.uk
www.hospitalradioreading.org.uk
Programme controller:
Stephen Ham
945 AM

Hospital Radio Rossendale
01706 233334
945 AM

Hospital Radio Yare
01493 842613
www.radioyare.com
Chairman: Gerry Jarvis
1350 AM. James Paget, Northgate,
Lowestoft Hospitals

IC Radio
020 7594 8100
info@icradio.com
www.icradio.com
Station manager: Mike Jones
999 AM
Imperial College halls of residence

Jam 1575
01482 466289
email@jam1575.com
www.jam1575.com
Station manager: Gareth Morris
1575 AM. Student radio

Kendal Radio
01539 795420
Info@kendalhospitalradio.com
www.kendalhospitalradio.org.uk
Studio manager: John Williamson
Hospital radio

Junction 11
0118 931 8698
www.1287am.com
Station manager: Joff Hopkins
1287 AM. Student radio

Kingstown Radio
01482 327711
onair@kingstownradio.com
www.kingstownradio.co.uk
Station manager: Nick Palmer
1350 AM. Hull hospital radio

Kool AM
020 8373 1072
pfmnews@email.com
www.koolam.co.uk
Programme controller: Joe Bone
1134 AM

Livewire
01603 592512
livewireradiouk@yahoo.co.uk
www.livewire1350.com
Station manager: Chris Davis
1350 AM. Union of UEA students

Loughborough Campus Radio
01509 635050
station@lcr1350.co.uk
www.lcr1350.co.uk
Head of media: Lucy Pritchard;
station manager: Oliver Folkerd
1350 AM. Student radio

Manchester United Radio
0161 8721 413
Contact: Kenneth Ramsden
1413 AM. Manchester United
matchday service

Mid-Downs Hospital Radio
01444 441350
studio@ndr.org.uk
Station manager: Alan French
1350 AM

Nevill Hall Sound
07771 722738
Station manager: Colin Palmer
1287 AM

Oakwell 1575 AM
01226 215753
enquiries@oakwell1575am.co.uk
www.oakwell1575am.co.uk
Station manager: Stuart Cocker
1575 AM. Matchday service for
Barnsley FC

Palace Radio
020 8653 5799
info@palaceradio.net
www.palaceradio.net
Communications manager:
Terry Byfield
1278 AM. Matchday service for
Crystal Palace FC

Portsmouth Hospital
Broadcasting
023 9228 6299
studio@phb945.co.uk
www.phb945.co.uk
Station manager: Barrie Swann
945 AM

Radio Airthrey
01786 467166
stationManager@airthrey.co.uk
www.airthrey.co.uk
Station manager: Matt Ludlow
1350 AM

Radio Branwen
01766 781911
radiobranwen@yahoo.co.uk
Station manager: Trevor Andrews
87.7 FM

Radio Brockley
020 8954 6591
studio@radiobrockley.org
www.radiobrockley.org
999 AM. The wards within
Stanmore's Royal National
Orthopaedic Hospital

Radio Brunel
01895 462238
studio@b1000.brunel.ac.uk
www.b1000.brunel.ac.uk
999 AM

Radio Cavell
0161 620 3033
info@radiocavell1350.org.uk
www.radiocavell.org.uk
Broadcasting manager:
Phil Edmunds
1350 AM

Radio Donnington
01869 336200
enquiries@event-tech.biz
www.event-tech.biz
Liaison: Diane Smith
1602 AM. Motor racing

Radio Glangwili
01267 227504
87.7 FM

Radio Gosh
020 7405 9200 x5205
peter@radiogosh.co.uk
Chairman: Peter Losch
999 AM

Radio Heatherwood
01344 625818
www.radioheatherwood.org.uk
Station manager: Dave Smith
999 AM

Radio Hotspot
01473 326287
www.royalhospitalschool.org
Manager: Don Topley
1287 AM

Radio Knockhill
01383 723337
aardvark@pitlochry.org
Station manager: Garry Stagg
1602 AM. Motor racing

Radio Lonsdale
01229 877877
studio@radiolonsdale.co.uk
www.southlakes-uk.co.uk
Station manager: Julian Ackred
87.7 FM

Radio Nightingale
01709 304244
Admin@radionightingale.org.uk
www.radionightingale.org.uk
1350 AM

Radio North Angus
01382 424095
info@radionorthangus.co.uk
www.radionorthangus.co.uk
Secretary: Malcolm Finlayson
87.7 FM

Radio North Tees
01642 624337
info@radionorthtees.com
www.radionorthtees.com
Station manager: Elliot Kennedy
1575 AM

Radio Northwick Park
020 8869 3959
info@radionorthwickpark.org.uk
www.radionorthwickpark.org.uk
Programme controller: David Reece
945 AM

Radio Rainbow
01224 681818
radiorainbowinternational@
hotmail.com
www.radio-rainbow.tnpod.com
945 AM

Radio Redhill
01737 768511
studio@radioredhill.co.uk
www.radioredhill.co.uk
Station manager: Nigel Gray
1287 AM

Radio Rockingham
01869 336200
enquiries@event-tech.biz
www.event-tech.biz
Liaison: Diane Smith
1602 AM. Rockingham speedway
commentary

Radio Rovers
01254 261413
alan.yardley@creatv.co.uk
www.gjmedia.co.uk
Station manager: Alan Yardley
1404 AM. Blackburn Rovers
matchday service

Radio Silverstone
01869 336200
enquiries@event-tech.biz
www.event-tech.biz
Liaison: Diane Smith
1602 AM. Motor racing

Radio Southlands
01273 446084
info@hospitalradiosouthlands.co.uk
www.hospitalradiosouthlands.co.uk
Programme controller: Adam James
846 AM

Radio Thruxton
01295 262000
enquiries@event-tech.biz
www.event-tech.biz
Liaison: Diane Smith
1602 AM. Motor racing

Radio Tyneside
0191 273 6970
info@radiotyneside.co.uk
www.radiotyneside.co.uk
1575 AM

Radio Warwick
024 7657 3077
studio@radiowarwick.ac.uk
www.radiowarwick.ac.uk
1251 AM

Radio West Suffolk
01284 713403
peteowen1350@hotmail.com
www.radiowestsuffolk.co.uk
Vice chairman: P Owen
1350 AM. West Suffolk Hospital

Radio Wexham
01753 570033
945 AM

Radio ysbty Glan Clwyd
01745 584229
Manager: Mrs M Jelly
1287 AM

Ram Air
01274 233267
studio@ramairfm.com
www.ramairfm.co.uk
Station manager: Mark Pickering
1350 AM

Range Radio
0161 861 9727
rap@whalleyrange.manchester.
sch.uk
www.whalleyrange.manchester.
sch.uk
Station manager: Roy Appleby
1350 AM

Red
01206 863211
red@essex.ac.uk
www.essexstudent.com
1404 AM

**Rookwood Sound Hospital
Radio**
029 2031 3796
programming@
rookwoodsound.co.uk
www.rookwoodsound.co.uk
Programme controller: Tim Evans
945 AM

Rugby Ref!Link
01225 835553
ppd@reflink.net
www.reflink.net
Managing director: Peter Downey
87.7 to 105 AM. Rugby referees

Solar AM
01744 733766
solar1287am@hotmail.com
Station manager: Terry Broughton
1287 AM

Sportslink UK
01225 835553
pd@officiallink.net
www.officiallink.net
Managing director: Peter Downey
87.7 to 105 AM. Tennis, dressage,
racing

**Stoke Mandeville Hospital
Radio**
01296 331575
info@smhr.co.uk
www.smhr.co.uk
1575 AM

Storm FM
01248 388000
admin@stormfm.com
www.stormfm.com
Manager: Alex Simpson
87.7 FM. University of Wales
Bangor

Storm Radio
01206 500700
storm@colchsfc.ac.uk
Station manager: Neil Kelly
999AM

Subcity Radio
0141 341 6222
www.subcity.org.uk
Station manager: Rosie Scott
1350 AM

Surge 1287 AM
0870 357 2287
office@surgeradio.co.uk,
studio@surgeradio.co.uk
www.surgeradio.co.uk
Station manager: Matt Treacy;
programme controller: Alex Duffy;
head of music: Andrew Bailey
1287 AM. Student radio

Trust AM
01909 502909
studio@trustam.com
www.trustam.com
1278 AM
Bassetlaw district general hospital

Tunbridge Wells Hospital radio
01892 528528
info@hrtw.org.uk
www.hrtw.org.uk
Programme controller: Mark Burgess
1350 AM

UCA
01292 886433
ucaradio@paisley.ac.uk
www.ucaradiopaisley.ac.uk
Station manager: Marcus Bowinan
87.7 FM

UKC Radio
01227 824201
ukcr@kent.ac.uk
www.ukcr.net
Programme controller:
Dan Thompson
1350 AM

Unity FM
01772 894876
info@unityfm.co.uk
Project manager: Paul Jenkins
107 FM. Culturally diverse music

University Radio Falmer
01273 678287
urf@sussex.ac.uk
Station manager: Fouad Sethra
999 AM

University Radio York
01904 433840
ury@york.ac.uk
www.ury.york.ac.uk
Programme controller: Adam Bell
1350 AM

URB
01225 386611
studio@bath.ac.uk
www.bath.ac.uk
Station manager: James Palmer
1449 AM

URF
01273 678999
Jonathan@urfonline.com
www.urfonline.com
Station manager: Jonathan Pascoe
1431 AM

URN
01273 678999
studio@urn1350.net
www.urn1350.net
Station manager: Phil Cotton
1350 AM

WCR AM
01902 317700
training@wcr1350.co.uk
www.wcr1350.co.uk
1350 AM

Whitechapel AM
020 7377 7000 x2928
info@whitechapelfm.org.uk
www.whitechapel.org.uk
999 AM

Withybush FM
01437 773562
studio@withybushfm.co.uk
www.withybushfm.co.uk
87.7FM

Xpression
01392 263568
stationManager@
Xpressionfm.com
www.Xpressionfm.com
Station manager: Dan Fowler;
programme controller: Ricky Bustin
87.7 FM

Xtreme
01792 295989
studio@xtremeradio.info
www.xtremeradio.info
1431 AM

Cable radio

Angel Radio
01983 242471
angelradio@37.com
www.angelfm.co.uk
Programme controller & Station
manager: Martin Kirby
Nostalgia before 1960

BCB 96.7FM
01274 771677
info@bcb.yorks.com
www.bcb.yorks.com
Station manager and programme
controller: Jonathan Pinfield;
project director: Mary Dowson
All types of music

Cablecom Investments
01638 532323
customer@cablecom.co.uk
www.cablecom.co.uk
Programme controller;
Robert Barnes
News, pop music and documentary

Cable Radio
01273 418181
office@cableradio.co.uk
www.cableradio.co.uk
Station manager: R Mustapha
Adult contemporary

CRMK
01908 265266
Station manager: Mike Barry

Kerrang!
0114 209 1034
natalie.johnson@emap.com
www.Emapdigitalradio.com
Manager: Natalie Johnson

Kiss
0114 209 1034
natalie.johnson@emap.com
www.Emapdigitalradio.com
Manager: Natalie Johnson

Kool AM
020 8373 1075
pfmnews@email.com
www.koolam.co.uk
Programme controller: Joe Bone
1134 AM. Harlow

Radio Forth
0131 556 9255
marketing@radioforth.com
www.forthonline.com
Managing director: Sandy Wilkie;
programme controller:
Nik Goodman
548 AM; 97.3 FM. Adult
contemporary

Radio Verulam
01442 398099
studio@radio-verulam.co.uk
www.radio-verulam.co.uk
Manager: Phil Richards

Smash! Hits
020 7436 1515
natalie.johnson@emap.com
www.Emapdigitalradio.com
Manager: Natalie Johnson

Satellite radio

Adventist World Radio
01344 401401
whitegates@AWR.org
www.awr.org
Programme controller: Bert Smit

All: Sports Live
0113 399 2043
cheryl.Westerman@teamtalk.com
Manager: Cheryl Westerman

Amrit Bani
020 8606 9292
info@amjritbani.com
www.amritbani.com
Operational director:
Surjit Singh Dusanjh
Religious Asian broadcasting

Apna Radio
0121 555 8238
info@apnaradio.net
www.apnaradio.net
Director: Arfan Younis
Asian/English

The Arrow
0121 695 0000
paul.fairburn@chryslis.com
www.thearrow.co.uk
Managing director: Paul Fairburn

Asian Gold
020 8571 7200
info@asiangoldradio.com
www.asiangoldradio.com
Chief executive director:
Zorawar Gakhal
Ethnic Asian

Assalam Radio
00 41 21 6476390
info@assalam.info
www.assalam.info
Manager: Mostepha Mohammed

Bloomberg Radio
020 7330 7575
digitalradio@bloomberg.net
www.bloomberg.co.uk
Radio Editor: Jack Reed

Calvary Chapel Radio
020 8466 5365/07779 507032
ccradio@btconnect.com
www.calvarychapelradio.co.uk
Managing director: Brian
Brodersen; programme controller:
Alison Johnstone-White;
programmer: Mark Seddon
Christian radio

Capital Gold
020 7766 6006
www.capitalradio.co.uk
Manager: Gills Hind

Club Asia
020 8594 6662
info@clubasiaonline.com
www.clubasiaonline.com
Programme controller:
Sumerad Ahmed
Young British Asians

Core
020 7911 7300
fresh@corefreshhits.com
www.corefreshhits.com
Digital content manager:
Nick Piggott

Cross Rhythms
0870 011 8008
admin@crossrhythms.co.uk
www.crossrhythms.co.uk
Managing director: Chris Cole;
Office manager: Jonathan Bellamy
Christian youth radio

Desi Radio – Southall
020 8574 9591
info@desiradio.org.uk
www.desiradio.org.uk
Chair of the trustees: Amarjit
Khera; programme controller:
Ajit Singh
Panjabi, satellite,digital

Easy Radio
020 8900 1035
info@easy1035.com
www.easy1035.com
Programme controller:
Natalie King

ETBC London
020 8795 0045
atbcradio@yahoo.co.uk
www.atbclondon.com
Programme controller: Karjhi Gesu
Asian

EWTN
00 1 205 271 2900
www.ewtn.com
Global Catholic network

Family Radio
00 1 800 543 1495
www.familyradio.com
Christian gospel

FCUK FM
020 8749 7272
ian@deliciousdigital.com
www.fcuk.com
Managing director: O Raphael;
director: Ian Taylor

Galaxy
0121 695 0000
www.galaxyfm.co.uk
Managing director: Paul Fair;
programme controller:
Neil Greenslade
Dance and R&B

Gaydar Radio
020 8893 9550
gary@qsoft.co.uk
Manager: Gary Frisch

Hallam FM
0114 209 1034
namesurname@hallamfm.co.uk
www.hallamfm.co.uk
Managing director: Ian Clasper;
news editor: Katy Henderson

Heart 106.2
020 7465 6100
enquiries@heart1062.co.uk
www.heart1062.co.uk
Managing director: Steve Parkinson
106.2 FM. Greater London

Holiday FM
info@holidayfmradio.com
www.holidayfmradio.co.uk
Gran Canaria, Lanzarote, Tenerife,
Fuerteventura, Katerini

Jazz FM
020 7298 7209
alistair@jazzfm.com
www.jazzfm.co.uk
Manager: Stuart Kilby

Laser Radio
01342 327842
laser@ukmail.com
www.laserradio.net
Managing director: Andrew Yeates
1557 AM. Greater Amsterdam and
Sky subscribers

LBC
020 7314 7300
newsroom@lbc.co.uk
www.lbc.co.uk
Managing director: Mark
Flanagan; programme director:
Steve Kyte

Magic
0114 209 1142
natalie.johnson@emap.com
www.emap.com
Station manager: Natalie Johnson

McColls FM
0113 399 2211
www.teamtalkbroadcast.com
Manager: Helen Jacklin

Mean Country
0870 150 0044
www.meanfiddler.com
Station manager: Dean James

The Mix
020 7911 7300
mail@themix.musicradio.com
www.musicradio.com
Station manager: Nick Piggott

Mojo
020 7436 1515
mojo@emap.com
www.mojo4music.com
Radio programme director:
Scott Armstrong

Music Choice
020 7014 8700
contactus@musicchoice.co.uk
www.musicchoice.com
Station manager: Margo Daly;
Head of News: Hannah Aiken

NPR Worldwide (National Public Radio)
00 1 202 513 2000
worldwide@npr.org
www.npr.org
Senior VP for programming:
Jay Kernis; VP programming:
Margaret Low Smith

On Air
020 7896 9000
voanews@voanews.com
www.voa.gov
Managing director: Tim Eris

Oneword
020 7976 3030
general@oneword.co.uk
www.oneword.co.uk
Managing director:
Simon Blackmore

Panjab Radio
020 8848 8877
info@panjabradio.co.uk
www.panjabradio.co.uk
Station manager:
Paramjit Kaur Nizzar
Panjab radio

Planet Rock
020 7911 7300
joinus@planetrock.com
www.planetrock.com
Digital content manager:
Nick Piggott

Primetime Radio
0870 050 5050
david.atkey@primetimeradio.org
www.primetimeradio.org
Managing director Ron Coles;
operations director: David Atkey

Premier Christian Radio
020 7316 1300
reception@premier.org.uk
www.premier.org.uk
Managing director: Peter Kerridge;
programme controller: Charmain
Noble-McLean
Christian & variety of styles

Q
0114 209 1142
natalie.johnson@emap.com
www.q4music.com
Managing director: Mark Story;
programme director: Simon Long

Radio Al Mahabba
01274 721810
rthurgoo@hcjb.org.uk
www.hcjb.org
Managing director: RW Thurgood
Arabic music

Radio Caroline
020 8340 3831
caroline-pirate@btconnect.com
www.radiocaroline.co.uk
Programme controller & station
manager: Peter Moore
Album rock music

Radio France Internationale (RFI)
00 33 1 5640 1212
www.rfi.fr

Radio London
01296 425644
sales@radiolondon.co.uk
www.radiolondon.co.uk
Station manager: Ray Anderson

Radio Telefis Eireann
info@rte.ie
www.rte.ie
Managing director of Radio:
Adrian Moynes
Ireland's public service broadcaster

Real Radio
029 2031 5100
sarahgraham@realradio.com
www.realradiofm.com
Managing director: Andy Carter;
programme director:
Sarah Graham
60s to present day

SBN
020 7691 4777
info@campusmedia.co.uk
www.sbn.co.uk
Station manager: Marina Lois;
assistant programmer:
Deidre Melvin
Rock, hip-hop, Indian punk

Sky Radio 100.7 FM
00 31 35 699 1005
skyradio@skyradio.nl
www.skyradio.com

Smash Hits
020 7436 1515
info@emap.com
www.emap.com
Station manager: Andy Roberts

Spectrum Digital 1 and 2
020 7627 4433
enquiries@spectrumradio.net
www.spectrumradio.net
General manager: Paul Hogan

The Storm
020 7911 7300
reception@stormradio.co.uk
www.stormradio.co.uk
Station manager: Heidi Hanson
Adult contemporary

Sukh Sagar Radio
020 8571 7200
info@asiangoldradio.co.uk
www.asiangoldradio.co.uk
Chief executive: Zorawar Gakhal
Ethnic Asian

Sunrise Radio (UK and Europe)
020 8574 6666
reception@sunriseradio.com
www.sunriseradio.com
Managing director: Tony Lit;
news editor: David Landau;
programme controller: Tony Patti
Asian

talkGospel.com
020 7316 1300
enquiries@talkgospel.com
www.talkgospel.com
Chairman: Noble McLean

The Talking Bible
www.talkingbible.com

TBC Radio
07817 063682
info@tbcuk.com
www.tbcuk.com
Managing director: V. Ramarag
Asian music

TotalRock
020 7731 6696
bs@totalrock.com
www.totalrock.com
Station manager: Tony Wilson

Trans World Radio UK
01225 831390
web@twr.org.uk
www.twr.org.uk
Chief executive: Russell Farnworth;
programme controller: Michael
Pfundner
Christian music

Voice of America
020 7896 9000
voanews@voanews.com
www.voa.gov
Station manager: Tim Ayrisnger

WorldSpace UK
020 7494 8200
ukservice@worldspace.com
www.worldspace.com
Senior vice-president: Safia Safwat
XFM
020 7766 6606
firstname.lastname@xfm.co.uk
www.xfm.co.uk
Managing director: Garham Bryce;
programme controller:
Andy Ashton
Guitar-based

Radio associations

Assoc. for international
Broadcasting
POBox 990, London SE3 9XL
020 8297 3993
info@aib.org.uk
www.aib.org.uk
Managing director:
Simon Spandwick
Trade organisation for
international broadcasters,
manufacturers and consultants

Broadcasting Press Guild
Tiverton, The Ridge
Woking, Surrey GU22 7EQ
01483 764895
torin.douglas@bbc.co.uk
Managing director: Richard Last
Promotes professional interests of
journalists who write or broadcast
about the media

Commercial Radio Companies
Association
The Radio Centre
77 Shaftesbury Avenue
London W1D 5DU
020 7306 2603
info@crca.co.uk
www.crca.co.uk
Trade body for commercial radio

Creators' Rights Alliance
British Music House
26 Berners Street
London W1T 3LR
020 7436 7296
info@creatorsrights.org
www.creatorsrights.org
Campaigns to protect creators'
rights; operates in all media areas

Digital Radio Development
Bureau (DRDB)
The Radiocentre
77 Shaftesbury Avenue
London W1D 5DU
020 7306 2630
info@drdb.org
www.drdb.org
Trade body; funded and supported
by BBC and commercial radio
multiplex operators

Musicians Union
60–62 Clapham Road
London SW9 0JJ
020 7582 5566
webmaster@
 musiciansunion.org.uk
www.musiciansunion.org.uk

Office of Communications
(Ofcom)
Riverside House
2A Southwark Bridge Road
London SE1 9HA
020 7981 3000
mediaoffice@ofcom.org.uk
www.ofcom.gov.uk
New broadcasting super-regulator

Performing Right Society
29–33 Berners Street
London W1T 3AB
020 7580 5544
info@prs.co.uk
www.prs.co.uk
Collects and distributes royalties

Rad10
rad10@rad10.com
www.rad10.com
Free training resource for radio
volunteers looking at going
professional; offers advice for
community radio groups

The Radio Academy
5 Market Place
London W1W 8AE
020 7255 2010
info@radioacademy.org
www.radioacademy.org
Professional body for radio; aims to
encourage pursuit of excellence and
a greater understanding of the
medium

Radio Joint Audience Research
(Rajar)
Gainsborough House
81 Oxford Street, London
W1D 2EU
020 7903 5350
info@rajar.co.uk
www.rajar.co.uk

Voice of the Listener and Viewer
(VLV)
101 Kings Drive
Gravesend, Kent DA12 5BQ
01474 352835
vlv@btinternet.com
www.vlv.org.uk
Independent, non-profit society
working to ensure independence,
quality and diversity in
broadcasting

Women's Radio Group
27 Bath Road
London W4 1LJ
Fax: 020 8995 5442
wrg@zelo.demon.co.uk
www.womeninradio.org.uk
Training and networking charity

World Radio Network
PO Box 1212
London SW8 2ZF
020 7896 9000
email@wrn.org
www.wrn.org
Home to series of global radio
networks; hosts transmission
services for world's leading
broadcasters

Radio trade press

Advance Production News
Crimson Communications
211a Station House,
Greenwich Communication
Centre
Greenwich High Road
London SE10 8JL
020 8305 6905
www.crimson.uk.com
Monthly. Listings for production
companies. Editor: Alan Williams

Audio Media
IMAS Publishing UK
Atlantica House,
11 Station Road
St Ives, Cambs PE27 5BH
01480 461555
pr@audiomedia.com
www.audiomedia.com
Monthly. Professional audio.
Editor: Paul Mac

Broadcast
Emap Media
33–39 Bowling Green Lane
London EC1R 0DA
020 7505 8000
bcletters@emap.com
www.broadcastnow.co.uk
Weekly. TV & radio industry.
Editor: Conor Dignam

Broadcast Hardware
International
Hardware Creations
48 The Broadway
Maidenhead, Berks
SL6 1PW
01628 773935
cathy@hardwarecreations.tv
www.hardwarecreations.tv
10 pa. Editor: Dick Hobbs

Commonwealth Broadcaster
Commonwealth Broadcasting
Association, 17 Fleet Street
London EC4Y 1AA
020 7583 5550
cba@cba.org.uk
www.cba.org.uk
Quarterly. Editor: Elizabeth Smith

Contacts
The Spotlight, 7 Leicester Place
London WC2H 7RJ
020 7437 7631
info@spotlightcd.com
www.spotlightcd.com
Annual. Contacts for stage, film, TV
and radio. Editor: Kate Poynton

Line Up
Line Up Publications
The Hawthornes
4 Conference Grove
Crowle WR7 4SF
01905 381725
editor@lineup.biz
www.ibs.org.uk
6pa. Journal of the Institute of
Broadcast Sound. Editor:
Hugh Robjohns

Pro Sound News
CMP Information, Ludgate House
245 Blackfriars Road
London SE1 9UR
020 7921 8319
info@cmpinformation.com
www.cmpinformation.com
12pa. Audio industry. Editor:
David Robinson

QSheet
10 Northburgh Street
London EC1V 0AT
020 7253 8888
Monthly. Support material for
presenters and producers.
Contact: Nik Harta

Radcom
Radio Society of Great Britain
Lambda House
Cranbourne Road
Potters Bar EN6 3JE
01707 659015
radcom@rsgb.org.uk
www.rsgb.org
Monthly. Radio enthusiasts.
Editor: Steve Telenius-Lowe

Radio Magazine
Radio Magazine
Crown House,
25 High Street
Rothwell, Northants
NN14 6AD
01536 418558
info@theradiomagazine.co.uk
www.theradiomagazine.co.uk
Weekly. Radio news for industry.
Editor: Paul Boon

Stage Screen and Radio
Bectu,
373–377 Clapham Road
London
SW9 9BT
020 7346 0900
janice@
stagescreenandradio.org.uk
www.bectu.org.uk
10pa. Broadcasting union.
Editor: Janice Turner

VLV Bulletin
Voice of the Listener and Viewer
101 Kings Drive
Gravesend
DA12 5BQ
01474 352835
vlv@btinternet.com
www.vlv.org.uk
Quarterly. Consumer campaigning
body. Editor: Jocelyn Hay

TV and radio awards

Amnesty International Media Awards
020 7814 6278
www.amnesty.org.uk/
    mediaawards
Human rights journalism

Bafta Awards
020 7734 0022
www.bafta.com
*Film, TV and interactive
industries*

British Comedy Awards
020 7605 1200
www.britishcomedy
    awards.co.uk

Broadcast Awards
020 7505 8452
www.broadcastnow.co.uk
Programme ideas and execution

Emmas (Ethnic Multicultural Media Academy awards)
020 7636 1233
www.emma.tv
Multicultural media

Indie Awards (Pact)
020 7331 6000
www.pact.co.uk

National TV Awards
020 7241 8000
Winners picked by viewers

NTL Commerical Radio Awards
020 7306 2603
www.crca.co.uk

Plain English Media Awards
01663 744409
www.plainenglish.co.uk/
    mediaawards
Campaign against gobbledygook

Race in the Media Awards
020 7939 0000
www.cre.gov.uk
*Organised by Commission for
Racial Equality*

Royal Television Society Awards
020 7691 2470
www.rts.org.uk

Sony Radio Academy Awards
020 7255 2010
www.radioacademy.org/awards

Student Radio Awards
www.studentradio.org.uk

Media training bodies

BBC Training and development:
Broadcast Training
BBC Training & Development
35 Marylebone High Street
London W1U 4PX
0870 122 0216
training@bbc.co.uk
www.bbctraining.com
All strands of broadcast training

BKSTS – The Moving Image Society
Pinewood Studios
Iver Heath
Bucks SL0 0NH
01753 656656
training@bksts.com
www.bksts.com
Film foundation, TV and digital tech, foundation sound for film and video, broadcasting engineering

British Universities Film & Video Council
77 Wells Street
London W1T 3QJ
020 7393 1500
ask@bufvc.ac.uk
www.busvc.ac.uk
To promote the use of media within higher education

Broadcast Journalism Training Council
The Secretary
18 Miller's Close
Rippingale
Lincolnshire PE10 0TH
01778 440025
Sec@bjtc.org.uk
www.bjtc.org.uk
Accredits courses

City & Guilds
1 Giltspur Street
London EC1A 9DD
020 7294 2800
enquiry@city-and-guilds.co.uk
www.city-and-guilds.co.uk
Vocational qualifications

Film Education
21–22 Poland Street
London W1F 8QQ
020 7851 9450
postbox@filmeducation.org
www.filmeducation.org

Film First Foundation
9 Bourlet Close
London W1W 7BP
020 7580 2111
info@firstfilm.co.uk
www.firstfilm.co.uk
Training for new film writers, producers and directors

FT2 – Film and Television Freelance Training
Fouth Floor, Warwick House
9 Warwick Street
London W1B 5LY
020 7734 5141
info@ft2.org.uk
www.ft2.org.uk
Training for new broadcast freelancers

National Council for the Training of Journalists
Latton Bush Centre
Southern Way
Harlow
Essex CM18 7BL
01279 430009
info@NCTJ.com
www.nctj.com
Runs schemes for print journalists. Accredits courses

Skillset
Skillset: The Sector Skills Council for the Audio Visual Industries
Prospect House
80–110 New Oxford Street
London WC1A 1HB
020 7520 5757
info@skillset.org
www.skillset.org
Owned by broadcast industry; accredits courses, publishes handbooks and runs Skillsformedia service (www.skillsformedia.com)

Aberdeen, University of
King's College
Aberdeen AB24 3FX
01224 272000
www.abdn.ac.uk
MLitt visual culture. BA film studies with various other options; Mlitt/ MPhil/PhD film and visual studies (by research).

Barnsley College
PO Box 266, Church Street
Barnsley S70 2YW
01226 216569/216287
programme.enquiries@
barnsley.ac.uk
www.barnsley.ac.uk
Fdg journalism & media production (with University of Huddersfield).

Bath, University of
Claverton Down
Bath BA2 7AY
01225 383019
admissions@bath.ac.uk
www.bath.ac.uk
HND audio and visual tech (at Salisbury college); HND media production (at Wiltshire College, Chippenham); HND multimedia and design (at Wiltshire College, Chippenham).

Bath Spa University College
Newton Park
Newton Street Low
Bath BA2 9BN
01225 875875
enquiries@bathspa.ac.uk
www.bathspa.ac.uk
Fdg/BA (Hons) commercial music; BA (Hons) creative music tech; Fdg design for digital technologies.

Bell College
Almada Street
Hamilton
Lanarkshire ML3 0JB
01698 283100
enquiries@bell.ac.uk;
r.bergman@bell.ac.uk
www.bell.ac.uk
PGDip in broadcast journalism (BJTC).

Birkbeck , University of London
Malet Street, Bloomsbury
London WC1E 7HX
0845 601 0174
info@bbk.ac.uk
CertDip/BA film and media; MA/MA(Res)history of film and visual media; MPhil/PhD film/ TV/media studies; Dip new media management; Dip web design and development.

Blackburn College
Feilden Street
Blackburn BB2 1LH
01254 55144
studentservices@
blackburn.ac.uk
www.blackburn.ac.uk
Pre-entry media production.

Bolton Institute of Higher Education
Deane Road
Bolton BL3 5AB
01204 900600
enquiries@bolton.ac.uk
www.bolton.ac.uk
BA (Hons) photography and video/ media, writing and production/ writing for stage, screen and radio; BA (Hons) animation and illustration; HND/BSc (Hons) multimedia and website development.

Arts Institute at Bournemouth
Wallisdown, Poole
Dorset BH12 5HH
01202 533011
general@aib.ac.uk
www.aib.ac.uk
BA (Hons) film and animation production.

Bournemouth University
Bournemouth Media School,
Weymouth House, Fern Barrow
Poole, Dorset
BH12 5BB
01202 524111
bms@bournemouth.ac.uk
www.bournemouth.ac.uk
BA/MA TV production; MA radio production/ broadcast and film management.

Bradford College
Great Horton Road
Bradford BD7 1AY
01274 433004
admissions@bilk.ac.uk
www.bradfordcollege.ac.uk
PGDip/MA politics of visual representation/ representation in film; BA (Hons) graphic media communication.

Bradford, University of
Richmond Road
Bradford BD7 1DP
01274 232323; media: 01274 233084
eimcugadmissions@
bradford.ac.uk
www.eimc.brad.ac.uk
BSc media tech and production; BSc computer animation and special effects/ electronic imaging and media comms (with pre-entry year)/ multimedia computing/ creative media. and technologies; BA digital media; MSc creative media and technologies with computer animation and special effects/ creative media and technologies with multimedia systems.

Bristol, University of
Senate House, Tyndall Avenue
Bristol BS8 1TH
0117 928 9000
admissions@bristol.ac.uk
www.bristol.ac.uk
MA film and TV production; MA TV studies.

Brunel University
Uxbridge
Middlesex
UB8 3PH
01895 274000
admissions@brunel.ac.uk
www.brunel.ac.uk
BA creative music tech/ film and TV studies (also with American studies/drama/English/history/ music); MA documentary practice.

Bucks Chilterns University College
Queen Alexander Road
High Wycombe
Bucks HP11 2JZ
01494 522141
marketing@bcuc.ac.uk
www.bcuc.ac.uk
BA (Hons) media studies (with drama production/video production/film studies).

Canterbury Christ Church University College
Department of Media
North Holmes Road
Canterbury
Kent CT1 1QU
01227 767700
admissions@cant.ac.uk
www.cant.ac.uk
BA (Hons) film, radio and TV studies (single, joint and combined); MA media production.

Cardiff University
Dept of Journalism and Media
Studies, PO Box 927
King Edward VII Avenue
Cardiff CF10 3NB
029 2087 4000
jomec@cardiff.ac.uk
www.cardiff.ac.uk/jomec
BA (Hons) journalism, film and media (single and joint); PGDip broadcast journalism.

Cardonald College
690 Moss Park Drive
Glasgow G52 3AY
0141 272 3333
enquiries@cardonald.ac.uk
www.cardonald.ac.uk
HNC/HND TV operations and production.

Carmarthenshire College (Coleg Sir Gar)
Pibwrlwyd Campus
Carmarthen
SA31 2NH
01554 748000
admissions@colegsirgar.ac.uk
www.colegsirgar.ac.uk
Short course in DJ tech; NatDip media production/ music tech; BA (Hons) media production.

Central England in Birmingham, University of
Corporation Street
Birmingham B4 7DX
0121 331 5000
media@uce.ac.uk
www.uce.ac.uk
BA (Hons) media and communication (culture and society/ radio and TV and video); PGDip broadcast journalism (BJTC); MA international broadcast journalism; MA media production.

Central Lancashire, University of
Department of Journalism
Preston, Lancashire PR1 2HE
01772 894730
meward@uclan.ac.uk
www.ukjournalism.org
PGDip/MA broadcast journalism (BJTC).

University College Chester
Parkgate Road
Chester CH1 4BJ
01244 375444
enquiries@chester.ac.uk
www.chester.ac.uk
BA media (commercial music production/ multimedia journalism/ radio production/ TV production (Granada Media & Education Partnership Scheme)) (single and combined); MA radio production/ screen studies/ TV production.

Chichester College
Westgate Fields, Chichester
West Sussex PO19 1SB
01243 536196
www.chichester.ac.uk
BTEC HND media (radio production).

University College Chichester
Bishop Otter Campus
College Lane
Chichester
West Sussex PO19 6PE
01243 816002
admissions@ucc.ac.uk
www.ucc.ac.uk
Fdg/BA (Hons) media production.

City Of Wolverhampton College
Wulfrun Campus, Paget Road
Wolverhampton WV6 0DU
01902 836000
mail@
    wolverhamptoncollege.ac.uk
www.wolverhamptoncollege.ac.uk;
www.mediacove.com
HND media design (video) (W'ton Uni); Fdg broadcast journalism (W'ton Uni).

City University, London
Department of Journalism,
Northampton Square
London EC1V 0HB
020 7040 5060; journalism dept:
020 7040 8221
ugadmissions@city.ac.uk
www.city.ac.uk
PGDip broadcast journalism (BJTC)/ TV current affairs journalism (BJTC).

Cleveland College of Art & Design
Green Lane, Linthorpe
Middlesbrough TS5 7RJ
01642 288888
admissions@ccad.ac.uk
www.ccad.ac.uk
Fdg TV and film production.

Cornwall College
Trevenson Campus, Pool
Redruth
Cornwall TR15 3RD
01209 611611
enquiries@cornwall.ac.uk
www.cornwall.ac.uk
Fdg graphic and communication design; Fdg multimedia design.

Coventry University
Priory Street
Coventry CV1 5FB
024 7688 7050
rao.cor@coventry.ac.uk
www.coventry.ac.uk
BA media production/ media studies and music or theatre; BA multimedia & communication design; PGCert/PGDip/MA design and digital media.

Darlington College Of Technology
Cleveland Avenue, Darlington
County Durham DL3 7BB
01325 503127
enquire@darlington.ac.uk
www.darlington.ac.uk
BTEC NatCert media (audio production); BTEC NatDip media (moving image).

De Montfort University
The Gateway
Leicester LE1 9BH
0116 255 1551
enquiry@dmu.ac.uk
www.dmu.ac.uk
HND music tech; BA (Hons) (single and joint)/BSc (Hons) music, tech and innovation; BSc (Hons) audio and recording tech/ broadcast tech/ media production; BA (Hons) film studies/ photography and video.

Derby, University of
School of Arts, Design & Technology, Kedleston Road
Derby DE22 1GB
01332 590500
admissions@derby.ac.uk
www.derby.ac.uk
Fdg commercial video and photography/ video production; BA (Hons) film and TV studies/ film and video.

Dundee, University of
Nethergate
Dundee DD1 4HN
01382 344000
srs@dundee.ac.uk
www.dundee.ac.uk
BA time-based art/ animation and electronic media; BSc interactive media design; PGDip/MSc electronic imaging; MSc animation and visualisation.

Ealing, Hammersmith and West London College
Gliddon Road, Barons Court
London W14 9BL
0800 980 2175
Marketing@wlc.ac.uk
www.wlc.ac.uk
Fdg digital animation.

East Anglia, University of
Norwich
Norfolk NR4 7TJ
01603 456161
admissions@uea.ac.uk
www.uea.ac.uk
BA film and TV studies/ film and English or American studies; MA film studies/ film studies with archiving.

University of East London
Docklands Campus
Longbridge Road
Dagenham E16 2RD
020 8223 3000
admiss@uel.ac.uk
www.uel.ac.uk
MA independent film, video and new screen media/ film, TV and history/ sonic culture: sound, arts and media in the digital age.

East Surrey College
Reigate School of Art Design and Media, Gatton Point
Claremont Road
Redhill, Surrey RH1 2JX
01737 772611
studentservices@esc.ac.uk
www.esc.ac.uk
C&G Dip media techniques – TV and video; HND moving image (documentary and drama production).

Edge Hill College of Higher Education
St Helen's Road, Ormskirk
Lancashire
L39 4QP
01695 584274
enquiries@edgehill.ac.uk
www.edgehill.ac.uk
BA (Hons) film studies/ with film and TV production/ media (film and TV).

Falmouth College of Arts
Woodlane Campus, Falmouth
Cornwall TR11 4RH
01326 370400
admissions@falmouth.ac.uk
www.falmouth.ac.uk
*BA (Hons) broadcasting/ film
studies; PgDip/MA broadcast
journalism (BJTC)/ TV
production.*

**Glasgow College of Building
and Printing**
60 North Hanover Street
Glasgow G1 2BP
0141 332 9969
enquiries@gcbp.ac.uk
www.gcbp.ac.uk
*HNC/HND journalism: broadcast
and print; HNC/HND
journalism: broadcast and print.*

Gloucestershire University
The Park
Cheltenham GL50 2QF
01242 532700
gthatcher@glos.ac.uk
www.glos.ac.uk
*BA (Hons) broadcast journalism/
video; BA/BSc (Hons) film studies;
PGCert/PGDip/MA film and
media.*

Goldsmiths College
Dept. of Media and
Communications,
University of London
New Cross, London SE14 6NW
020 7919 7171
media-comms@gold.ac.uk
www.goldsmiths.ac.uk
*Short courses: introduction to
video/ to TV studio/ to single-
camera production and video
editing/ surrealism in the cinema;
MA feature film/ radio (BJTC,
NUJ)/ screen doc/ screen drama
direction/ TV journalism (BJTC).*

Greenwich University
Old Royal Naval College
Park Row
Greenwich, London SE10 9LS
020 8331 8000
courseinfo@greenwich.ac.uk
www.gre.ac.uk
*HND lens-based media/ TV
production tech; Fdg creative
industry (music tech); BA film
studies (with options); HND/BA
graphic and digital design; BA
design tech/ 3D digital design.*

Grimsby College
Nuns Corner
Grimsby DN34 5BQ
01472 311222
infocent@grimsby.ac.uk
www.grimsby.ac.uk
*HNC/HND media production/
music production; HND moving
image; BA (Hons) digital media
production (TV, film and video)
(with Lancaster University).*

**Guildford College of Further and
Higher Education**
Stoke Park, Guildford
Surrey GU1 1EZ
01483 448500
info@guildford.ac.uk
www.guildford.ac.uk
*NatDip/HND/BA (Hons) media
production.*

Harrow College
Brookshill, Harrow Weald
Middlesex HA3 6RR
020 8909 6000
www.harrow.ac.uk
*Short courses: film
studies/introduction to video
production and editing.*

Henley College Coventry
Henley Road, Bell Green
Coventry CV2 1ED
024 7662 6300
info@henley-cov.ac.uk
www.henley-cov.ac.uk
BTEC media (moving image).

Hertfordshire, University of
College Lane
Hatfield AL10 9AB
01707 284000
admissions@herts.ac.uk
www.herts.ac.uk
*BA (Hons) film (combined)/
digital and lens media; BSc
(Hons) music: commercial
composition and tech/ music tech/
sound design tech; MA interactive
broadcast media; BA (Hons)
digital publishing (combined)/
digital animation/ digital
modelling/ digital and lens
media/ model design and special
effects; MA 3D digital animation/
3D modelling and special effects/
hyperfictions.*

Highbury College, Portsmouth
Dept. of Media and Journalism,
Dovercourt Road
Portsmouth
Hampshire PO6 2SA
023 9238 3131
info@highbury.ac.uk
www.highbury.ac.uk
*PGDip in broadcast journalism
(BJTC).*

Hopwood Hall College
St Mary's Gate
Rochdale OL12 6RY
01706 345346
enquiries@hopwood.ac.uk
www.hopwood.ac.uk
*BTEC FirstDip/NatDip media
(moving image).*

University of Huddersfield
Queensgate
Huddersfield HD1 3DH
01484 422288
admissions@hud.ac.uk
www.hud.ac.uk
*BA(Hons) media and TV
production/ media and radio
journalism.*

Hull College
Queens Gardens
Hull HU1 3DG
01482 329943
info@hull-college.ac.uk
www.hull-college.ac.uk
*BTEC NatAward/NatDip media
(moving image/audio).*

**Kensington and Chelsea
College**
Hortensia Road
London SW10 0QS
020 7573 3600
l.gibbons@kcc.ac.uk
www.kcc.ac.uk
*LOCN music tech/ video
production.
LOCN sound design for
multimedia; BTEC NatCert/HNC
multimedia.*

Kent Institute of Art and Design
Oakwood Park, Maidstone
Kent ME16 8AG
01622 620000
info@kiad.ac.uk
www.kiad.ac.uk
*BA (Hons) video media arts; MA
artists' film, video and
photography; Fdg graphic design
and interactive media; BA (Hons)
animation.*

Kent, University of
The Registry, Canterbury
Kent CT2 7NZ
01227 764000
recruitment@kent.ac.uk
www.kent.ac.uk
BA (Hons) film and contemporary arts; BSc (Hons) music tech; MA/MPhil/PhD film studies.

King's College London
School of Humanities, Strand
London WC2R 2LS
020 7836 5454
ceu@kcl.ac.uk
www.kcl.ac.uk
BA film studies with various options; MA visual and performing arts – National Film Theatre/ contemporary cinema cultures.

Kingston University
River House, 53–57 High Street
Kingston-upon-Thames
Surrey KT1 1LQ
020 8547 2000
admissions-info@kingston.ac.uk
www.kingston.ac.uk
BA(Hons) film studies (combined)/ TV studies (combined); BA (Hons)/ DipHE/CertHE audio tech and music industry studies; MA production design for film and TV/ screen design for film and TV (motion graphics)/ film studies/ composing for film and TV; MA/DPhil media, film and drama (by research); Fdg/MA graphic comms; MA illustration and animation/ composing for new media.

Lambeth College
Belmore Street, Wandsworth Road
London SW8 2JY
020 7501 5010
courses@lambethcollege.ac.uk
www.lambethcollege.ac.uk
BTEC NatDip media (moving image); C&G Cert video production techniques; BTEC NatAward radio; BTEC NatCert music tech and audio electronics; NCFE Cert music tech.

Lancaster University
Bailrigg
Lancaster LA1 4YW
01524 65201
ugadmissions@lancaster.ac.uk
www.lancs.ac.uk
BA (Hons) film and cultural studies/ film with sociology or philosophy; PGDip/MSc media production and distribution.

Leeds Metropolitan University
Civic Quarter
Leeds LS1 3HE
0113 283 2600
course-enquiries@lmu.ac.uk
www.lmu.ac.uk
CertHE/Fdg film and TV production; HNC/HND moving image production; BA (Hons)/MA film and moving image production; BSc (Hons) creative music and sound tech/ music tech; PGDip/MA screenwriting (fiction).

Leeds Trinity & All Saints University College
School of Media, Brownberrie Lane, Horsforth
Leeds LS18 5HD
0113 283 7100
enquiries@tasc.ac.uk
www.tasc.ac.uk
MA/PgDip in bimedia journalism (BJTC)/ radio journalism (BJTC).

Leeds, University of
Institute of Communications Studies
Leeds LS2 9JT
0113 243 1751
admissions@leeds.ac.uk
www.leeds.ac.uk
BA broadcasting.

Lincoln, University of
Brayford Pool
Lincoln LN6 7TS
01522 882000
enquiries@lincoln.ac.uk
www.lincoln.ac.uk
BA (Hons) journalism – print, internet, radio and TV; PGDip/MA journalism; BA (Hons) media production/ TV and film design/ digital and interactive TV; MA documentary and factual programme production; MPhil/PhD film studies/ media production; BA (Hons) animation/ interactive multimedia/ interactive and screen-based graphics. Short courses: basic and specialist copy-editing, proofreading, e-Publishing, introduction to book commissioning/ introduction to book marketing/issues with electronic or digital publishing/ book arts/ design for print/ introduction to the print process/ writing for specialists; BA/BA (Hons) publishing media; PGDip/MSc publishing.

Liverpool Community College
Journalism School
The Arts Centre
9 Myrtle Street
Liverpool L7 7JA
0151 252 1515
www.liv-coll.ac.uk
FCert broadcast journalism (BJTC provisional).

Liverpool John Moores University
JMU Tower, 24 Norton Street
Liverpool L3 8PY
0151 231 5090
recruitment@livjm.ac.uk
www.livjm.ac.uk
BA/BA(Hons) media professional studies with TV/ media professional studies with radio (subject to validation)/ screen studies/ popular music studies; MA screenwriting.

Liverpool, University of
Liverpool L69 3BX
0151 794 2000
uksro@liv.ac.uk
www.liv.ac.uk
BA (Hons) European film studies and modern languages (joint).

London College of Communication, School of Media
Elephant & Castle
London SE1 6SB
020 7514 6569
info@lcc.arts.ac.uk
www.lcc.arts.ac.uk
PGDip broadcast journalism; MA documentary research.

London College of Fashion
20 John Prince's Street
London W1G 0BJ
020 7514 7344
enquiries@fashion.arts.ac.uk
www.fashion.arts.ac.uk
BA (Hons) fashion promotion – pathways in broadcast; MA fashion media.

London Film School
24 Shelton Street
London WC2H 9UB
020 7836 9642
info@lfs.org.uk
www.lfs.org.uk
MA filmmaking.

London Metropolitan University
31 Jewry Street
London EC3N 2EY
020 7320 1616
enquiries.city@londonmet.ac.uk
www.londonmet.ac.uk
*Fdg audio production for
broadcast media; BA (Hons)
film and broadcast production/
film studies (single and joint)/
sound and media;
MA film-making.*

London South Bank University
103 Borough Road
London SE1 0AA
020 7928 8989
enquiries@lsbu.ac.uk
www.lsbu.ac.uk
*BA (Hons) digital video
production/ sonic media/ film
studies (combined); BA (Hons)
digital media arts; BSc (Hons)
special effects; MA new media.*

Luton, University of
Park Square
Luton, Beds LU1 3JU
01582 734111
enquiries@luton.ac.uk
www.luton.ac.uk
*Fdg media, art and design (also
at Dunstable College)/ media
production (at Barnfield College,
Milton Keynes College and
Bedford College)/ music tech (at
Dunstable College); BA (Hons)
media performance/ media
production/ music tech/ TV
production; PGCert/PGDip/MA
media production (doc); Fdg
digital imaging and design for
media (at Milton Keynes College).*

**Manchester Metropolitan
University**
Faculty of Art & Design
Ormond Building
Lower Ormond Street,
Manchester M15 6BX
0161 247 1701
www.mmu.ac.uk
*MA media arts/ visual culture;
BA (Hons) contemporary film
and video; BA (Hons) illustration
with animation.*

Mid-Cheshire College
Hartford Campus, Chester Road
Northwich, Cheshire CW8 1LJ
01606 744444
info@midchesh.ac.uk
www.midchesh.ac.uk
*Short course: sound recording
studio techniques; NatDip media
(moving image)/ music tech.
NCFE multimedia design.*

Middlesex University
White Hart Lane
London N17 8HR
020 8411 5000
admissions@mdx.ac.uk
www.mdx.ac.uk
*BA (Hons) recording arts and BA
digital film arts/ film making
(apply directly to SAE Institute
020 7609 2653); BA TV
production; BA (Hons) film
studies (single and joint); BA/BSc
(Hons) sonic arts. BA (Hons)
multimedia arts and BA digital
film arts (apply directly to SAE
Institute 020 7609 2653);
HNC/HND multimedia; BSc
(Hons) information tech (with
multimedia pathway).*

Napier University
School of Communication Arts,
Craighouse Campus
Craighouse Road
Edinburgh EH10 5LG
0131 455 6150
www.napier.ac.uk
*Short courses: intro to
screenwriting/ project
management for film production/
science fiction and comic culture/
working in TV and film art
departments/ handling the media
– TV/ writing for the press and
broadcast media; BA/BA (Hons)
photography, film and imaging;
MA screen project development.*

National Broadcasting School
The Innovation Centre
University of Sussex
Brighton BN1 9SB
01273 704510
www.nationalbroadcasting
school.com
*Cert radio presentation and
programming (CRCA)/ radio
journalism and news presentation
(CRCA/NCTJ).*

**National Film and Television
School**
Beaconsfield Studios
Station Road
Beaconsfield
Bucks HP9 1LG
01494 671234
admin@nftsfilm-tv.ac.uk
www.nftsfilm-tv.ac.uk
*ExecDip script development;
Dip digital post-production/
sound recording for film and TV/
TV production: factual
entertainment/ special effects;
MA animation direction/
cinematography/ composing for
film and TV/ documentary
direction/ editing/ fiction
direction/ sound post-production/
producing/ production design/
screenwriting/ TV production:
factual entertainment (subject to
validation).*

**NE Wales Institute of Higher
Education**
Plas Coch, Mold Road
Wrexham
LL11 2AW
01978 290666
enquiries@newi.ac.uk
www.newi.ac.uk
*HND film and TV design; BA
(Hons) film studies (with
options)/ design: moving image;
HND/Fdg/BEng (Hons)/BSc
(Hons) sound broadcast and
production; Fdg/BEng (Hons)
digital technologies; BA (Hons)
design: multimedia design; MA
animation.*

Neath Port Talbot College
Dwr-y-Felin Road
Neath SA10 7RF
01639 648000
enquiries@nptc.ac.uk
www.nptc.ac.uk
*HNC/HND broadcast media;
BA(Hons) music performance and
production (popular music).*

New College Nottingham
City Campus, Adams Building
Stoney Street
Lace Market
Nottingham NG1 1NG
0115 910 0100
enquiries@ncn.ac.uk
www.ncn.ac.uk
C&G TV and video production.

Newcastle College
Rye Hill Campus
Scotswood Road
Newcastle Upon Tyne NE4 5BR
0191 200 4000
enquiries@ncl-coll.ac.uk
www.ncl-coll.ac.uk
BTEC HND music production;
Fdg stage management and
technical production/ TV and
media practice; Fdg illustration
and animation/ multimedia
design.

Newcastle Upon Tyne University
Newcastle Upon Tyne NE1 7RU
0191 222 6000
admissions-enquiries@ncl.ac.uk
www.ncl.ac.uk
MA/PGDip film studies.

North East Surrey College of Technology – Nescot
Reigate Road, Ewell
Epsom
Surrey KT17 3DS
020 8394 3038
info@nescot.ac.uk
www.nescot.ac.uk
NatDip media production/ music
tech; NatDip multimedia; Fdg
media and multimedia (OUVS).

North East Worcestershire College
Peakman Street
Redditch, Worcestershire
B98 8DW
01527 570020
info@ne-worcs.ac.uk
www.ne-worcs.ac.uk
HNC/HND media (moving
image); NatDip music tech.

North Tyneside College
Embleton Avenue, Wallsend
Tyne and Wear NE28 9NJ
0191 229 5000
infocent@ntyneside.ac.uk
www.northtyneside.ac.uk
HNC/HND TV and video
production; BTEC NatDip media
production (moving image).

North West Kent College
Oakfield Lane, Dartford
Kent DA1 2JT
0800 074 1447
course.enquiries@
nwkcollege.ac.uk
www.nwkcollege.ac.uk
NatDip media studies; Dip
advanced music tech (joint).

Northbrook College Sussex
Little Hampton Road, Worthing
West Sussex BN12 6NU
01903 606060
admissions@nbcol.ac.uk
www.nbcol.ac.uk
HND media – the moving image.

Northumbria University
Ellison Place
Newcastle Upon Tyne NE1 8ST
0191 232 6002
ca.marketing@northumbria
.ac.uk
www.northumbria.ac.uk
BA (Hons) media production/
English and film studies;
BA (Hons) multimedia design.

Norwich School of Art and Design
St George Street, Norwich
Norfolk NR3 1BB
01603 610561
info@nsad.ac.uk
www.nsad.ac.uk
MA writing the visual;
BA (Hons) animation; MA
animation and sound design/
digital practices.

Nottingham Trent University
Burton Street
Nottingham NG1 4BU
0115 941 8418
cbj@ntu.ac.uk
www.ntu.ac.uk
BA (Hons) design for TV; BSc
(Hons) audio-visual tech/ audio
visual production; PGDip/MA TV
journalism/ TV journalism
(international)/ radio
journalism/ radio journalism
(international).

Nottingham, University of
University Park
Nottingham NG7 2RD
0115 951 5151
undergraduate-enquiries@
nottingham.ac.uk
www.nott.ac.uk
BA (Hons) music with film
studies/ film studies with options;
MA film studies.

Paisley University
Paisley
Scotland PA1 2BE
0800 027 1000
uni-direct@paisley.ac.uk
www.paisley.ac.uk
BA (Hons) cinema/commercial
music; BSc (Hons) computer
animation and multimedia; BA
(Hons) digital art/ computer
animation and digital art.

Peterborough Regional College
Park Crescent
Peterborough PE1 4DZ
01733 767366
info@peterborough.ac.uk
www.peterborough.ac.uk
NCFE studio recording and music
tech; BTEC NatDip media
(audio/radio)/ media (moving
image/video).

Plymouth College of Art and Design
Tavistock Place
Plymouth PL4 8AT
01752 203434
enquiries@pcad.ac.uk
www.pcad.ac.uk
Fdg moving image.
Fdg animation and creative
media/ multimedia design.

Plymouth, University of
Drake Circus, Plymouth
Devon PL4 8AA
01752 600600
prospectus@plymouth.ac.uk
www.plymouth.ac.uk
HND sound engineering and
multimedia integration; HND
media moving image (taught at
Truro College); HND media
production (taught at South
Devon).

Portsmouth, University of
University House, Winston
Churchill Avenue
Portsmouth
Hampshire PO1 2UP
023 9284 8484
info.centre@port.ac.uk
www.port.ac.uk
BA (Hons) media studies with
drama/ entertainment tech.

Queen Margaret University College, Edinburgh
Corstophine Campus
Clerwood Terrace
Edinburgh EH12 8TS
0131 317 3000
marketing@qmuc.ac.uk
www.qmuc.ac.uk
BA (Hons) film and media.

Queen Mary, University of London
Mile End Road
London E1 4NS
020 7882 5555
external-relations@qmw.ac.uk
www.qmw.ac.uk
BA film studies and drama.

Queen's University of Belfast
University Road
Belfast BT7 1NN
028 9024 5133
www.qub.ac.uk
BA (Hons) film studies; BSc (Hons)
music tech; MA film studies.

The Radio and TV School
High Street, Staplehurst
Kent TN12 0AX
01580 895256
mail@radioandtvschool.com
www.radioandtvschool.com
Broadcast certificates of
achievement – one-to-one courses
in radio presentation and
production techniques; also
courses in TV and voice-over.

Ravensbourne College of
Design and Communication
Walden Road, Chislehurst
Kent BR7 5SN
020 8289 4900
info@rave.ac.uk
www.ravensbourne.ac.uk
Fdg/BA broadcasting courses.
BA interaction and moving image
design.

Robert Gordon University
School Hill
Aberdeen AB10 1FR
01224 262000
admissions@rgu.ac.uk
www.rgu.ac.uk
BSc (Hons) computing for internet
and multimedia (British
Computer Society)/ computing for
graphics and animation (BCS).

Roehampton University of
Surrey
Erasmus House
Roehampton Lane
London SW15 5PU
020 8392 3000
enquiries@roehampton.ac.uk
www.roehampton.ac.uk
BA TV studies/ film studies/ film
studies and screen practice/
journalism and news media.

Royal Holloway, University of
London
Egham
Surrey TW20 0EX
01784 434455
undergrad-office@rhul.ac.uk
www.rhul.ac.uk
BA German/French/Italian with
film studies; MA TV production/
feature film screenwriting/ screen
studies/ documentary by practice.

Salford, University of
Salford
Greater Manchester M5 4WT
0161 295 5000
ugadmissions-exrel@
    salford.ac.uk
www.salford.ac.uk
BSc (Hons) journalism and
broadcasting (NCTJ); HND audio
and video systems/ professional
sound and video tech/ media
production; BSc (Hons) acoustics/
audio tech/ audio, video and
broadcast tech/ journalism and
broadcasting (NCTJ); BA (Hons)
media and performance/ TV and
radio/ popular music
and recording; PGDip/MA TV
documentary production/
TV and radio scriptwriting.

Salisbury College
Southampton Road, Salisbury
Wiltshire SP1 2LW
01722 344344
enquiries@salisbury.ac.uk
www.salisbury.ac.uk
C&G 1820 (parts 1 & 2) sound
engineering; BTEC NatDip music
tech; HND TV and film; BA (Hons)
photomedia (film and TV).
Fdg computer aided design (3D
modelling and animation)/
multimedia.

Sandwell College
Oldbury Business Centre
Pound Road
Oldbury, West Midlands
B68 8NA
0800 622006
enquiries@sandwell.ac.uk
www.sandwell.ac.uk
NatDip music tech; HNC
professional sound and video;
HNC/HND media production
(moving image)/ music
production; HND professional
sound engineering; BSc (Hons) TV
tech and production (with
University of Central England,
Birmingham).

Sheffield College
The Norton Centre, Dyche Lane
Sheffield S8 8BR
0114 260 3603
mail@sheffcol.ac.uk
www.sheffcol.ac.uk
BTEC HND media production.

Sheffield Hallam University
Psalter Lane Campus
Sheffield S11 8UZ
0114 225 5555
admissions@shu.ac.uk
www.shu.ac.uk
BA (Hons) film and literature/
film and media production; BA
(Hons)/PGCert/PGDip/MA film
studies; PGCert/PGDip/MA
broadcast journalism/ film and
digital production.

Sheffield University
Department of Journalism
Studies, 18–22 Regent Street
Sheffield S1 3NJ
0114 222 2500
journalism@sheffield.ac.uk
www.sheffield.ac.uk/journalism
PGDip/MA broadcast journalism
(BJTC).

South Birmingham College
Cole Bank Road
Birmingham B28 8ES
0121 694 5000
info@sbc.ac.uk
www.sbirmc.ac.uk
Short course: introduction to
digital video editing; NOCN
sound engineering;
NCFE/OCN/BTEC
NatCert/NatDip music tech;
OCN/BTEC NatCert/NatDip
media production; CollegeCert
scriptwriting for film and TV
(fiction).

South Devon College
Newton Road, Torquay
Devon TQ2 5BY
01803 400700
www.southdevon.ac.uk
NatDip media moving image;
HND media production.

172

South East Essex College
Carmarvon Road
Southend-on-Sea
Essex SS2 6LS
01702 220400
marketing@southend.ac.uk
www.southend.ac.uk
Short courses: TV presenting
skills/ radio broadcasting skills/
sound engineering (stage 1 and 2)/
video production and editing;
NCFE intermediate music tech;
BTEC NatDip moving image;
HNC/HND performing arts
(music production); BA (Hons) TV
production and screen media/
music production.
Short course in basic 3D
animation; BSc (Hons) e-media/
digital animation.
Centre of Vocational Excellence for
media technology

South Nottingham College
Greythorn Drive, West Bridgford
Nottingham NG2 7GA
0115 914 6464
enquiries@south-nottingham
.ac.uk
www.south-nottingham.ac.uk
HNC/HND media production.
HNC/HND multimedia/
photography and digital imaging.

South Thames College
Wandsworth High Street
London SW18 2PP
020 8918 7777
studentservices@south-
thames.ac.uk
www.south-thames.ac.uk
Short courses: introduction to low-
budget film production/
scriptwriting/ final cut – desktop
video/ 16mm film production;
HNC media (inc 16mm film
making)/ media production;
NCFE/NatCert/HNC/NatDip
music tech; NatAward music for
media. Centre of Vocational
Excellence for Music Business,
Design and Production

Southampton Institute
East Park Terrace,
Southampton
Hampshire SO14 0RB
023 8031 9000
fmas@solent.ac.uk
www.solent.ac.uk
BSc (Hons) audio tech (BKSTS)/
film and video tech (BKSTS)/
media tech/ music studio tech
(BKSTS); BA (Hons) film and TV
studies/ film studies; PGDip/MA
film; BA (Hons) animation/
digital media/ multimedia
design; MA interactive
production.

St Helen's College
St Helens
Merseyside WA10 1PZ
01744 623580
enquire@sthelens.ac.uk
www.sthelens.ac.uk
Fdg factual TV and video
production; BA (Hons) TV and
video production (both through
Liverpool John Moores
University); BA (Hons) digital
graphic communication (subject
to validation).

Staffordshire University, Faculty
of Arts, Media and Design
College Road, Stoke-on-Trent
Staffordshire ST4 2XW
01782 294869
amdadmissions@staffs.ac.uk
www.staffs.ac.uk
BA (Hons) broadcast journalism
(NCTJ)/ broadcasting factual/
broadcasting music/ film, TV and
radio studies/ film studies/
design: media production; MA
broadcast journalism (NCTJ).

Stevenson College Edinburgh
Bankhead Avenue
Edinburgh EH11 4DE
0131 535 4700
info@stevenson.ac.uk
www.stevenson.ac.uk
HNC/HND TV operations/ audio-
visual tech; Fdg film and TV.

Stirling, University of
Stirling FK9 4LA
01786 467046
recruitment@stir.ac.uk
www.stir.ac.uk
BA (Hons) film and media studies
(single and combined)/ European
film and media/ journalism
studies (single and combined).

Stockport College of Further
and Higher Education.
Wellington Road South
Stockport, Cheshire SK1 3UQ
0845 230 3106
admissions@stockport.ac.uk
www.stockport.ac.uk
BTEC NatDip media
broadcasting; HND media:
broadcasting/ media
broadcasting (moving image).

Stratford Upon Avon College
The Willows North
Alcester Road
Stratford-upon-Avon
Warwickshire CV37 9QR
01789 266245
college@stratford.ac.uk
www.stratford.ac.uk
BTEC NatDip media (moving
image).

Sunderland, University of
Langham Tower, Ryhope Road
Sunderland SR2 7EE
0191 515 2000 (media dept:
0191 515 2112)
student-helpline@
sunderland.ac.uk
www.sunderland.ac.uk
BA (Hons) media production
(TV and radio or video and new
media); MA media production
(TV and video); MA radio
(production and management);
BA (Hons) media production
(video and new media).

Surrey Institute of Art and
Design
Falkner Road, Farnham
Surrey GU9 7DS
01252 722441
registry@surrart.ac.uk
www.surrart.ac.uk
BA (Hons) film and video
(BKSTS).
BA (Hons) digital screen arts.

Sussex, University of
Falmer
Brighton BN1 9RH
01273 606755
information@sussex.ac.uk
www.sussex.ac.uk
Film studies cert (centre for
continuing education); BA film
studies (with options)/ music and
media studies; MA/MPhil film
studies.

Teesside, University of
Middlesbrough
Tees Valley TS1 3BA
01642 342015
hotline@tees.ac.uk
www.tees.ac.uk
Fdg TV and Film Production;
BA (Hons) TV production
professional practice/ media
production professional practice/
media and music tech.

Thames Valley University
London College of Music & Media
St Mary's Road
Ealing, London W5 5RF
0800 036 8888
www.tvu.ac.uk
BA (Hons) film: video production
with film studies; MA film and the
moving image: video: feature film
production/ video production
with film studies; BA (Hons)
digital broadcast media.

Trinity College
Carmarthen
Wales SA31 3EP
01267 676767
registry@trinity-cm.ac.uk
www.trinity-cm.ac.uk
BA media studies/ film studies/
theatr, cerdd a'r cyfryngau
(theatre, music and media); MA
cyfryngau (media).

UHI Millennium Institute
Caledonia House,
63 Academy Street
Inverness IV1 1LU
01463 279000
eo@uhi.ac.uk
www.uhi.ac.uk
HNC media production – offered
at Inverness College UHI; HND
TV and multimedia – fluency in
Gaelic required, offered at Sabhal
Mòr Ostaig UHI; HND video
production – offered at Perth
College UHI.

Ulster, University of
Cromore Road
Co Londonderry
Northern Ireland
BT52 1SA
0870 040 0700
online@ulster.ac.uk
www.ulster.ac.uk
BA (Hons) film studies (single and
combined)/ media (single and
combined); MA film and TV
management (proposed).

University College London
Gower Street
London
WC1E 6BT
020 7679 2000
www.ucl.ac.uk
MA film studies.

University College Northampton
Boughton Green Road
Northampton NN2 7AL
01604 735500
study@northampton.ac.uk
www.northampton.ac.uk
BA (Hons) film and TV studies.

**University College Winchester
(formerly King Alfred's College)**
Hampshire SO22 4NR
01962 841515
admissions@winchester.ac.uk
www.winchester.ac.uk
BA drama, community theatre
and media/ film and american
studies/ film studies/ screen
production.

University College, Worcester
Henwick Grove
Worcester WR2 6AJ
01905 855000
admissions@worc.ac.uk
www.worc.ac.uk
HND film-making/ music for the
moving image.

**University of Wales Institute,
Cardiff**
PO Box 377, Western Avenue
Cardiff CF5 2YB
029 2041 6070
uwicinfo@uwic.ac.uk
www.uwic.ac.uk
BA (Hons) broadcast media and
popular culture; BA (Hons)
graphic communication; BA
(Hons)/BA/BSc (Hons) design for
interactive media.

**University of Wales,
Aberystwyth**
Old College, King Street
Aberystwyth, Ceredigion
SY23 2AX
01970 623111
www.aber.ac.uk
BA/MA/PhD theatre, film and TV
studies (with Welsh, French,
Spanish, German, English, IT,
international politics or politics).

University of Wales, Bangor
Gwynedd
LL57 2DG
01248 351151
admissions@bangor.ac.uk
www.bangor.ac.uk
BA (Hons) astudiaethau ffilm a'r
cyfryngau (film & the media)/
astudiaethau theatr a'r cyfryngau
(theatre and media studies (also
with Welsh))/ English with
film studies or theatre studies;
BA (Hons) English language/
French/German with film studies;
PGDip/MA cynhyrchu cyfryngol
(media production).

University of Wales, Lampeter
Ceredigion SA48 7ED
01570 422351
dept of film and media:
01570 424790
admissions@lamp.ac.uk
www.lamp.ac.uk
BA/PGDip/MA media production.

University of Wales, Newport
Caerleon Campus, PO Box 179
Newport
South Wales NP18 3YG
01633 430088
uic@newport.ac.uk
www.newport.ac.uk
BA (Hons) cinema studies and
scriptwriting/ creative sound and
music (both subject to validation);
BA (Hons) film and video/
documentary film and TV; MA
documentary photography/ film;
MA/MSc sports media (subject to
validation); BA (Hons)
animation/ multimedia; MA
animation/ design (new media
and tech).

University of Wales, Swansea
Singleton Park
Swansea SA2 8PP
01792 205678
admissions@swansea.ac.uk
www.swansea.ac.uk
BA (Hons) screen studies.

Warwickshire College
Leamington Centre
Warwick New Road
Leamington Spa
Warwickshire CV32 5JE
0800 783 6767
www.warkscol.ac.uk
HND visual communication.

West Herts College
Hampstead Road
Watford WD17 3EZ
01923 812000
admissions@westherts.ac.uk
www.westherts.ac.uk
NatDip media (moving image);
Fdg media, design and production
– media production.
Short course: 3D computer
animation.

West Kent College
Brook Street, Tonbridge
Kent TW9 2PW
01732 358101
marketing@wkc.ac.uk
www.wkc.ac.uk
HNC/HND TV production tech;
BA (Hons) broadcast journalism.

**West of England, University
of the**
Frenchay Campus
Coldharbour Lane
Bristol BS16 1QY
0117 965 6261
enquiries@uwe.ac.uk
www.uwe.ac.uk
BA (Hons) time-based media; BSc
(Hons) music systems engineering/
music systems with mathematics;
PGDip/MA communication
media (screenwriting); MA film
and video.

Westminster, University of
309 Regent Street
London W1B 2UW
020 7911 5000
www.wmin.ac.uk
BA media studies with pathways
in TV production or radio
production/film and TV
production/commercial music;
PGDip broadcast journalism
(BJTC); MA film: culture and
industry/screenwriting and
producing/audio production/
music business management;
Cert/Dip media and
communication studies; BA media
studies with pathway in PR; MA
comms/communication policy/
public communication and PR;
BA animation; BSc digital and
photographic imaging/
multimedia computing; MSc
digital and photographic
imaging/interactive multimedia/
computer animation; MA
hypermedia studies/design for
interaction.

Wirral Metropolitan College
Conway Park Campus
Europa Boulevard
Conway Park, Birkenhead
Wirral CH41 4NT
0151 551 7777
enquiries@wmc.ac.uk
www.wmc.ac.uk
MOCN radio and sound
production.

Wolverhampton, University of
Wulfruna Street
Wolverhampton WV1 1SB
01902 321000
enquiries@wlv.ac.uk
www.wlv.ac.uk
HND digital media (design for
screen)/digital media – video
production; Fdg broadcast
journalism; BA (Hons) film
studies/literary, film and theatre
studies/TV graphics/video; MA
art and design network – video;
BA (Hons)/MA animation/design
for multimedia/digital media/
graphic communication/
multimedia communication.

York St John College
Lord Mayor's Walk
York YO31 7EX
01904 624624
admissions@yorksj.ac.uk
www.yorksj.ac.uk
BA (Hons) film and TV
production.

**Yorkshire Coast College of
Further Education**
Lady Edith's Drive, Scarborough
North Yorks YO12 5RN
01723 372105
admissions@ycoastco.ac.uk
www.yorkshirecoast
     college.ac.uk
Fdg applied digital media
(design) (University of Hull/NTI);
HND graphic and multimedia
design.